OECD Environmental Performance Reviews: Poland 2015

OECD
BETTER POLICIES FOR BETTER LIVES

Please cite this publication as:
OECD (2015), *OECD Environmental Performance Reviews: Poland 2015*, OECD Publishing.
http://dx.doi.org/10.1787/9789264227385-en

ISBN 978-92-64-08190-1 (print)
ISBN 978-92-64-22738-5 (PDF)

Series: OECD Environmental Performance Reviews
ISSN 1990-0104 (print)
ISSN 1990-0090 (online)

Photo credits: © Pyty/Shutterstock.com, © Pawel Kazmierczak/Sutterstock.com.

Corrigenda to OECD publications may be found on line at: *www.oecd.org/publishing/corrigenda*.

Preface

This third *OECD Environmental Performance Review of Poland* assesses progress achieved since the last review carried out in 2003, the year before Poland joined the European Union. It shows that EU membership not only stimulated the economy, but it also supported improved environmental management and enhanced the quality of life of Poland's citizens. Environmental policies and institutions were strengthened. Increased investment extended access to water, sanitation and other environmental services and helped to reduce pollution.

Despite this progress, this *Environmental Performance Review* highlights that the Polish economy remains among the most resource- and carbon-intensive in the OECD, largely due to heavy reliance on coal. It calls for further efforts to decouple environmental pressures from economic growth and to reduce people's exposure to hazardous pollutants.

The *Review* also provides useful guidance on how to continue improving the process of environmental policy making. Until recently, Poland's public policies were organised around a large number of strategies and policy documents. To give a better focus and sense of priorities, these have been significantly reduced. As a result, environmental policy is now articulated within the framework of the Energy Security and the Environment Strategy. This provides a good opportunity for integrating environment into Poland's development policy and for addressing the challenges related to the use of coal. At the same time, it requires new institutional mechanisms for monitoring environmental policies to ensure that they are on track to achieve agreed objectives.

Poland has made good progress in enhancing the efficiency of its environmental policy mix through greater use of market-based instruments. In 2012, the revenues generated by environmentally related taxes as a share of GDP and total tax revenues were noticeably above the corresponding OECD averages. However, as in many other OECD countries, these instruments could be designed in a way that provides better incentives for reducing environmental pressures. For example, passenger vehicle tax rates are not based on environmental criteria; a broad range of exemptions to taxes on coal and natural gas remain; and major water users are exempt from water abstraction fees.

The report also draws lessons from Poland's long tradition of sustainable forest management practices, which have allowed the potential timber harvest to increase while conserving biodiversity. Among other natural endowments, Poland hosts the only primeval forest remaining in Europe: the Białowieża. These forests are both an important source of income and valuable repositories of biodiversity. The achievements in terms of management and conservation were recognised in 2013 by the award of the UNESCO Prize for Environmental Preservation to the Polish public forest management agency for its outstanding contributions in the areas of research, education and awareness raising. Nevertheless, there is scope to better align forestry and biodiversity policies: spatial planning legislation should be amended to prevent further encroachment into forests, and the management of protected forests must be significantly strengthened to meet EU obligations.

Another focus of the report is waste management. For much of the review period, Poland had made slow progress in establishing an effective system of municipal waste management. A major reform undertaken in 2013 is a welcome step forward and provides a better basis for establishing collection service for all inhabitants and increasing separate collection of recyclable waste. Nevertheless, municipal capacities will need to be strengthened to promote compliance with waste legislation.

This review presents 28 policy recommendations to improve the environmental performance of Poland. It suggests, for example, strengthening the institutional arrangements for co-ordinating and assessing environmental policies, strengthening capacities for analysing the economic aspects of environmental policies, and clearly specifying the measures needed to move toward a low-emission economy. It calls for better pricing of environmental externalities while providing targeted support to households that may be adversely affected. It proposes use of payments for ecosystem services to support the effective management of protected forests. It also recommends strengthening efforts to improve resource productivity and to develop a coherent investment approach for municipal waste treatment.

The *Environmental Performance Review* is the result of a constructive policy dialogue between Poland and the other members and observers of the OECD Working Party on Environmental Performance. Beyond the support provided to Poland, I am confident that this collaborative effort will help to improve the management of the environmental challenges faced by other OECD members and partner countries.

Angel Gurría

OECD Secretary General

Foreword

The principal aim of the OECD Environmental Performance Review programme is to help member and selected partner countries improve their individual and collective performance in environmental management by:

- *helping individual governments assess progress in achieving their environmental goals;*
- *promoting continuous policy dialogue and peer learning;*
- *stimulating greater accountability from governments towards each other and public opinion.*

This report reviews the environmental performance of Poland since the previous OECD Environmental Performance Review in 2003. Progress in achieving domestic objectives and international commitments provides the basis for assessing the country's environmental performance. Such objectives and commitments may be broad aims, qualitative goals or quantitative targets. A distinction is made between intentions, actions and results. Assessment of environmental performance is also placed within the context of Poland's historical environmental record, present state of the environment, physical endowment in natural resources, economic conditions and demographic trends.

The OECD is indebted to the government of Poland for its co-operation in providing information, for the organisation of the review mission to Warsaw and Izabelin municipality (2-8 March 2014) and for facilitating contacts both inside and outside government institutions.

Thanks are also due to all those who helped in the course of this review, to the representatives of member countries participating in the OECD Working Party on Environmental Performance and especially to the examining countries: Austria and Switzerland. The team that prepared this review comprised experts from reviewing countries: Ms Ana Jakil (Austria) and Mr Christoph Dürr (Switzerland); members of the OECD Secretariat: Mr Gérard Bonnis, Mr Peter Borkey, Mr Brendan Gillespie, Mr Krzysztof Michalak, Ms Sara Moarif, Ms Alexa Piccolo and Ms Frédérique Zegel; and Mr Tony Zamparutti (consultant). Ms Carla Bertuzzi, Ms Clara Tomasini (OECD Secretariat) and Ms Rebecca Brite (consultant) provided statistical and editorial support during the preparation of the report. Preparation of this report also benefitted from comments provided by other members of the OECD Secretariat.

The OECD Working Party on Environmental Performance discussed the draft Environmental Performance Review of Poland at its meeting on 28 October 2014 in Paris, and approved the Assessment and Recommendations.

Table of contents

Part II

Progress towards selected environmental objectives

Tables

Figures

Follow OECD Publications on:

http://twitter.com/OECD_Pubs

http://www.facebook.com/OECDPublications

http://www.linkedin.com/groups/OECD-Publications-4645871

http://www.youtube.com/oecdilibrary

http://www.oecd.org/oecddirect/

This book has...

StatLinks

A service that delivers Excel® files from the printed page!

Look for the *StatLinks* at the bottom of the tables or graphs in this book. To download the matching Excel® spreadsheet, just type the link into your Internet browser, starting with the *http://dx.doi.org* prefix, or click on the link from the e-book edition.

General notes

Signs

The following signs are used in Figures and Tables:

. . : not available

– : nil or negligible

. : decimal point

Country aggregates

OECD Europe: This zone includes all European member countries of the OECD, i.e. Austria, Belgium, the Czech Republic, Denmark, Estonia, Finland, France, Germany, Greece, Hungary, Iceland, Ireland, Italy, Luxembourg, the Netherlands, Norway, Poland, Portugal, the Slovak Republic, Slovenia, Spain, Sweden, Switzerland, Turkey and the United Kingdom.

OECD: This zone includes all member countries of the OECD, i.e. the countries of OECD Europe plus Australia, Canada, Chile, Israel, Japan, Korea, Mexico, New Zealand and the United States.

Country aggregates may include Secretariat estimates.

Currency

Monetary unit: Polish zloty (PLN).

In 2013, USD 1.00 = PLN 3.16.

Cut-off date

This report is based on information and data available up to November 2014.

Executive summary

Poland's EU accession helped improve environmental performance

Since its accession to the European Union in 2004, Poland has experienced impressive economic growth. This has allowed living standards and environmental performance to improve. Supported by EU funds, increased investment in infrastructure has extended access to water services. Greenhouse gas (GHG) emissions, waste generation, water withdrawal and emissions of several air pollutants have been decoupled from economic growth. More than half of Polish citizens consider the state of the environment in their neighbourhood to be good. However, Poland's GDP per capita still ranks among the bottom five OECD countries, and economic and environmental disparities remain within and among regions. The Polish economy is among the most resource- and carbon-intensive in the OECD due to heavy reliance on coal. In 2012, average air concentrations of health-damaging fine particulate matter were the highest in Europe.

The environmental governance system should be further adjusted to support policy implementation

Poland has made impressive efforts to transpose EU environmental legislation but now faces significant implementation challenges, particularly in the areas of water and waste management. The environmental compliance assurance system has been strengthened through the decentralisation of compliance monitoring and inspections. It has also been made more efficient by streamlining inspection procedures, reducing administrative burdens and increasing the effectiveness of non-compliance responses. Nevertheless, Poland must embed its enforcement efforts in a complex multilevel system of environmental governance. This system would benefit from an independent review. New institutional arrangements and updated legislation have helped rationalise environmental impact assessment (EIA) procedures, which helped reduce the time for issuing EIA decisions from 300 to 100 days. However, opportunities exist to further improve and harmonise the methodology for conducting EIA and to make the process more transparent by facilitating public participation at all stages.

Poland should clarify its pathway to a low-carbon economy

Poland's main policy priorities have been consolidated in a relatively small number of strategies, including the 2014 Energy Security and the Environment Strategy. This provides opportunities for better integrating environment into the strategically important energy sector and addressing its heavy reliance on coal. However, without appropriate mechanisms for co-ordinating and assessing policies, there is a risk that the previous strong focus on environmental issues could be lost. As in many EU countries, the low allowance price in the EU Emissions Trading System has not provided sufficient incentives to invest in lower-carbon energy sources. Adopting the National Programme for the Development of a Low-Emission Economy would help in managing the trade-offs between energy security and climate change policies. Achieving the 2020 EU GHG emission targets will require measures to mitigate the growing emissions from the transport sector. These emissions have been stimulated in part by significant investment in road transport infrastructure and insufficient support for less carbon-intensive modes of transport.

There is scope for economic instruments to better reflect environmental costs

Poland has made progress in expanding the use of economic instruments in its environmental policy mix. While revenue from environmentally related taxes has increased and, as a share of GDP, was above the OECD average in 2012, these and other economic instruments could provide better environmental incentives for firms and households. The excise duty on diesel is still below that of petrol even though diesel combustion emits more CO_2 and local pollutants per litre. Passenger vehicle tax rates are not based on environmental criteria despite large imports of polluting second-hand vehicles. A broad range of exemptions from taxes on coal and natural gas remain. Although Poland has very limited freshwater resources, major water users are exempt from water abstraction fees. Reviewing the system of environmentally related taxes and charges could help Poland identify more efficient and effective ways of tackling its environmental challenges.

Poland has a long tradition of sustainable forest management practices

Poland's forests are both an important source of income and valuable repositories of biodiversity. The Białowieża is the only primeval forest remaining in Europe. The management of public forests (80% of total forests) and biodiversity has benefitted from a high-quality, stable institutional framework. However, implementation of Natura 2000 will require a further alignment of forestry and biodiversity objectives, amendments to spatial planning legislation and significant investment. Wider use of access charges and the development of payments for ecosystem services could help in this regard.

Recent reforms provide a better basis for more effective municipal waste management

For most of the review period, Poland's municipal waste management was hampered by a system that placed the main responsibility on households rather than municipalities. A 2013 reform reversing this serves as a better basis for providing waste service to all inhabitants and increasing the separate collection of recyclable waste. Preliminary results are encouraging but municipal capacities will need to be strengthened and the accuracy of waste data improved to ensure compliance with waste legislation. Updating national and regional waste management plans can also help in developing a coherent investment approach for municipal waste treatment and diverting waste from landfill. As a relatively materials-intensive country, Poland should strengthen efforts and innovation to improve resource productivity.

PART I

Progress towards sustainable development

PART I

Chapter 1

Key environmental trends

This chapter provides a snapshot of key environmental trends in Poland over the period since 2000, and describes progress towards green growth. It shows the positive impact that Poland's accession to the EU has had on living standards and environmental performance. The chapter describes Poland's progress in reducing the carbon, energy and material intensities of its economy; in managing its natural asset base; and in improving its people's environmental quality of life.

The statistical data for Israel are supplied by and under the responsibility of the relevant Israeli authorities. The use of such data by the OECD is without prejudice to the status of the Golan Heights, East Jerusalem and Israeli settlements in the West Bank under the terms of international law.

1. Introduction

This chapter provides a snapshot of key environmental trends in Poland. It highlights some of the main environmental achievements and remaining challenges on the path towards green growth and sustainable development, focusing on the period since 2000. Drawing on indicators from national and international sources, it broadly follows the OECD framework for monitoring progress towards green growth (OECD, 2011). After a brief overview, the chapter describes Poland's progress in using energy and natural resources efficiently, in managing its natural asset base and in improving its people's environmental quality of life. To the extent possible, it compares the state of the environment and key environmental trends with those of other OECD countries and in relation to Poland's national and international commitments. It thus provides a baseline for chapters that assess the effectiveness of Poland's environmental policies in influencing these trends and in using environmental objectives to generate economic opportunities.

Poland joined the European Union in 2004 and this has had a positive impact on living standards and environmental performance. EU membership also stimulated the economy, which has grown at a substantially higher rate than the OECD average over the past decade. Poland's is the only European economy that did not shrink during the global economic crisis, though it slowed sharply in 2012-13, worsening the fiscal deficit. The income gap with the OECD average narrowed, and income inequality and relative poverty decreased more than in most OECD countries. However, gross domestic product (GDP) per capita still ranks among the bottom five in the OECD and disparities remain within and among regions. Despite progress in decoupling environmental pressures from economic growth, the Polish economy is among the most resource- and carbon-intensive in the OECD due to heavy reliance on coal (Figure 1.1, Box 1.1, Table 1.1).

Poland reduced greenhouse gas (GHG) emissions by significantly more than it was required to under the Kyoto Protocol. The main drivers of this success were improved energy efficiency in heavy industry and structural changes in the economy in the late 1980s and early 1990s. Between 2000 and 2012, Poland achieved a significant but relative decoupling of GHG emissions from economic growth. Manufacturing industries and construction have reported the largest decrease in emissions. Although the energy industry is by far the largest emitter, the transport sector has been the fastest growing source of GHG emissions. The energy and carbon intensities of the economy decreased faster than in most OECD countries. Improved energy efficiency and the moderate shift from coal to natural gas are among the main factors.

Material productivity has varied with the cycles of investment in infrastructure. In 2011, the Polish economy was among the most resource-intensive in the OECD, reflecting the relatively high share of industry in economic activity, an important mining sector and buoyant construction activity. Progress has been made in decoupling waste generation from economic growth, and municipal waste generation per capita remains well below the OECD average. However, in 2012, about 20% of the population was not covered by municipal

Figure 1.1. **Economic performance in Poland and the OECD, 2000-13**

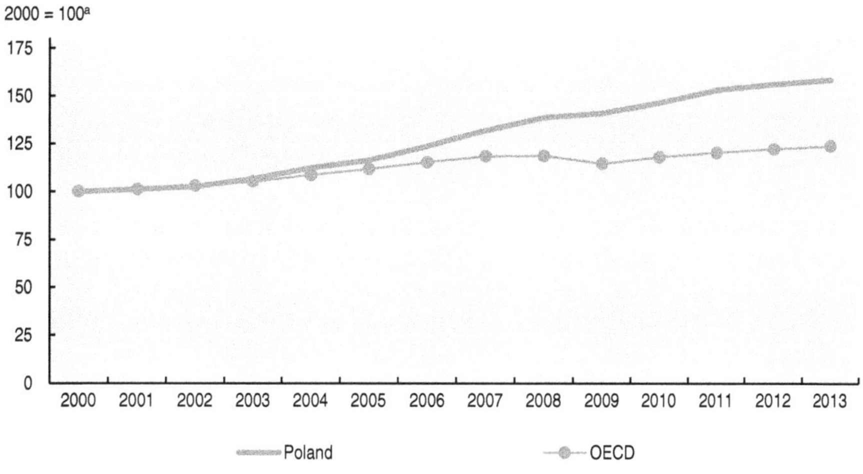

a) Index of relative change based on GDP values expressed at 2005 prices and purchasing power parities.
Source: OECD (2014), *OECD Economic Outlook No. 95* (database).

StatLink http://dx.doi.org/10.1787/888933197503

Box 1.1. **The economic and social context**

The economy

- Economic growth has been strong in Poland over the past decade. The Polish economy is the only one in Europe that did not shrink during the global economic crisis. Between 2000 and 2013, the annual GDP growth rate was 3.6%, compared to 1.7% in the OECD. In 2012-13, the economy slowed sharply, but GDP is projected to grow by 3.0% in 2014 and 3.4% in 2015 (OECD, 2014a).
- Although the income gap with the OECD average narrowed, in GDP per capita Poland is still among the bottom five OECD countries (Annex I.A). Economic disparities remain within and among voivodships (regions). Income per capita in the capital region of Mazowieckie exceeds the EU average, while eastern regions (Lubelskie, Podkarpackie) are among the poorest in the EU (Table 1.1).
- Poland has a strong industrial base. Industry and construction account for 33% of GDP, above the OECD average of 27%. Services account for around 63%, while agriculture represents nearly 4% (OECD, 2014b).
- Output of the environmental goods and services sector is estimated at 5-6% of GDP (Chapter 3).
- International trade plays a significant role in the economy. In 2012, exports amounted to 47% of GDP, while imports represented about 46%, above the OECD averages of less than 30% for both (Annex I.A). Motor vehicles and related parts and accessories are the largest export commodities. They are primarily shipped to EU countries. Crude oil is the largest import commodity. Most oil and gas imports come from the Russian Federation.
- Unemployment decreased significantly in the past decade but started rising again in 2009 to reach 10.4% in 2013, above the OECD average of 7.9% (OECD, 2014a).
- Since 2004, income inequality (as measured by the Gini coefficient) and relative poverty have decreased more than most of OECD countries and Poland is now in line with the OECD averages (Annex I.B).

Box 1.1. **The economic and social context** *(cont.)*

Public finance

- The general government deficit worsened slightly in 2013 to 4.3% of GDP.* The fiscal slippage resulted from lower-than-expected tax receipts due to the sharp economic slowdown and higher social expenditure and public consumption. Public debt gradually increased from 37% of GDP in 2000 to 57% in 2013 (OECD, 2014a, 2014b).
- General government spending has generally been high in the last decade, varying with EU financial cycles. In 2013, it accounted for about 42% of GDP, in line with the OECD average. Public environmental expenditure increased from 0.8% of GDP in 2006 to 1.0% in 2011, reflecting Poland's effort to meet EU environmental requirements (Chapter 3).
- The tax to GDP ratio has been below the OECD average since 2000. In 2011 it was 32.3%, while the OECD average was 34.1% (OECD, 2013b).
- In 2012, revenue from environmentally related taxes accounted for 2.2% of GDP and 6.8% of total tax revenue, above the respective OECD averages (Chapter 3).

The population

- In 2012, the population in Poland was about 38.5 million. Population density is 123 inhabitants per square kilometre, slightly higher than the OECD Europe average of about 109.
- About 22% of the population lives in urban regions, which occupy 2% of the land area; more than 72% of the territory is classified as rural and is home to 47% of the population (OECD, 2014c).**
- In 2012, life expectancy at birth was 77 years, below the OECD average of 80 years. At 1.3 children per woman, the fertility rate is among the lowest in the OECD.
- The population is ageing: the share of people aged 65 and over increased to 14% in 2012, just under the OECD average of 15%. Youth (under age 15) represent about 15%, while the OECD average is 18%.
- The population is generally well educated: 90% of working-age people (25-64 years old) have at least upper secondary education, among the highest rates in the OECD (Annex I.B). However, the share of tertiary graduates within the same age group, at 25%, is lower than the OECD average (32%).

* In 2014, pension changes reversed part of the 1999 reform and created a one-off budget surplus for 2014.
** The remainder falls under the intermediate category.

waste collection service and landfilling remained the predominant type of treatment of municipal waste.

Since 2000, agricultural land area has decreased while land for a range of other uses increased, notably for housing, services, infrastructure and forests. Poland is among the few OECD countries where environmental pressures from nutrients have not been decoupled from agricultural production. However, the levels of nutrient surpluses remain below the OECD averages. The intensity of forest resource use declined to a low level compared to other OECD countries. Areas under strict protection cover a relatively small part of Poland's territory and the conservation status of habitats and species is relatively unfavourable. Further efforts will be required to achieve the Aichi targets of protecting 17% of terrestrial area and 10% of marine area by 2020.

Table 1.1. **Selected regional indicators, 2012**

Voivodship (region)	Population density (inh./km²)	GDP per capita[a] (Poland = 100)	Unemployment (%)	Municipal waste generation (kg per capita)	Pop. covered by municipal waste collection (%)	Pop. connected to wastewater treatment plants (%)	Pop. connected to water supply (%)
Lodzkie	139	93	11.1	351	71	67	90
Mazowieckie	149	163	8.0	362	77	64	84
Malopolskie	221	86	10.4	300	77	58	76
Slaskie	374	108	9.4	334	84	76	94
Lubelskie	86	68	10.5	233	64	55	82
Podkarpackie	119	68	13.3	201	82	69	76
Podlaskie	59	72	9.2	291	70	66	88
Swietokrzyskie	109	75	13.2	180	77	54	85
Lubuskie	73	83	9.0	345	91	70	90
Wielkopolskie	116	104	8.5	314	83	66	93
Zachodniopomorskie	75	84	10.9	336	89	81	94
Dolnoslaskie	146	113	11.1	364	93	77	92
Opolskie	107	80	9.5	293	86	69	95
Kujawsko-Pomorskie	117	82	11.9	305	80	71	91
Pomorskie	125	95	9.5	331	86	82	93
Warmińsko-Mazurskie	60	72	11.0	309	80	73	89
Poland	**123**	**100**	**10.1**	**314**	**80**	**69**	**88**

a) 2011 data.
Source: CSO (2014), *Local Data Bank* (database); Eurostat (2014), *Science and Technology Statistics* (database); OECD (2014), *OECD Regional Statistics* (database).

Poland is poorly endowed with freshwater resources and its water use intensity is about twice the OECD average. Since 2000, water withdrawal has been further decoupled from economic growth. However, insufficient treatment of municipal and industrial sewage, saline water discharged from coal mines and pollution loads from diffuse agricultural sources continue to affect water quality. More than two-thirds of surface water bodies fail to meet the good-status objectives of the EU Water Framework Directive (WFD). Increased investment in infrastructure has extended access to water services and helped both to reduce pollution loads and to provide good quality drinking water. Nevertheless, the connection rate for public wastewater treatment plants is well below the OECD average, in part because it is uneconomic to provide networked services to dispersed rural communities.

Over the past decade, emissions of several air pollutants have been further decoupled from economic growth, though to a much lesser extent than in the 1990s. Sulphur oxide (SO_X) emissions per unit of GDP are triple the OECD Europe average and nitrogen oxide (NO_X) emissions double. Significant additional efforts will be required to achieve the proposed 2020 emission reduction targets in the revised EU National Emission Ceilings Directive. In 2012, Poland recorded the highest level of $PM_{2.5}$ pollution in Europe, partly due to small scale combustion of biomass and coal and concentrated local pollution. The country has one of the EU's highest levels of mortality from respiratory and heart diseases, which are linked to ambient air pollution, though the level decreased in the second half of the last decade. Power plants are among the EU's largest contributors to health and environmental damage costs from industrial air pollution.

The majority of Polish people assign high importance to climate change issues, although only one-tenth consider environmental protection an important issue. More than half consider the state of the environment in their neighbourhood to be good.

2. Transition to a low-carbon, energy- and resource-efficient economy

2.1. Carbon and energy intensities

Greenhouse gas emissions

- In 2012, GHG emissions, excluding emissions and removals from land use, land-use change and forestry, totalled 399 million tonnes of carbon dioxide equivalent (CO_2 eq). Average domestic emissions in 2008-12 were 30% below the level set in 1988, the Polish base year under the Kyoto Protocol. Thus Poland went beyond its commitment of limiting GHG emissions to 6% below the 1988 level (Figure 1.2). The main drivers of this success were improved energy efficiency in heavy industry and structural changes in the economy in the late 1980s and early 1990s.
- Over 2000-12, total GHG emissions increased by only 1%, while overall GDP growth was around 56%. Hence Poland achieved a significant, but still relative, decoupling of emissions from economic growth. According to national projections, emissions should be 5% lower in 2020 than in 2012, then increase to the 2012 level in 2030 (Figure 1.2). However, meeting Poland's 2020 GHG emission target[1] may pose a challenge (IEA, 2011; World Bank, 2011; Chapter 3).
- As in many other OECD countries, energy-related emissions make up the largest share of total GHG emissions. The energy industry accounts for 42%, compared with 32% in OECD Annex I countries. Since 2000, manufacturing industries and construction have reported the largest decrease in emissions (-35%), while emissions from transport have risen by almost 70% (Figure 1.2).
- CO_2 emissions account for 80% of GHGs emissions, followed by methane (10%) and nitrous oxide (7%). F-gases account for the remainder. Since 2000, these shares have remained stable.
- CO_2 intensity (the ratio of CO_2 emissions from fuel combustion per unit of GDP) has decreased by 35% since 2000 but it remains one of the highest among OECD countries (Annex I.C), largely due to the heavy reliance on coal.

Energy intensity

- Total primary energy supply (TPES) has increased by 9% since 2000. It slightly declined in 2009 due to the economic slowdown, rose again in 2010 with the recovery and cold winter, and dropped once more in 2012-13. Although its share is declining, coal continues to dominate the energy mix, accounting for 54% of TPES and 85% of electricity generation in 2013 (Figure 1.3).
- As a result of the relatively slow increase in energy supply and consumption in the context of economic growth of more than 56%, energy intensity decreased faster than in most OECD countries over the last decade (Figure 1.3, Annex I.A). Improved efficiency in energy transformation and final energy use (notably in the iron/steel and chemical industries) is among the main factors. In 2013, however, energy intensity was still 19% higher than the OECD Europe average (Annex I.A). Achieving the indicative target for 2020 of stabilising primary energy consumption at about the 2010 level is challenging because of projected economic growth (European Commission, 2013a).
- Total final energy consumption (TFC) increased by 15% over 2000-12, mainly because of increased demand for road transport (Figure 1.4). Since 2000, the transport sector has been the fastest growing consumer of energy (+73%), followed by the commercial sector (+65%). Energy consumption decreased in the industry, agriculture and forestry sectors (Figure 1.4).

Figure 1.2. **GHG emissions**

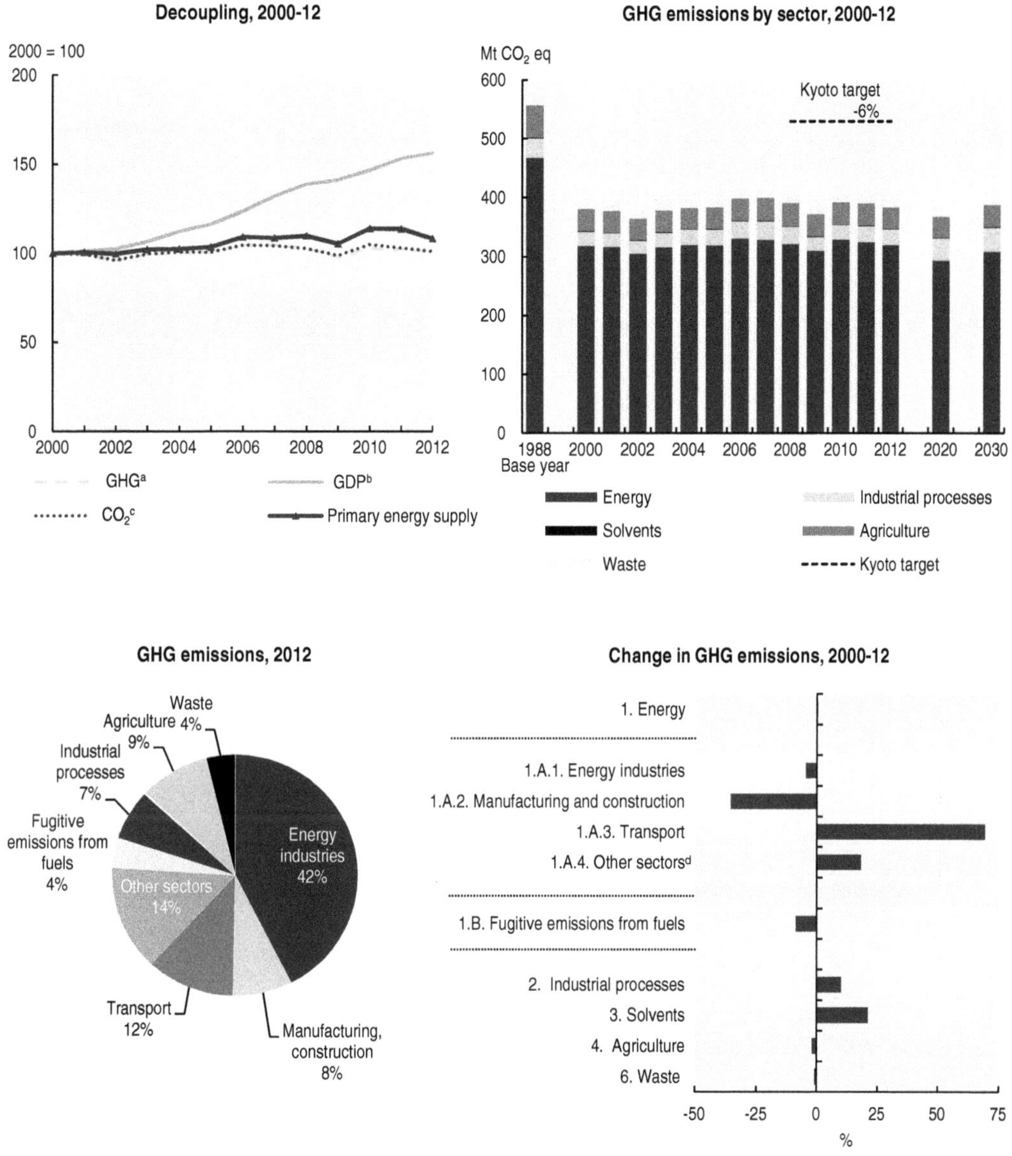

a) Excluding emissions/removals from land use, land-use change and forestry.
b) GDP at 2005 prices and purchasing power parities.
c) CO_2 emissions from energy use only; sectoral approach; excludes international marine and aviation bunkers.
d) Emissions from fuel combustion of residential, commercial/institutional and agriculture/forestry/fisheries sectors.
Source: IEA (2014), *IEA CO_2 Emissions from Fuel Combustion Statistics* (database); IEA (2014), *IEA World Energy Statistics and Balances* (database); OECD (2014), *OECD Economic Outlook No. 95* (database); UNFCCC (2014), "National Inventory Report 2014".

StatLink http://dx.doi.org/10.1787/888933197517

- The residential sector was the largest energy user in 2012, accounting for 29% of TFC, followed by transport (25%) and industry (21%) (Figure 1.4).

Energy mix

- Poland has a higher share of fossil fuels in its energy mix than most other OECD countries (Annex I.A). Coal, oil and natural gas together accounted for more than 90% of TPES in 2013. As a result, the carbon intensity of energy is comparatively high. Since 2000, there has been a shift from coal to renewable energy sources as well as to oil and gas.

Figure 1.3. **Energy structure and intensity, 2000-13**

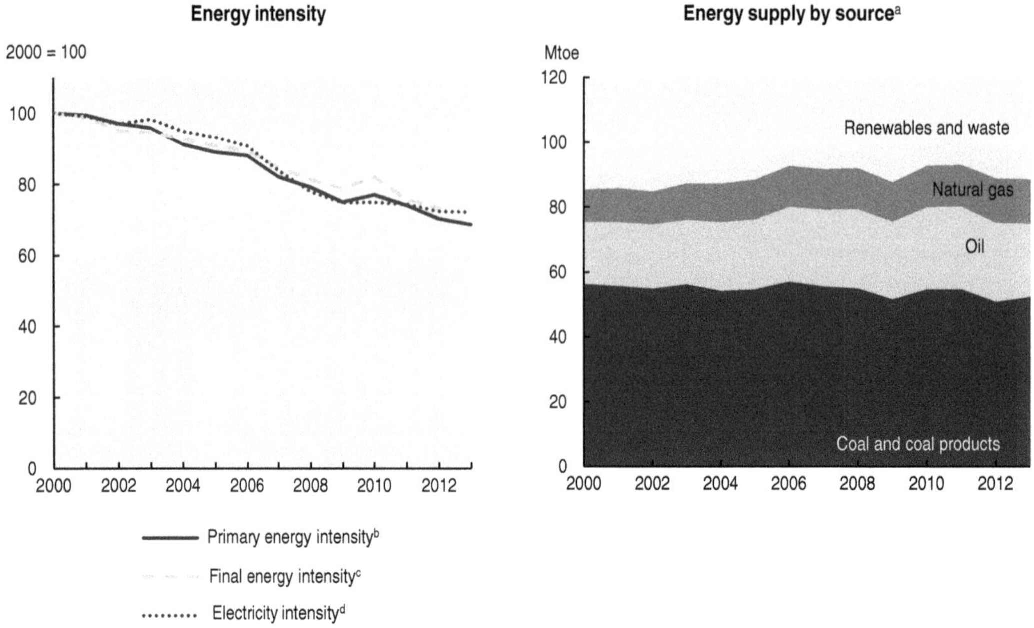

a) Total primary energy supply. Breakdown excludes trade of electricity and heat.
b) Total primary energy supply per unit of GDP at 2005 prices and purchasing power parities.
c) Total final consumption of energy per unit of GDP at 2005 prices and purchasing power parities.
d) Electricity consumption per unit of GDP at 2005 prices and purchasing power parities.
Source: IEA (2014), *IEA World Energy Statistics and Balances* (database); OECD (2014), *OECD Economic Outlook No. 95* (database).

StatLink http://dx.doi.org/10.1787/888933197529

Figure 1.4. **Final energy consumption**

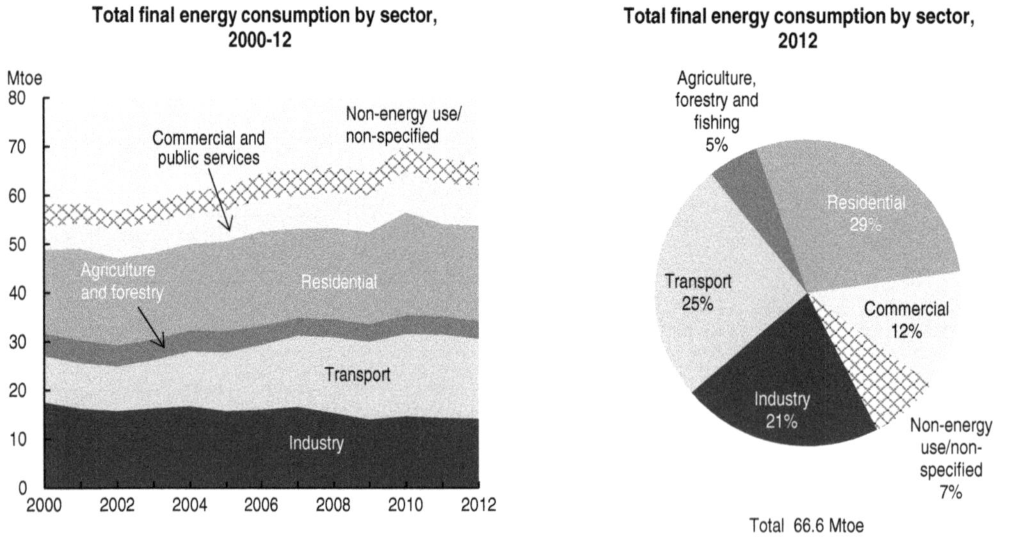

Source: IEA (2014), *IEA World Energy Statistics and Balances* (database).

StatLink http://dx.doi.org/10.1787/888933197539

- The share of renewables in the energy supply grew from 4% in 2000 to 8% in 2013, mainly as a result of increased use of biomass (direct use in the residential sector for heating and use for heat and electricity in the energy industry), of transport biofuels and of wind (Figure 1.5).

Figure 1.5. **Energy from renewable sources**

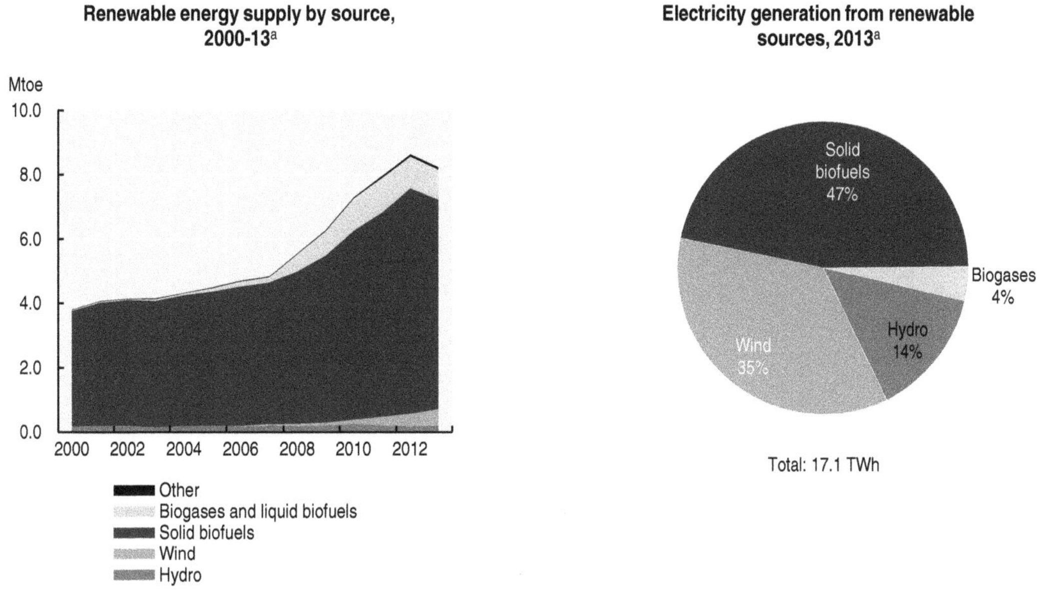

a) 2013 data are preliminary.
Source: IEA (2014), *IEA World Energy Statistics and Balances* (database).

StatLink http://dx.doi.org/10.1787/888933197545

- Poland's energy policy aims to diversify the energy mix towards gas, nuclear power and renewables. The construction of two nuclear power plants is planned, each of 3 000 MW, with the first unit scheduled for operation in 2024 (Ministry of Economy, 2014a).
- In 2013, renewables contributed 10% of electricity generation, half the OECD average. Since 2000, wind power has been the fastest growing renewable source of electricity, followed by solid biomass, while the share of hydropower has steadily decreased (Figure 1.5).
- Poland was on track in 2012 to achieve its target of 15% of gross final energy consumption from renewables by 2020 (Ministry of Economy, 2014b). However, the system to support use of renewables favoured co-firing of biomass with coal in existing power plants and did not foster investment in more innovative technologies (Chapter 3).

Transport

- Between 2000 and 2012, the transport sector was the fastest growing consumer of energy, and consequently the fastest growing source of GHG emissions.
- Since 2000, road freight traffic has almost tripled while freight haulage by rail and pipeline has grown at a much slower pace than GDP (Figure 1.6). Passenger transport by road more than doubled, whereas traffic by rail, bus and coach declined.
- As a result, the modal split has further shifted towards road, which represented 75% of freight and 95% of passenger transport in 2011. Despite significant EU support for transport infrastructure, rail infrastructure remains underdeveloped (OECD, 2014b; Chapter 3).
- At 49 private cars per 100 persons, the car ownership rate is below the OECD average, but the vehicle fleet has had one of the OECD's strongest growth rates since 2000 (Annex I.A).
- The passenger car fleet is ageing (Figure 1.6). The number of vehicles aged ten years or over has grown steadily to reach 71% of the fleet in 2012, among the highest shares in the

Figure 1.6. **Transport trends**

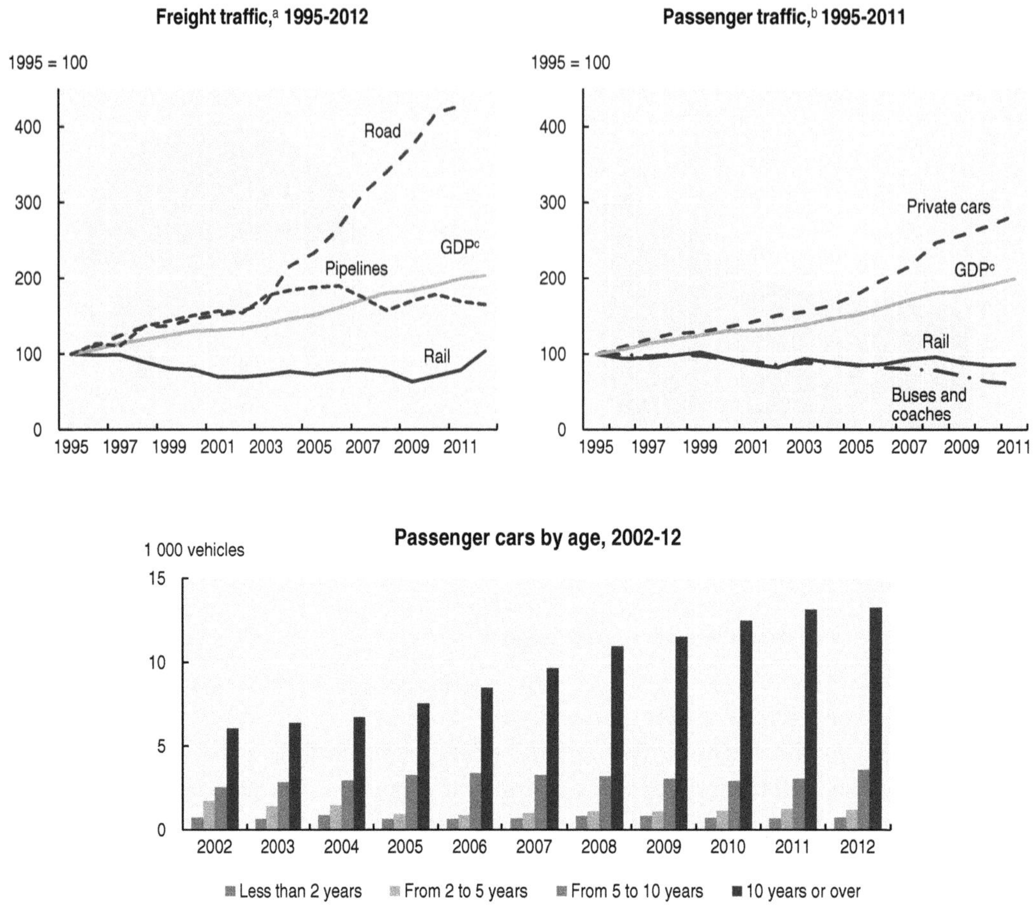

a) Based on values expressed in tonne-km.
b) Based on values expressed in passenger-km.
c) GDP at 2005 prices and purchasing power parities.
Source: Eurostat (2014), *Transport Statistics* (database); OECD (2014), *OECD Economic Outlook No. 95* (database); OECD (2014), *OECD Environment Statistics* (database).

StatLink http://dx.doi.org/10.1787/888933197558

European Union.[2] Partly due to a lack of environmental considerations in car taxation, Poland imports large numbers of polluting second-hand vehicles (Chapter 3).

2.2. *Resource efficiency*

Material productivity

- In 2011, per capita domestic material consumption (DMC)[3] was 24% higher than the OECD average. The economy was among the OECD's most resource intensive, reflecting a relatively high share of industry, a large mining sector and buoyant construction activity (Annex I.C)
- Construction minerals are dominant in DMC, accounting for half of material use, followed by fossil fuels and biomass at about 20% each (Figure 1.7).
- Between 2000 and 2010, material consumption increased but at a slower rate than economic activity, so material productivity improved by 22%. However, productivity gains were offset by a sharp rise in DMC in 2011 (Figure 1.7, Annex I.C). This was due to high demand

Figure 1.7. **Resource productivity**

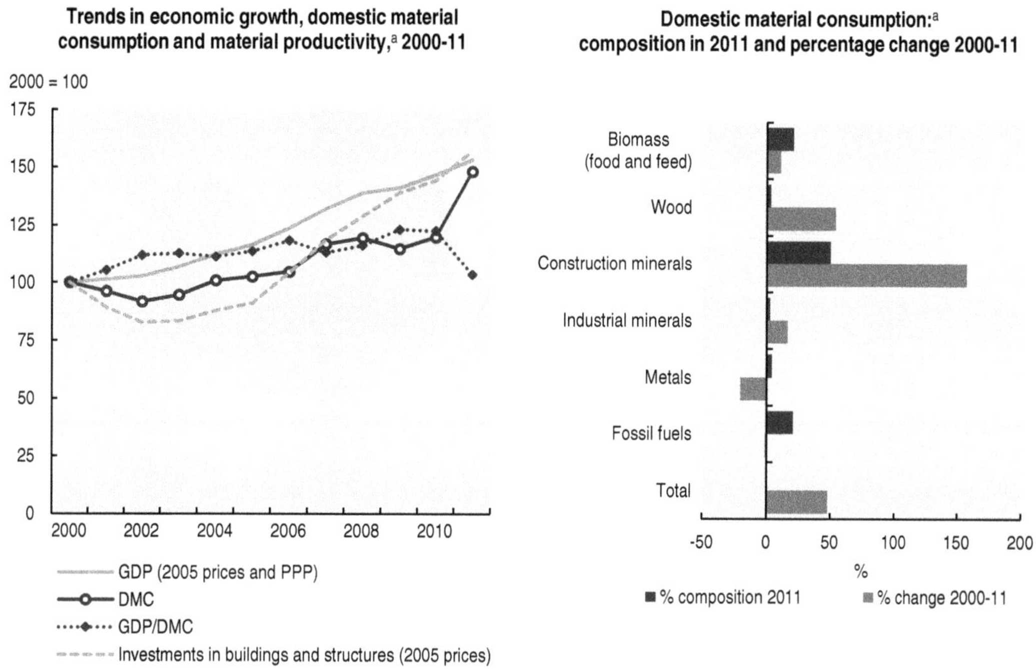

a) Domestic material consumption (DMC) is the sum of domestic raw material extraction used by an economy and its physical trade balance (imports minus exports of raw materials and manufactured products). Material productivity designates the amount of GDP generated per unit of materials used. It refers to the ratio of GDP to domestic material consumption. A rise in material productivity is equivalent to a decline in material intensity (i.e. DMC/GDP).

Source: OECD (2014), *OECD Environment Statistics* (database); OECD (2014), *OECD National Accounts Statistics* (database).

StatLink http://dx.doi.org/10.1787/888933197564

for construction minerals, driven by new investment in infrastructure, particularly in road transport and preparation of the 2012 European football championship (Chapter 5).

Waste generation and recovery

- Between 2000 and 2012, Poland made progress in decoupling waste generation from economic growth:[4] total amounts generated remained stable while GDP grew by over 50%. The mining and quarrying sector accounts for about 40% of total waste generated, followed by manufacturing (19%) and the energy production and construction sectors (13% each) (Figure 1.8).
- With about 310 kg of municipal waste generated per capita in 2012, Poland is well below the OECD average of 520 kg per capita, reflecting the remaining gap in income level (Annex I.C).
- About 80% of the population is covered by a municipal waste collection service, among the lowest rates in the OECD. Poland failed to achieve the goal of universal coverage by 2007, set in the 2010 National Waste Management Plan. Coverage ratios range from 64% in Lubelskie region to 93% in Dolnoslaskie (Table 1.1; CSO, 2013; MoE, 2006).
- Collected amounts of municipal waste declined until the mid-2000s and remained broadly stable afterwards. Poor waste management is among the factors driving this trend (MoE, 2006, 2010).[5] The municipal waste management system was recently reformed to address key problems (Chapter 5).

Figure 1.8. **Waste management**

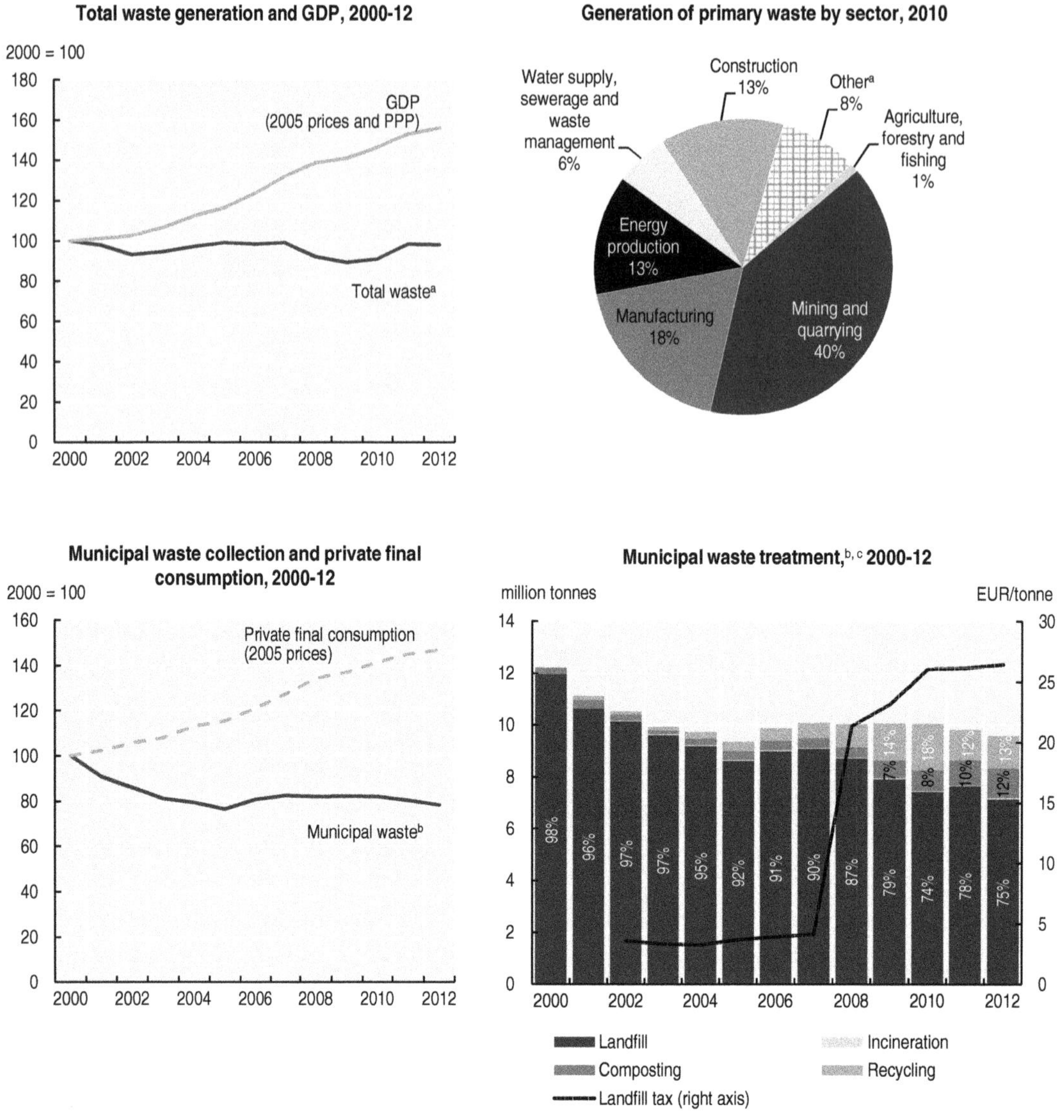

a) Including municipal waste.
b) Waste collected by or for municipalities including household, bulky and commercial waste, and similar waste handled at the same facilities.
c) Break in time series in 2011.
Source: CSO (2013), *Environment 2013;* OECD (2014), *OECD Economic Outlook No. 95* (database); OECD (2014), *OECD Environment Statistics* (database).

StatLink http://dx.doi.org/10.1787/888933197575

- Landfilling is the predominant type of treatment of municipal waste, accounting for 75% of total treatment. Although the proportion has decreased steadily since the landfill tax was raised in 2008, it remains much higher than the OECD average of 45% (Figure 1.8, Annex I.C). Poland missed the 2010 and 2013 EU Landfill Directive targets on reducing the percentage of biodegradable municipal waste disposed of in landfills (Chapter 5).
- Recycling accounts for 13% of treatment of municipal waste and composting for 12%. A major effort will be needed to recycle 50% of glass, metals, paper and plastics in household waste by 2020 (Chapter 5).

Nutrient balance and agricultural inputs

- Gross nutrient surpluses grew between 2000-02 and 2010-12 (Eurostat, 2014a). Poland is among the few OECD countries where environmental pressures from nutrients have not been decoupled from agricultural production over the past decade. However, their levels expressed in terms of nitrogen or phosphorus per hectare of agricultural land remained below the OECD averages in 2007-09 (OECD, 2013c).
- Between 2002 and 2012, use of nitrogenous and phosphorous fertiliser increased at a faster pace than agricultural production. This trend, combined with the decrease in area of agricultural land, resulted in Poland ranking among the ten OECD countries with the highest intensity of commercial fertiliser use (FAO, 2014; Annex I.C).

3. Managing the natural asset base

3.1. Biodiversity and ecosystems

Forests and agricultural land

- Agricultural land decreased from 60% of the total land area in 2000 to 47%[6] in 2012. Over the same period, other uses of land, including for housing, services and infrastructure, increased from 10% to 22% (FAO, 2014).
- Since 2003, the amount of agricultural land under organic farming has increased more than tenfold to 4.6% of the total in 2012, compared with the EU average of 5.7% (Eurostat, 2014b).
- Forest (of which 80% is publicly owned) covers about 30% of the total land area, a proportion roughly on a par with the OECD average. It increased by 3% between 2000 and 2012. Good timber harvest management and afforestation have contributed to the growth in volume of standing wood (Chapter 4).
- Though removal has continuously increased over the last decade, it has remained lower than incremental growth. As a result, the intensity of use of forest resources (felling as a share of annual growth) declined to the current 55%, which is low compared to levels in other OECD countries (Chapter 4).
- Nearly all public forests are certified under the Forest Stewardship Council (FSC) system or the Programme for the Endorsement of Forest Certification. Poland ranks fifth in the world in terms of FSC-certified area (Chapter 4).
- The Białowieża Forest is the only primeval forest remaining in Europe. About two-thirds of the flora and fauna found in Poland are associated with forest environments. Programmes aimed at preserving forest gene resources have helped in increasing or maintaining populations of protected forest mammals. However, populations of some protected forest birds, such as black grouse, have significantly decreased (Figure 1.9, Chapter 4).

Protected areas

- Protected areas in IUCN categories I and II, i.e. strict nature reserves and wilderness areas, and national parks account for about 1% of the total area, below the OECD average of 4% (Figure 1.10). Areas which have less strict management requirements, such as protected landscape areas and landscape parks, represent the largest categories of areas protected under national law, which covered 32.5% of the territory in 2012 (CSO, 2013).
- Natura 2000 sites, established at EU level, include 145 Special Protected Areas for birds and 845 Sites of Community Importance for habitats in Poland. The network covers almost

Figure 1.9. **Population of protected forest mammals and forest birds, 2000-13**

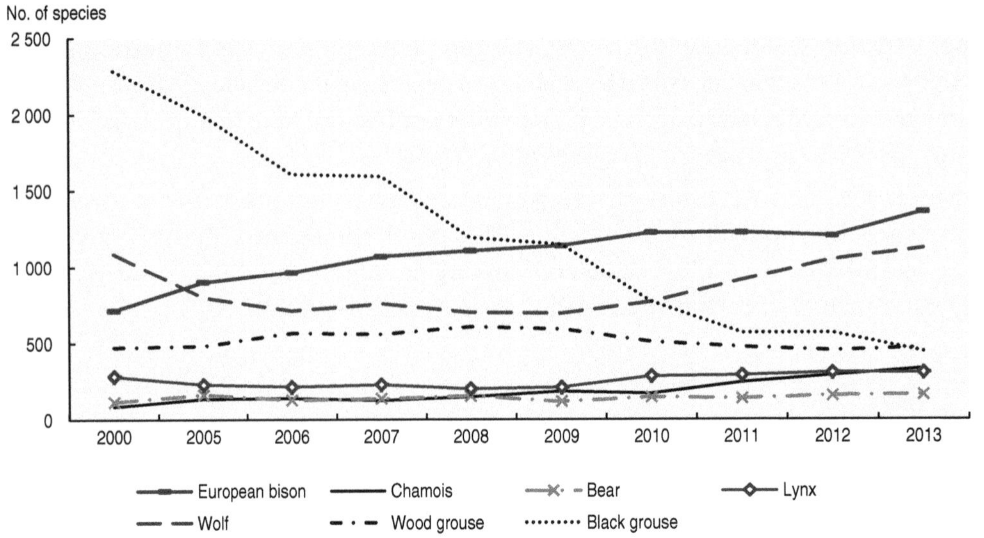

Source: CSO (2013), *Environment 2013.*

StatLink http://dx.doi.org/10.1787/888933197581

Figure 1.10. **Nature reserves and national parks, 2010**

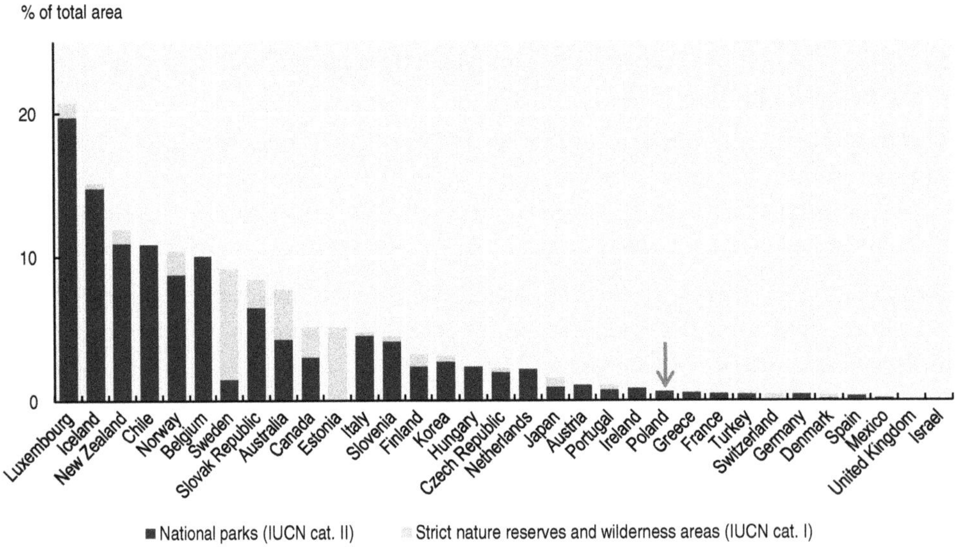

Source: OECD (2013), *Environment at a Glance 2013: OECD Indicators.*

StatLink http://dx.doi.org/10.1787/888933197597

20% of the territory and largely overlaps with the national protection system (Government of Poland, 2014).

- As of 2012, 10 areas had been recognised by the UNESCO Man and the Biosphere Programme, and 13 wetlands had been designated under the Convention on Wetlands of International Importance (Ramsar) (Government of Poland, 2014).
- Further effort will be required to achieve the Aichi targets of protecting 17% of terrestrial areas and 10% of marine areas by 2020. This will require implementation of management

plans and a significant increase in the number and size of areas under strict protection (Government of Poland, 2014).

Ecosystems and species

- Some 12% of mammals, 8% of birds and 11% of vascular plant species are threatened, which is lower than in many other OECD countries. However, the shares of freshwater fish and reptiles that are threatened are comparatively high (Figure 1.11) (Annex I.C).

Figure 1.11. **Threatened species of flora and fauna, late 2000s**

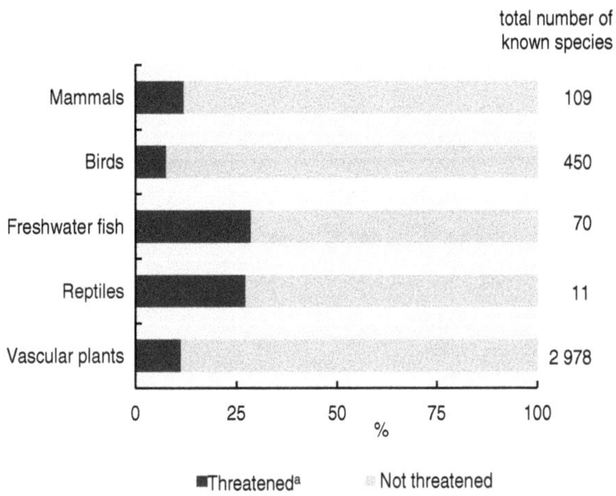

a) IUCN categories "critically endangered", "endangered" and "vulnerable" in % of known species.
Source: OECD (2014), *OECD Environment Statistics* (database).

StatLink http://dx.doi.org/10.1787/888933197604

- The conservation status of a large part of the natural habitats and plant and animal species is inadequate under the Natura 2000 programme. Heathlands were evaluated as the best preserved, while bogs and dunes were the types of natural habitats whose conservation status was assessed as the weakest (Government of Poland, 2014).
- Between 2000 and 2012, total fish production (mostly marine captures) declined by 9% due to the decommissioning programme after EU accession and the Fishing Effort Adjustment Plan adopted in 2010 (FAO, 2014; Eurofish, 2014). The fish processing sector (mainly imported fish) has become one of the largest in Europe. Fish farming is carried out in traditional land-based freshwater farms. Poland has the largest area of carp farms in Europe.

3.2. *Water resources*

- With about 1 600 m^3 available per capita annually, Poland is among the OECD countries with the most limited freshwater resources. As a result, although abstraction levels are relatively low, freshwater resources are under medium to high stress. Intensity of water use is about twice the OECD average (Annex I.C).
- Surface water from rivers and lakes meets nearly 80% of existing needs. Groundwater resources are mainly used for drinking water (public supply and self-supply of households).
- Freshwater is mostly used in industry, particularly for cooling in electricity production. Abstractions for public supply account for 18% of total water withdrawal (Figure 1.12).

Figure 1.12. **Freshwater resources and abstractions**

Decoupling, 2000-12 | Abstraction by main use, 2012

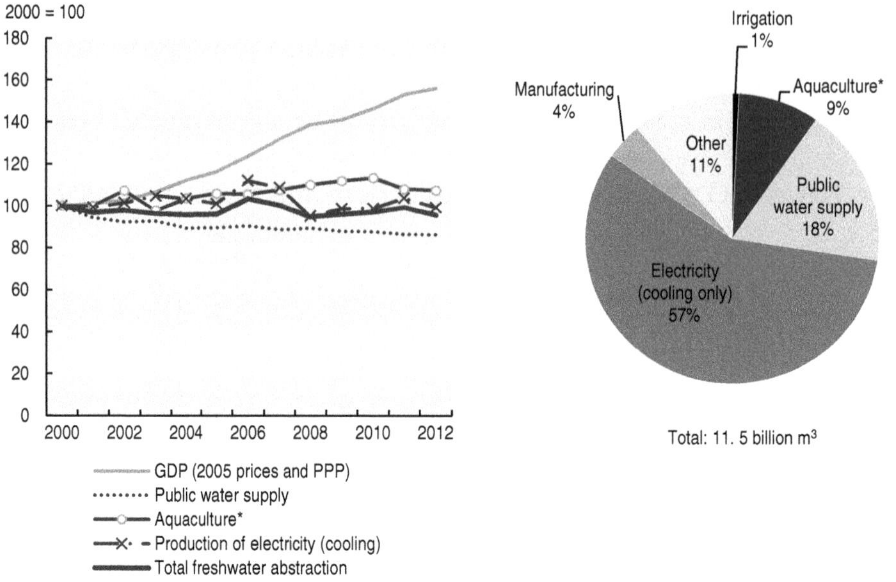

*Water abstraction for filling fishponds exceeding 10 ha.
Source: OECD (2014), *OECD Environment Statistics* (database).

StatLink http://dx.doi.org/10.1787/888933197611

- Between 2000 and 2012, total water withdrawal decreased by 4%. Water use for industry, irrigation, mining and public supply was further decoupled from economic growth, whereas abstractions for aquaculture increased (Figure 1.12). Industry modernisation, water metering, reduction of leakage and water pricing are among the factors explaining this progress.
- The longest Polish rivers are the Vistula and Odra, whose river basin districts cover almost 97% of the country. Both flow into the Baltic Sea (European Commission, 2012).
- Insufficient treatment of municipal and industrial sewage, saline water discharged from coal mines and pollution loads from diffuse agriculture are the main sources of water quality problems (Chief Inspectorate for Environmental Protection, 2010).
- Around 69% of river water bodies[7] fail to meet the "good ecological status" or "good ecological potential" required by the EU Water Framework Directive (Chief Inspectorate for Environmental Protection, 2014).
- In addition, 66% of natural lakes fail to meet the "good ecological status" and 55% of heavily modified or artificial lakes fail to meet the "good ecological potential" required by the WFD.
- In 2012, the chemical status of groundwater (classes I, II, III) was good at around 80% of the stations examined.
- Drinking water quality is generally good. Large water suppliers show high rates of compliance with the WFD microbiological and chemical parameters. As in other EU countries, small suppliers perform less well regarding compliance rates for microbiological parameters below 90% (European Commission, 2014).

- In 2008-11, about 43% of freshwater bodies with monitoring stations were classified as eutrophic or hypertrophic. Poland has one of the EU's highest proportions (86%) of eutrophic and hypertrophic lakes. In 2012, about 4.5% of the territory was designated as nitrate vulnerable zones under the Nitrates Directive. Measures to prevent and reduce nitrate pollution include spatial and temporal limitation of fertiliser application and increased manure storage capacity. Their effect on water quality has not yet been evaluated (European Commission, 2013b).
- Nitrate concentrations in freshwater bodies seem to have declined: in 2012, only 4% of groundwater stations exceeded 50 mg of nitrate per litre (compared with 14% in the EU over 2008-11), while 80% were below 10 mg per litre. In 2008-11, annual averages indicate that 69% of surface water monitoring stations were below 10 mg per litre (as against 63% in the EU), while 1% exceeded 50 mg per litre (compared with 2% in the EU) (Chief Inspectorate for Environmental Protection, 2014).
- Bathing waters (of which 40% are coastal and 60% inland) account for about 1% of total EU bathing waters. In 2013, all coastal bathing waters and 97% of inland bathing waters achieved the minimum quality standards established by the relevant EU directives (EEA, 2014a).

4. Improving the environmental quality of life

4.1. *Environment and well-being*

- In 2014, the majority of people surveyed viewed climate change as a threat and supported a 40% cut in GHG emissions by 2030; 88% were in favour of developing renewables to improve energy security (EurActiv, 2014).
- A 2013 survey by the Ministry of the Environment (MoE) indicated that only 11% of respondents considered environmental protection an important issue, a higher share than in previous surveys (MoE, 2013).
- More than half the people surveyed considered the state of the environment in their neighbourhood to be good (MoE, 2013). In another survey, 79% said they were satisfied with water quality, compared with the OECD average of 84% (OECD, 2012).
- Other surveys have shown increased awareness of waste management issues and concern about access to green spaces (MoE, 2013; OECD, 2012).

4.2. *Air emissions and air quality*

- Over the past decade, emissions of several air pollutants have been further decoupled from economic growth but to a much lesser extent than in the 1990s (Figure 1.13). Between 2000 and 2012, while GDP grew by 56%, emissions of SO_X decreased by 41%, NO_X by 3% and ammonia (NH_3) by 7% (Figure 1.13). Emissions of $PM_{2.5}$ and PM_{10} were unchanged. Emissions of non-methane volatile organic pollutants (NMVOC) increased by 10% and carbon monoxide (CO) by 6%.
- In 2012, SO_X emissions per unit of GDP were triple the OECD Europe average and NO_X emissions double (Annex I.C).
- Poland met the 2010 targets under the EU National Emission Ceilings (NEC) Directive. However, significant additional effort will be required to achieve the proposed 2020 emission reduction targets under the revised NEC Directive (Figure 1.13; European Commission, 2013c).

Figure 1.13. **Air pollutant emissions**

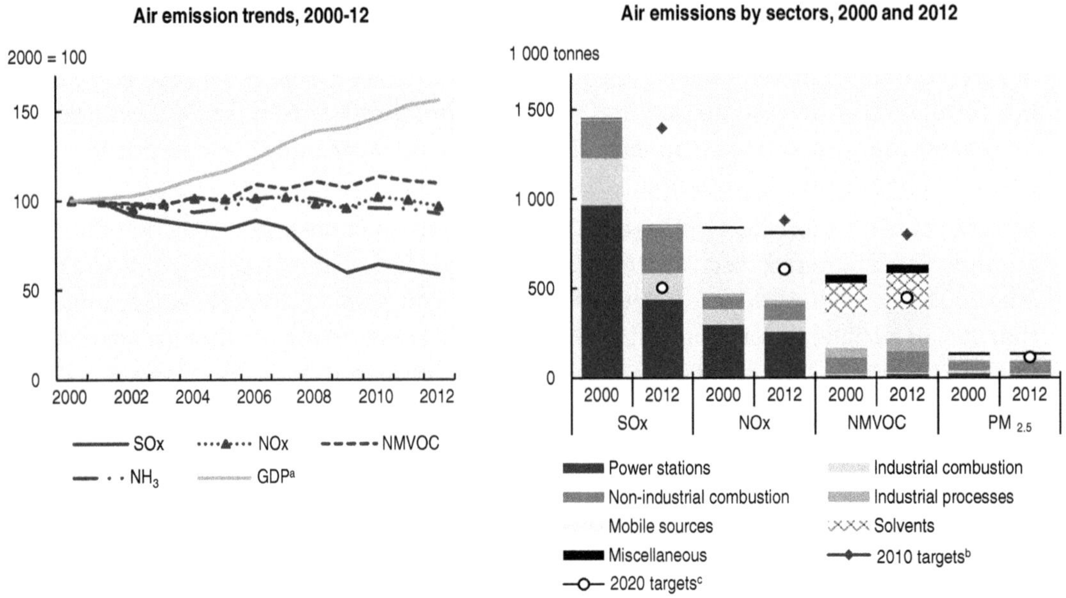

a) At 2005 prices and purchasing power parities.
b) Targets set by EU Directive 2001/81/EC (NEC Directive) on national emission ceilings for certain atmospheric pollutants.
c) Proposed targets under the revised NEC Directive.
Source: EMEP (2014), *WebDab* (database); OECD (2014), *OECD Economic Outlook No. 95 (database);* OECD (2014) *OECD Environment Statistics* (database).

StatLink http://dx.doi.org/10.1787/888933197627

- The main factors that have influenced trends since 2000 include implementation of EU air quality legislation after accession in 2004, the lower share of coal in TPES and increased use of desulphurisation equipment at power plants (Government of Poland, 2013).
- Power stations account for 51% of total SO_X emissions and non-industrial combustion (e.g. for residential heating) for 30%. Transport is the largest source of NO_X, accounting for 46% of total emissions, followed by power stations at 31% (Figure 1.13).
- In 2012, Poland recorded the highest level of average concentrations of $PM_{2.5}$ in Europe and exceeded recommended levels at a number of sites (EEA, 2014b). Small scale combustion of coal and biomass and concentrated local pollution (particularly in heating season) are the main factors in these compliance issues (European Commission, 2013d).
- Since 2000, there has been no clear progress in exposure levels to PM_{10} and concentrations exceed recommended levels in many urban areas (Figure 1.14). Full application of available end-of-pipe technical emission control measures at industrial plants will not be sufficient to achieve compliance without dedicated action to shift from solid fuels in the household sector to cleaner forms of energy (IIASA, 2012).
- Poland ranks low for several other air quality measures, such as concentrations of arsenic, mercury, benzene and benzo(a)pyrene (EEA, 2014b).
- Urban exposure to ozone air pollution has decreased by 32% since 2003, and Polish levels were lower than the EU average in the early 2010s (Figure 1.14).

Figure 1.14. **Population exposure to air pollution, 2000-12**

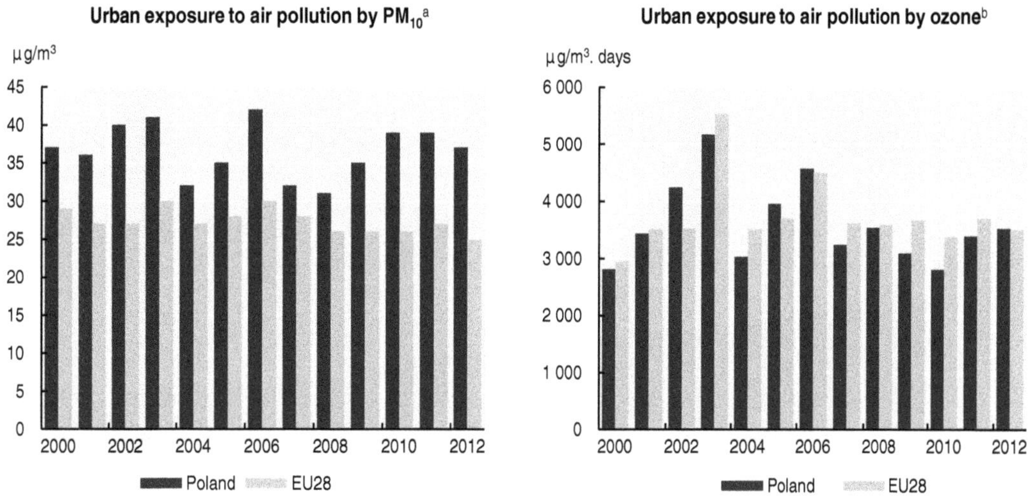

a) Population weighted annual mean concentrations of particulate matter at urban background stations in agglomerations.
b) Population weighted annual sum of maximum daily 8-hour average ozone concentrations greater than 70 µg/m³ at urban background stations in agglomerations.
Source: Eurostat (2014), *Environment Statistics* (database).

StatLink http://dx.doi.org/10.1787/888933197630

4.3. *Water supply and sanitation*

- The share of the population connected to the water supply network increased from 84.8% in 2002 to 87.9% in 2012, while connection to public sewerage improved from 56.7% to 64.3% (Chapter 3). However, there are wide variations between regions and between rural and urban areas (Table 1.1).
- Since 2002, the share of the population connected to public wastewater treatment plants has increased by 12 percentage points to reach 69%[8] in 2012, which has helped reduce pollution loads. More than 50% of the population is now connected to a wastewater treatment facility with tertiary treatment (Figure 1.15). Nevertheless, the connection rate for public wastewater treatment plants is well below the OECD average (Annex I.C).

4.4. *Health impacts*

- In 2010, Poland had one of the highest levels of mortality from ambient particulate matter and ozone pollution in the OECD (OECD, 2014d). About 25 000 deaths were attributable to outdoor air pollution, though the level has decreased in the second half of the last decade. Between 2005 and 2010, the economic cost of deaths from ambient air pollution increased[9] by 10% (compared with 7% in the OECD) to reach USD 53 billion.
- Polish power plants are among the EU's largest contributors to costs of damage to health and the environment from industrial air pollution (EEA, 2011).

4.5. *Exposure to chemicals*

- Emissions of metals have increased since 2000 (e.g. lead by some 5% and cadmium by about 8%). Mercury emissions are almost 5% lower than in 2000.
- Levels of polychlorinated biphenyls (PCBs)[10] in the muscle tissue of all species of fish except cod decreased until 2002-03, but in later years such reduction was no longer

Figure 1.15. **Population connected to wastewater treatment facilities, 2000-12**

Percentage share by type of treatment[a]

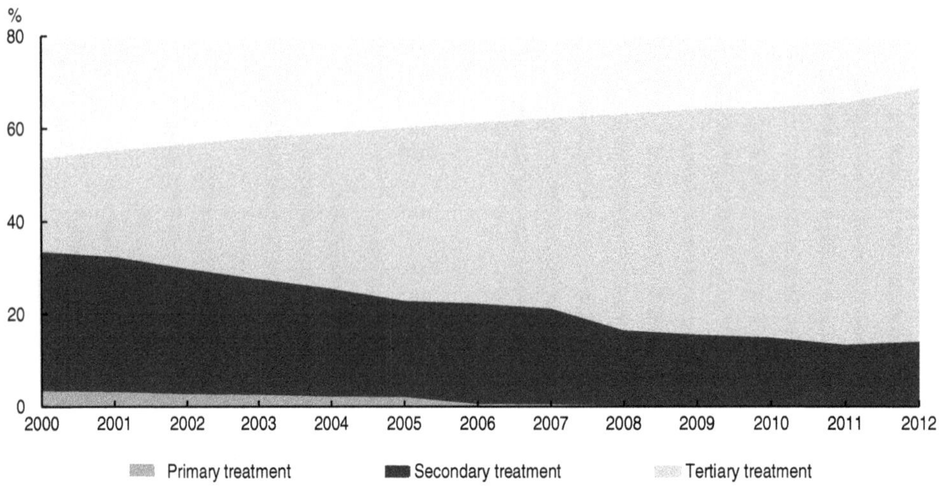

a) Data include population not connected by pipe (whose wastewater is transported from independent storage to urban wastewater treatment plants by means of trucks).
Source: OECD (2014), *OECD Environment Statistics* (database).

StatLink http://dx.doi.org/10.1787/888933197642

observed. However, a decline in the total content of PCBs has been noticeable in the case of salmon (Government of Poland, 2011).

- Among persistent organic pollutants,[11] only benzo(a)pyrene is monitored as a representative of polycyclic aromatic hydrocarbons (PAHs).[12] At most sites, average annual concentrations of benzo(a)pyrene exceeded the target level (EEA, 2014b).
- While an international study from Krakow showed links between prenatal exposure to PAHs and reduced birth weight, and suggested adverse effects on cognitive development (EEA, 2014b), other analyses in Poland are as yet inconclusive (Government of Poland, 2013).

Notes

1. In addition to its participation to the EU Emissions Trading System (ETS), Poland is required to limit the increase in GHG emissions not covered by the ETS to 14% by 2020 compared to 2005 levels.
2. To some extent this may be caused by incomplete deregistration, leading to an overestimation of the growth of the national fleet (Mehlhart et al., 2011).
3. DMC is the sum of domestic raw material extraction used by the economy and the physical trade balance (imports minus exports of raw materials and manufactured products).
4. Data inaccuracy may also contribute to this trend.
5. Data inaccuracy may be another contributing factor.
6. Break in time series due to a change in definition in the 2010 agricultural census (CSO, 2014). According to the previous definition, in 2009, agricultural land accounted for 53% of the total land area (excluding inland water).
7. Out of the 4 594 river water bodies designated, 36% are heavily modified or artificial.
8. Includes households not connected by pipe but whose wastewater is collected in septic tanks and delivered to urban wastewater treatment plants by truck.
9. Largely due to Poland's rapid rate of growth, which resulted in a higher Value of a Statistical Life (OECD, 2014d).

10. PCBs were synthetic chemicals first produced in the late 1920s. They were used as cooling fluids in electrical equipment and machinery because of their durability and resistance to fire. They are now banned.

11. Among these are PCBs, formerly used in transformer oil, benzo(a)pyrene, found in coal tar, and pesticides such as DDT, endrin, dieldrin, aldrin, chlordane, toxaphene, heptachlor, mirex and hexachlorobenzene.

12. PAHs are fused aromatic rings that do not contain heteroatoms or carry substituents; they occur in oil, coal and tar deposits, and as by-products of fuel burning.

References

Chief Inspectorate for Environmental Protection (2014), *State of the Environment Report 2014*, Chief Inspectorate for Environmental Protection, Warsaw.

Chief Inspectorate for Environmental Protection (2010), *The State of the Environment in Poland 2008*, Chief Inspectorate for Environmental Protection, Warsaw.

CSO (2014), *Agriculture in 2013*, Central Statistical Office, Warsaw.

CSO (2013), *Environment 2013*, Central Statistical Office, Warsaw.

EEA (2014a), *European bathing water quality in 2013*, European Environment Agency, Copenhagen.

EEA (2014b), *Air quality in Europe: 2014 Report*, European Environment Agency, Copenhagen.

EEA (2011), *Revealing the costs of air pollution from industrial facilities in Europe*, European Environment Agency, Copenhagen.

EMEP (2013), *WebDab* (database), European Monitoring and Evaluation Programme, *www.ceip.at/webdab-emission-database* (accessed April 2014).

EurActiv (2014), "Polish public swings behind EU climate plan", EurActiv, 19 March, *www.euractiv.com/energy/polish-public-swings-eu-climate-news-534245* (accessed April 2014).

Eurofish (2014), Overview of the Polish fisheries and aquaculture sector, Eurofish, Copenhagen, *www.eurofish.dk/index.php?option=com_content&view=article&id=120%3Apoland&catid=37&Itemid=27*.

European Commission (2014), *Report from the Commission, Synthesis Report on the Quality of Drinking Water in the EU examining the Member States' reports for the period 2008-2010 under Directive 98/83/EC*, COM(2014) 363 final, European Commission, Brussels.

European Commission (2013a), *Assessment of the 2013 National Reform Programme and Convergence Programme for Poland*, Commission Staff Working Document, SWD(2013) 371 Final, European Commission, Brussels.

European Commission (2013b), *Commission Staff Working Document, Accompanying the document: Report from the Commission to the Council and the European Parliament on the Implementation of Council Directive 91/676/EEC concerning the protection of waters against pollution caused by nitrates from agricultural sources based on Member State reports for the period 2008-2011*, {SWD(2013) 405 final}, COM(2013) 683 final, European Commission, Brussels.

European Commission (2013c), *Annexes to the Proposal for a Directive of the European Parliament and of the Council on the reduction of national emissions of certain atmospheric pollutants and amending Directive 2003/35/EC*, COM(2013) 920 final, European Commission, Brussels.

European Commission (2013d), *Commission Staff Working Document, Accompanying the documents: Communication from the Commission to the Council, the European Parliament, the European Economic and Social Committee and the Committee of the Regions – a Clean Air Programme for Europe, Proposal for a Directive of the European Parliament and of the Council on the limitation of emissions of certain pollutants into the air from medium combustion plants, Proposal for a Directive of the European Parliament and of the Council on the reduction of national emissions of certain atmospheric pollutants and amending Directive 2003/35/EC, Proposal for a Council Decision on the acceptance of the Amendment to the 1999 Protocol to the 1979 Convention on Long-Range Transboundary Air Pollution to Abate Acidification, Eutrophication and Ground-level Ozone*, {COM(2013)917} {COM(2013)918} {COM(2013)919} {COM(2013)920}{SWD(2013)532}, SWD(2013)531, European Commission, Brussels.

European Commission (2012), *Commission Staff Working Document, Member State: Poland, Accompanying the document: Report from the Commission to the European Parliament and the Council on the Implementation of the Water Framework Directive (2000/60/EC): River Basin Management Plans*, {COM(2012) 670 final}, SWD(2012) 379 final, European Commission, Brussels.

Eurostat (2014a), Database, *http://appsso.eurostat.ec.europa.eu/nui/show.do?dataset=aei_pr_gnb&lang=en* (accessed October 2014).

Eurostat (2014b), Database, *http://appsso.eurostat.ec.europa.eu/nui/show.do?dataset=food_in_porg1&lang=en* (accessed July 2014).

Eurostat (2013), *Energy, Transport and Environment Indicators,* Publications Office of the European Union, Luxemburg.

FAO (2014), FAOSTAT (database).

Government of Poland (2014), "Fifth National Report on the Implementation of the Convention on Biological Diversity", Warsaw, *www.cbd.int/doc/world/pl/pl-nr-05-en.pdf.*

Government of Poland (2013), "Answers to OECD Environmental Performance Review Questionnaire on Poland" (internal document).

Government of Poland (2011), *National Implementation Plan for the Stockholm Convention on Persistent Organic Pollutants for Poland 2011*, Warsaw.

IEA (2011), *Energy Policies of IEA Countries: Poland 2011*, OECD Publishing, Paris, *http://dx.doi.org/10.1787/9789264098190-en.*

IIASA (2012), *TSAP-2012 Baseline: Health and Environmental Impacts*, TSAP Report #6 Version 1.0, International Institute for Applied Systems Analysis, Laxenburg, *http://ec.europa.eu/environment/air/pdf/tsap_impacts.pdf.*

Mehlhart G. et al. (2011), *European second-hand car market analysis*, Darmstadt, *www.oeko.de/oekodoc/1114/2011-005-en.pdf.*

Ministry of Economy (2014a), Polish Nuclear Power Programme, Warsaw, *www.pgeej1.pl/english/files/154140128_MG_PPEJ.pdf.*

Ministry of Economy (2014b), *Interim Report on progress in the promotion and use of energy from renewable sources in Poland in 2011-2012*, Warsaw, *http://ec.europa.eu/energy/renewables/reports/doc/2013_article_22_progress_reports_inenglish_language.zip.*

MoE (2013), *Badanie świadomości izachowań ekologicznych mieszkańców Polski – Badanie trackingowe–pomiar: październik 2013* [The study of ecological awareness and behaviour of the Polish population – Measurement tracking study: October 2013], Ministry of the Environment, Sopot, Poland.

MoE (2010), *2014 National Waste Management Plan*, Ministry of the Environment, Warsaw, *www.mos.gov.pl/g2/big/2013_11/2328f96819e9bda79bf26d0e00728080.doc.*

MoE (2006), *2010 National Waste Management Plan*, Ministry of the Environment, Warsaw, *www.mos.gov.pl/g2/big/2009_06/e97e2a07ce29b48c19f462f83a6bf1a9.pdf.*

OECD (2014a), *OECD Economic Outlook*, Vol. 2014/1, OECD Publishing, Paris, *http://dx.doi.org/10.1787/eco_outlook-v2014-1-en.*

OECD (2014b), *OECD Economic Surveys: Poland 2014*, OECD Publishing, Paris. *http://dx.doi.org/10.1787/eco_surveys-pol-2014-en.*

OECD (2014c), *OECD Factbook 2014: Economic, Environmental and Social Statistics*, OECD Publishing, Paris, *http://dx.doi.org/10.1787/factbook-2014-en.*

OECD (2014d), *The Cost of Air Pollution: Health Impacts of Road Transport*, OECD Publishing, Paris, *http://dx.doi.org/10.1787/9789264210448-en.*

OECD (2013a), *Environment at a Glance 2013: OECD Indicators*, OECD Publishing, Paris, *http://dx.doi.org/10.1787/9789264185715-en.*

OECD (2013b), *Revenue Statistics 2013*, OECD Publishing, Paris, *http://dx.doi.org/10.1787/rev_stats-2013-en-fr.*

OECD (2013c), *OECD Compendium of Agri-environmental Indicators*, OECD Publishing, Paris, *http://dx.doi.org/10.1787/9789264186217-en.*

OECD (2013d), "Briefing note Poland", *OECD Health Data 2013* (database), *www.oecd.org/health/healthdata* (accessed April 2014).

OECD (2012), *OECD Better Life Index*, OECD Publishing, Paris, *www.oecdbetterlifeindex.org.*

OECD (2011), *Towards Green Growth: Monitoring Progress: OECD Indicators*, OECD Green Growth Studies, OECD Publishing, Paris, *http://dx.doi.org/10.1787/9789264111356-en.*

OECD (2003), *OECD Environmental Performance Reviews: Poland 2003*, OECD Publishing, Paris, *http://dx.doi.org/10.1787/9789264100961-en*.

WHO (2009), *Country Profiles of Environmental Burden of Disease: Poland*, World Health Organization, Geneva.

WHO (2007), *Country Profiles of Environmental Burden of Disease: Poland*, World Health Organization, Geneva.

World Bank (2011), *Transition to a Low-Emissions Economy in Poland*, Poverty Reduction and Economic Management Unit, Europe and Central Asia Region, World Bank, Washington DC.

PART I

Chapter 2

Policy-making environment

Poland's new strategic framework provides opportunities and risks for promoting more coherence between environmental and other policies. This chapter analyses the Polish environmental governance system, including mechanisms for horizontal and vertical co-ordination. It reviews the regulatory framework for environmental management, including for environmental impact assessment and permitting, as well as enforcement and compliance assurance activities. The promotion of environmental democracy through access to information and public participation in decision making is also discussed.

Assessment and recommendations

From the early 1990s to 2012, Poland's environmental planning framework was grounded in a rolling series of National Environmental Policies (NEPs). Each four-year NEP was approved by the Council of Ministers and the Parliament, providing political support and a mandate for the environment ministry to oversee implementation. Progress reports were regularly presented to the Parliament. In 2009, Poland's approach to development planning was changed: it is now structured around three overarching development strategies and nine strategic policies. Environment was integrated into one of the nine strategic policies, Energy Security and the Environment. This strategy is overseen by the Ministry of Economy in co-operation with the Ministry of the Environment (MoE). From an environmental perspective, the new framework provides opportunities to integrate environment into the government's overall development strategy. However, there is a risk that the strong mandate and focus on environmental issues provided by the NEPs could be lost unless effective mechanisms are put in place to co-ordinate, monitor and adjust environmental policies.

Since Poland's accession to the EU in 2004, its environmental laws and policies have been largely driven by EU environmental law. Transposing the EU environmental directives was a major challenge, and the number of infringements increased between 2006 and 2010. Over time, the number of infringement cases concerning delays in transposing EU legislation was overtaken by cases related to non-compliance with EU requirements. Water and waste management are the areas where the most infringement procedures are pending. Although the 2001 Environmental Protection Law provided a framework for environmental legislation, transposition of EU directives has resulted in another 20 environmental laws and about 100 regulations. Efforts have been made to streamline this body of law and to reduce the associated administrative burden, but there are further opportunities for simplification and consolidation.

Environmental policy implementation is largely the responsibility of subnational authorities. In 1999, Poland's subnational governance structure was significantly reformed. The number of regions was reduced from 49 to 16, and regional governments were directly elected, though there would still be a representative of the national authorities in each region. The elected regional representatives are now responsible for regulatory matters such as permitting, while regional inspectorates (part of the regional representation of the national authorities) are responsible for environmental enforcement. Regional directorates that are subordinate to the MoE are responsible for environmental impact assessment (EIA) and Natura 2000; the latter responsibility is shared with State Forests. In principle the division of labour is clear, but in practice co-ordination is a challenge. The situation is further complicated by arrangements in the water sector, where there are seven Regional Water Management Boards, yet two river basins account for 97% of the national territory. In addition, the 380 counties and 2 479 municipalities have environmental responsibilities. The need to simplify and streamline the environmental governance system, including enforcement, has been recognised for some time. To this end, specific goals and measures have been included in the cross-cutting Efficient State Strategy.

Since the early 1990s, the Inspectorate for Environmental Protection has supported the development of an effective environmental monitoring system, which has been further strengthened over the last decade. In most areas, it provides solid support for environmental authorities at the different levels of government to develop and implement environmental policies, though data quality and quantity vary among environmental areas. Data on waste, which is collected by municipalities under MoE supervision, are particularly weak. There is very limited capacity for economic analysis, and environmental policy has generally not been informed by economic evaluation.

EU structural and cohesion funds have provided substantial support for the implementation of environmental policies. In 2008, the General Directorate for Environmental Protection was established under the MoE to streamline procedures and thereby facilitate the disbursement of EU funds. This and the 2008 EIA Act helped reduce the time for issuing EIA decisions from 300 to 100 days. However, opportunities exist to further improve and harmonise the methodology for conducting EIA, and to make the process more transparent by facilitating public participation at all stages of the process.

Although the EU Strategic Environmental Assessment (SEA) Directive was transposed into law in 2008, SEAs were undertaken over 2000-08, including for all operational programmes using EU structural and cohesion funds at the national and regional levels. There is evidence that SEA helped to make the development of some policies and programmes more transparent and to facilitate inputs from stakeholders. However, as in many countries, applying approaches that strike a good balance between efficient procedures and adequate participation has been difficult.

The Supreme Audit Office, which reports to the lower chamber of the Parliament, has played a useful role in *ex post* policy evaluation. In 2010-14, it carried out 22 audits of national and regional programmes related to environment. Reports prepared by the Supreme Audit Office include evaluations of the way financial resources are managed and proposals for administrative or legal changes to improve performance and accountability. Wide coverage of the reports in the media has helped increase their influence.

Poland has established an effective environmental regulatory system. Legal requirements for integrated environmental permits were established in advance of EU accession, and extensive support was provided to implementing agencies and industry. Currently, 99% of the 3 269 installations that require an integrated permit have received one. Requirements for small and medium-sized enterprises are tailored to their environmental impact. Compliance is monitored by regional inspectorates in a consistent way according to multiyear plans and detailed, risk-based methodologies developed and recently upgraded by the Chief Inspectorate. This has enabled efficient use of inspectorate resources and helped reduce compliance costs. A comprehensive set of non-compliance response instruments has been applied and appears to have been effective, though there is no information on the results.

In 2002, Poland was one of the first countries to ratify the Aarhus Convention. A dedicated environmental portal has become the main vehicle for providing a wide range of information concerning policies, the state of the environment and environmental requirements in investment processes, as well as links to environment-related databases and registers. A variety of institutions are involved in providing information, including at the local level. Nevertheless, there is scope to improve the administration's response to citizens' requests for environmental information. Environmental non-government organisations (NGOs) have made good use of mechanisms for public participation and have influenced decision making. However, there are still cases where opportunities for participation have been limited. Environmental organisations generally enjoy wider standing to appeal decisions than NGOs working in other policy sectors, yet very few cases have been brought before civil courts, perhaps because of difficulties in establishing the right to represent the public good. There have been cases where individuals have used access to environmental justice to block projects in order to secure financial gain upon withdrawing their objection. This has resulted in criticism of the environmental movement in some sections of Polish society.

Recommendations

- Put in place mechanisms to co-ordinate, monitor and adjust environmental policies in the context of the Energy Security and the Environment Strategy and the Mid-term National Development Strategy (e.g. establish an environmental subcommittee of the Co-ordinating Committee for Development Policy chaired by the environment minister; include an environment chapter in the annual reports on implementation of the Mid-term National Development Strategy).
- Carry out an independent review of environmental institutions at the different levels of government, including their funding, with a view to clarifying responsibilities, reducing complexity and enhancing their efficiency and effectiveness.
- Strengthen capacity for conducting *ex ante* and *ex post* economic analysis of environmental policies; strengthen co-operation with research institutions to this end.
- Strengthen EIA procedures by further standardising requirements, facilitating public participation at all stages of the process and ensuring that adequate consideration is given to alternatives; more closely link EIA and environmental permitting for large installations.
- Reinforce efforts to integrate SEA findings into the design of policies and programmes at national and local level, including by disseminating guidance and information on good practices.
- Further strengthen environmental compliance promotion by upgrading the supporting monitoring and analytical equipment; further strengthening co-operation between the national and regional inspectorates; developing indicators to monitor the results of compliance promotion activities; and strengthening communication with the public.

1. Environmental policy and regulatory framework

1.1. *Environmental planning at the national level*

Following good progress in implementing Poland's pioneering first National Environmental Policy (NEP, 1991), the framework for environmental policy planning for the first decade of the 21st century was set in the 2001 Environmental Protection Law. It required preparation of an NEP every four years. It also required each new NEP to be based on a review of progress on implementation of previous ones and to include longer-term outlooks. The second NEP, adopted in 2001, and the third, for 2003-06 (with outlook to 2010), met these requirements, providing an important basis for Poland's EU membership in 2004.

In 2006, the Council of Ministers submitted to the Sejm (Parliament) a draft NEP for 2007-10 (outlook to 2014). A shortened parliamentary term meant its adoption was postponed until 2008, when an NEP for 2009-12 (outlook to 2016) updated the main strategic directions and set new objectives, in many cases reflecting EU priorities. The 2009-12 NEP was constructed around two themes: i) protection of natural resources, covering nature protection, sustainable forestry, rational use of water resources, soil protection and sound management of geological resources; and ii) improving the state of the environment and environmental security, covering health and environment, air and water quality, waste management, noise and electromagnetic fields, and chemicals in the environment.

The NEPs were the principal documents providing the strategic environmental planning framework for most components of the environment. In some cases, NEP provisions were supported by separate plans identifying key problems in specific areas and setting policy objectives, targets and actions. Examples include a series of waste management plans,[1] the National Biodiversity Strategy 2007-13, the National Biodiversity Action Programme 2007-13, the 2010 National Water and Environmental Programme[2] and the 2013 National Adaptation Strategy.

In the area of climate change, planning efforts have not yielded the expected results. A climate change mitigation strategy, "Climate Policy of Poland: Strategy to Reduce Greenhouse Gas Emissions in Poland until 2020", was developed by the environment ministry in 2003 and adopted by the Council of Ministers. However, it has not been amended since Poland's accession to the EU introduced new targets related to climate change. In 2011, Poland started work on a National Programme for the Development of a Low-Emission Economy, which seeks to support low-emission technology to promote growth and competitiveness. It is expected to be completed in 2015.

Since 2007, the planning process has been supported by the Operational Programme Infrastructure and Environment (OPIE), which guides the use of EU financing from cohesion funds and the European Regional Development Fund, and matching national funds. OPIE includes objectives stemming from EU membership and the National Strategic Reference Framework.[3] Under OPIE 2007-13, which was the biggest operational programme in EU history, EUR 6.1 billion was allocated for environment (including water management). For 2014-20, under the new OPIE, EUR 4.5 billion is allocated for environmental protection and EUR 1.8 billion for a low-emission economy (Chapter 3).

In 2009, the government adopted Principles of the National Development Management System, a document drafted by the Ministry of Regional Development[4] in co-operation with the Office of the Prime Minister and Strategic Advisory Group of the Prime Minister. It envisaged a significant reform of the national development programming model. The model includes three overarching development strategies: a long-term one to 2030, a medium-term one to 2020 and the National Spatial Development Concept to 2030. These are to be supplemented by a limited number of national policies. Also in 2009, the government adopted a plan for streamlining development strategies, which restricted the number of strategic policy documents to nine. One was Energy Security and the Environment (ESE), drafted by the Ministry of Economy in co-operation with the Ministry of the Environment (MoE).

The other eight integrated strategies[5] had been adopted by the end of 2013, but the ESE was not adopted until April 2014. Its main objective is "to create conditions for the development of a competitive and efficient energy sector while respecting the principles of sustainable development and respect for the environment". The ESE outlines directions for developing the energy sector and ensuring energy security. The energy-related sections include several references to climate change mitigation and adaptation measures. The environmental part indicates priorities related to water, air and waste management, eco-innovation, environmental awareness raising and employment impacts.

Limiting the number of national planning documents is a step in the right direction, as it provides a good basis for better integration of strategic planning and opens up possibilities for better consideration of trade-offs between sectoral policies and for the adoption of win-win approaches. The new approach is also expected to result in more explicit and specific targets, which should strengthen environmental planning: the NEPs have often been criticised as too general and declarative, and lacking clear, quantitative and measurable targets. Several past strategies and policy documents in key areas lacked adequate cost-benefit analysis and review of the cost of inaction. Only limited studies of pollution's impact on human health and ecosystems have been carried out and taken into account in prioritising policy responses. The reform of the planning system aims to increase efficiency in programming and implementation and provides opportunities and risks regarding the integration of a green element into other strategies. However, it will require intensified monitoring of results and reporting on progress. Regular assessment should also offer opportunities to apply more explicit cost-benefit analysis of objectives and to identify trade-offs between policy measures. A strong, well-defined institutional framework for carrying out such assessment is also required, and has yet to be agreed.

1.2. Planning at subnational level

All subnational levels of government have been required to adopt their own environmental protection plans in line with NEP objectives.[6] These regional and local planning documents identify priorities, specific goals, the types of environmental investment required to achieve the goals, a timetable, and financing. In some areas, such as waste, regional (voivodship) management plans have been prepared in accordance with each NEP. Originally the planning cycle had a complex, cascading system on four levels, with plans from counties (powiats) and municipalities (gminas) having to be consistent with the those of the level above, and reporting in the opposite direction, from lower to higher levels. As this system proved complicated to co-ordinate, the most recent cycle takes a two-level approach. The change was driven by the need to better integrate planning with the OPIE and the 16 voivodship operational programmes.

Since 2003, air pollution prevention programmes have been prepared for areas where concentrations of air pollutants, mostly PM_{10} but also $PM_{2.5}$, benzo(a)pyrene and heavy metals, exceed allowable levels. Initially, 161 zones out of 362 were identified for such programmes but only 26 required them by 2007. In 2010, the overall number of zones was reduced to 46, most of which were required to prepare programmes. The self-government authorities (marshals' offices) at the voivodship level are responsible for preparing and implementing these programmes, which target low emission sources (individual household stoves and local heating boilers) and the transport sector.

Poland has ten river basin districts, although those of the Vistula and Odra, the longest Polish rivers, cover almost 97% of the country. In compliance with the EU Water Framework Directive (WFD), management plans were developed and adopted for all river basins in 2011. The scope and structure were the same for all river basin areas but those for the Vistula and Odra were more detailed, due to the higher number of users and the intensity of pressures. Under Polish law, there are instances where the plans are binding on other planning acts or individual decisions, notably national, regional and local land use plans, regional development plans, water law permits and decisions on environmental impact assessment (EIA).

One policy area where limited progress has been made is spatial planning at subnational levels. Despite the 2003 Spatial Planning Act, a comprehensive approach to land use planning across the country is still needed. The law requires local authorities to make studies of conditions and directions for local land use management, and most municipalities have done so, but the studies have no binding force. Many are outdated and do not reflect current development status. For example, they do not include constraints related to nature reserves and protected landscape areas (Chapter 4). The 2003 law provides for local authorities to adopt binding local land use plans, but only 28% of the land was covered by these plans in 2012, mostly due to unresolved ownership claims and planning costs (Śleszyński et al., 2014). Without such plans, landowners can develop their property as they like. For residential development on greenfield locations, just three conditions must be fulfilled for the local authority to allow the land use change: i) at least one adjacent plot has to have housing on it (the definition of "adjacent" is unclear); ii) the land must be accessible by public road; and iii) existing infrastructure must be sufficient for the project. The result has been spatial chaos and, in many cases, degradation of protected areas. A 2014 evaluation by the Supreme Audit Office (NIK) (Section 3) requested mayors and other municipal leaders to intensify work on local land use plans and make sure land use studies and local plans comply with the Spatial Planning Act and the Environmental Protection Law. The NIK also called for county construction inspectors to respond effectively in cases of non-compliance.

1.3. *Regulatory framework*

Poland is a unitary state, so all legal acts, including statutes adopted by the Sejm, executive regulations delegated to the Council of Ministers or relevant ministers, and ratified international agreements, are legally binding for the entire territory. The Constitution envisages local laws as well, binding only for a specific administrative unit. They can be adopted by administrative bodies at regional, county or municipal level, but must comply with national legislation.

The 2001 Environmental Protection Law, also called the Environmental Code, set out general principles of environmental protection policy, including the polluter-pays and precautionary principles; regulated specific environmental media; provided for policy instruments such as environmental permitting, the use of fees for environmental purposes and fines for non-compliance; outlined the functioning of environmental funds; and provided requirements for installations which are subject to industrial accident prevention systems. The law was supported by separate laws on key aspects of environmental policy, such as the 2001 Water Law, the 2001 Waste Act and the 2004 Nature Conservation Act.

The need to harmonise Polish and EU legislation, reinforced by the rapid development of new EU requirements, stimulated sector- and media-specific legal initiatives. The number of acts covering specific topics grew: the Sejm has now passed about 20 laws dealing exclusively with environmental issues, and the government has adopted about 100 executive regulations in this area. For example, the 2012 Waste Act is accompanied by eight statutes (in addition to the Environmental Protection Law) regulating various aspects of waste management.

Most of these instruments aimed to harmonise the legal framework with the substantial body of EU law predating Poland's EU accession. Although significant progress was made, the harmonisation process faced delays and some framework laws were not accompanied by implementing legislation. As a result, the number of infringements of EU environmental law rose from 10 in 2006 to 26 in 2010. Over time, the number of infringement cases related to transposition of EU legislation was overtaken by cases related to non-compliance with EU law. Examples of the latter concerned proper disposal of end-of-life vehicles, nitrate water pollution and the environmental impact of projects in Natura 2000 areas. Overall, Poland had the third highest number of environment-related infringements among EU countries in 2013 and fourth highest in 2012. However, in 2013 only two of the cases involved European Court of Justice rulings of failure to fulfil an obligation under EU law.

In light of the number of environmental regulations that had to be transposed into Polish law before or soon after accession, the progress achieved is impressive. Most of the infringement issues were related to new EU requirements. The MoE attaches special importance to addressing non-compliance cases despite significant constraints regarding technical and human capacity. The areas of water and waste management need particular attention.

At the same time, the increasing number of laws and regulations over the past decade has led to growing complexity in the legal system overall, and with regard to the environment in particular. Like many other OECD countries, Poland has launched initiatives aimed at simplifying the legislative framework, particularly as regards legislation that creates major obstacles to growth of entrepreneurship. A programme to this effect begun in 2010 was followed by measures both to improve lawmaking procedures and to improve and simplify existing legislation. A central participant in this process is the Government Legislation Centre (RCL), under the authority of the prime minister, which co-ordinates government legislative activity, provides legal advice to the Council of Ministers, prepares government bills and advises on parliamentary bills.[7] In addition, an interdepartmental group reviewing the impact of environmental legislation was recently established in the MoE.

2. Institutional and co-ordination framework

2.1. Key environmental institutions

National level

The national institutional framework for environmental management did not change over most of the review period. The MoE has primary responsibility for drawing up national policies, preparing legislation, including environmental standards, and monitoring policy implementation in almost all environmental areas, including air, waste, water and nature conservation, except as regards land use planning, most product controls and marine pollution. The portfolio also includes water administration, based on river basins, and policy making regarding forest and mineral resource management, including exploration and exploitation licences. The MoE co-ordinates the development of environmental policies within the government and supports their implementation at subnational levels.

The MoE oversees five central administrative authorities: the Chief Environmental Protection Inspectorate (GIOS), the Water Management Authority,[8] the Mining Authority,[9] the Atomic Energy Agency[10] and the General Directorate for Environmental Protection (GDEP). It is also responsible for two specialised organisations: the National Fund for Environmental

Protection and Water Management (NFEPWM) and State Forests, better known as Lasy Państwowe (LP). Finally, the MoE oversees the operations of the 23 national parks.

All these institutions play important roles in supporting implementation of environmental policies, but two have particular multilevel functions. The NFEPWM, together with 16 funds at the regional level, is the main instrument for financing environmental expenditure (Chapter 3). These funds draw their resources from pollution and user charges and taxes, along with the EU funds allocated in OPIE 2007-13. The national fund redistributes the money in the form of preferential loans and grants to municipalities, public utility companies, businesses and households. It also supports investment identified as NEP priorities.

The other key multilevel institution is the Inspectorate for Environmental Protection (IOS), which operates the national environmental monitoring system (e.g. carrying out measurements and preparing assessments of state of the environment, establishing reference laboratories, certifying methodology and measures), monitors compliance of the largest and most hazardous industrial facilities and regulates transboundary movements of waste. It consists of the Chief Inspectorate (GIOS) in Warsaw and 16 voivodship (regional) inspectorates (WIOSes), with 34 branch offices under the latter.[11]

In 2008, the environmental administration was restructured by the creation of the GDEP, with headquarters in Warsaw and 16 regional directorates (RDEPs). The GDEP's main tasks are managing EIA and strategic environmental assessment (SEA) and overseeing the Natura 2000 network.[12] Its establishment was an important factor in accelerating EIA of investment projects, especially infrastructure projects supported by EU funds. The allocation of dedicated staff and adoption of the EIA Act resulted in reduction of the time required to complete EIAs by as much as two-thirds. Making the GDEP the focal point on the Natura 2000 network brought its management closer to investment decision making. The RDEPs are independent from the regional administration (unlike the WIOSes), reporting to the GDEP, which provides autonomy and independence in decision making. However, creating the GDEP as an addition to existing environmental structures, such as the regional inspectorates and marshal's offices, has contributed to institutional complexity at the regional level. An in-depth review of environmental management responsibilities, especially at the regional level, has been launched but no results have been published. Completing and openly discussing the review could allow better calibration of relations between administrative units so as to simplify procedures, reduce administrative burdens and cut costs.

Subnational level

The subnational administrative governance system was subject to significant reforms in 1999. The number of regions was reduced from 49 to 16, and self-government structures were introduced (Box 2.1). The reform aimed to decentralise policy and decision making and improve the functioning of subnational government. The 2001 Environmental Protection Law reinforced the decentralisation of environmental responsibilities and outlined the powers at each level with respect to regulation, monitoring, inspection and enforcement.

Poland's accession to the EU in 2004 and related increased environmental requirements brought significant challenges to the functioning of the environmental protection system at subnational levels. The growing scope of duties, including planning, controlling and reporting obligations, imposed by the national level had to be reconciled with the

Box 2.1. **Poland's multilevel governance**

16 regions (voivodships)

Administration in each voivodship is shared by a governor (voivod), appointed by the central government, and a self-government structure consisting of a regional assembly (Sejmik), directly elected for a four year term, and, as the executive, a marshal elected by the Sejmik.

The voivod's office oversees the self-government bodies and makes sure national laws are observed and central government policies implemented. The self-government structure is responsible for regional economic development, higher education, hospitals and the labour market. The voivodships manage large scale regional and intermunicipal infrastructure, including waste management facilities through a permitting system. Although they have relatively limited responsibility for providing public services (mainly higher education and transport), their strategic role is important owing to the elaboration of regional development strategies and the management of EU funding.

380 counties (powiats)

Each voivodship is divided into smaller entities called powiats. The number of powiats per voivodship ranges from 12 in Opolskie to 42 in Mazowieckie. Local government authority is wielded by a council, directly elected for a four year term. The executive, chosen by the council, is called the starosta. In the 66 city-counties, the municipal council and executive carry out these functions.

Powiat self-government, essentially funded by the central government, executes programmes and service delivery that municipalities cannot carry out individually. Their main responsibilities include secondary schools, public health services, social welfare, culture, architecture and construction, and public safety. Powiats also manage most multi-municipality infrastructure, including collective transport, roads, water supply, wastewater and waste collection and small waste management facilities through a permitting system.

2 479 municipalities (gminas)

Municipalities, called gminas, are administrative units within counties. There are between 3 and 19 per county, aside from the city-counties, which each constitute a single gmina. A gmina may be classed as urban (consisting of a town or city), urban-rural (a town and its surrounding villages and countryside) or rural (not containing a town). A municipality has a directly elected council and executive. The executive is an administrator in rural municipalities, a mayor in urban-rural municipalities or a president in large urban municipalities.

Gminas bear the main responsibility for local development, including spatial planning, real property management, housing, social services, education and environmental protection. The urban and urban-rural gminas also manage infrastructure, including roads, water supply, wastewater and, since 2013, municipal waste collection and treatment (Chapter 5).

principles of self-governance and public participation in decision making. All these factors increased the system's complexity and need for effective co-operation, both horizontally and vertically.

The division of tasks between the gminas, powiats and voivodships is generally clear. Powiat and gmina self-government authorities issue development consents and pollution permits, including integrated pollution prevention and control permits for installations clearly assigned to various levels on the basis of their size. Voivodship environmental protection inspectorates handle routine inspections of large polluters, while powiats are responsible for inspecting small and medium-sized installations. Gminas are responsible for municipal waste management, but voivodships deal with large generators of waste, and powiats handle small and medium-sized waste generators, in both cases through a permitting system. Spatial planning and land development are carried out at the voivodship level, while gminas are in charge of local spatial development plans. Any disputes concerning the division of responsibilities between local and regional authorities and the central government are settled by administrative courts.

A key change in the functional organisation and division of competences came in 2008, when the voivodship marshal and assembly took over most of the voivod's responsibilities related to environmental protection, and the GDEP and RDEPs were created. The marshals now set environmental policies and are in charge of regional land use planning. They also acquired regulatory powers for individual matters, such as issuing environmental permits and collecting environmental fees and taxes. Although the marshals' environmental responsibilities are closely linked with the operation of the regional environmental protection inspectorates and directorates, the mechanisms for information exchange and co-ordination seem insufficient, as in cases of issuing environmental permits.

Institutional arrangements are particularly complicated in the water sector. At the national level the main authority is the National Water Management Authority, which is responsible for the co-ordination and preparation of river basin management plans. At the regional level, although the basins of two rivers account for 97% of the territory, there are seven Regional Water Management Boards, which are responsible for water management in their respective regions, including identification of significant pressures and assessment of their impact on the status of surface waters and groundwater, along with analysis, including economic and water use, preparation and maintenance of lists of protected areas, development of flood plans and co-ordination of flood protection activities. In addition, other institutions play an important role in water management, including the GIOS in water monitoring, voivodship and powiat authorities in water licensing and water infrastructure development, and powiat authorities for land improvement and water facilities. Discussions about clarifying and streamlining the institutional arrangements have been going on for some time but to date no decision has been reached.

Gminas have far-reaching responsibilities for setting their own development policy. The strongest instrument they have is the local land use plan, which is legally binding. Gminas also decide the direction of the policy for local development, e.g. by designating areas for certain purposes. Authorities at gmina level issue EIA decisions as well. These are the first, mandatory part of multistage decision making (development consent) for projects subject to compliance under the EU EIA Directive (2011/92/EU), for which an EIA decision is issued at the gmina level. In issuing these decisions, gminas must consult their RDEP.

Decentralisation of competences has not been followed by fiscal decentralisation on a comparable scale, however, so the regions are dependent on central government subsidies to implement programming not supported by EU funding.[13] Although regional and local government units have a limited right to set taxes and levies, all three subnational levels complain that increased competences and requirements stemming from EU regulations have not been matched by the provision of sufficient funds to carry out their duties.

2.2. Horizontal and vertical co-ordination

Government policies and regulations are developed through consultative frameworks, including formal interagency consultations of draft documents and dialogue with stakeholders. All NEP drafts, developed by the MoE, have been subject to extensive commenting by other ministries. Each NEP was approved by the Council of Ministers and the Sejm. All policy documents are also subject to consultation within the Interministerial Group for Programmes and Implementation of Structural and Cohesion Funds and by the Committee for European Affairs, which co-ordinates the government's work in matters related to Poland's EU membership.

Only in a limited number of cases has the development of environmentally related cross-cutting policies been entrusted to dedicated interministerial co-ordination bodies. The most recent examples include the establishment of the Interministrial Committee for the Implementation of the Energy Policy 2030 and the appointment of government plenipotentiaries to co-ordinate the development of policies on climate change and hydrocarbon extraction, both in 2010. At the working level, interministrial co-operation is sometimes carried out through topic-specific steering committees and working groups, which in most cases co-ordinate implementation of EU directives. For example, an extensive network of working groups and technical committees has been established on the WFD, including on environment, agriculture, economic analysis of water use, water quality assessment and public consultations.

Since 2009, the key long-term national development documents have been the National Spatial Development Concept 2030 and the Long-term National Development Strategy 2030. These, together with the operational programmes for use of EU structural and cohesion funds, became the unifying framework for co-ordinating sectoral policies, including those related to environmental management. An important co-ordination role is played by the Co-ordinating Committee for Development Policy. The recent adoption of the ESE strategy will require the MoE to reinforce co-ordination mechanisms with the Ministry of Economy to ensure appropriate implementation the policy and regular, in-depth monitoring of progress. Establishing a formal permanent body for interministerial co-ordination of environmental policies, headed by the MoE (e.g. as a subcommittee in the Co-ordinating Committee for Development Policy), could provide such a function.

The MoE is supported by independent bodies that advise on the minister on policy and legal development. They are composed of prominent scientists, other experts and representatives of the public (including NGOs and economic institutions). The State Council for Environmental Protection (PROS),[14] the National Council for Nature Conservation and the Forestry Council are the main ones; they played a particularly active role in preparing for EU accession. The councils operate through working groups. For example, PROS has working groups on such issues as biodiversity, energy and environment, agriculture and environment, environmental governance, sustainable development, water economy and, more recently, education for sustainable development.

A network of environmental agencies called Partnership: Environment for Development promotes implementation of national objectives at the regional level and develops harmonised methodologies and operational guidance for regional programming and management of EU funds. The network, co-financed by the EU in the framework of the European Network of Environmental Authorities-Managing Authorities for the Cohesion Policy, brings together representatives of the MoE, the Ministry of Infrastructure and

Development, the GDEP and RDEPs, and regional authorities in charge of regional operational programmes. The network holds regular plenary sessions and has seven working groups.[15] Since its inception in 2010, it has carried out analyses such as a review of regional waste installations and a study of local authority administrative tasks stemming from the WFD. It has prepared guidance, e.g. on the procedural aspects of EIA, and conducted study tours to other EU countries. Reinforcing its activities and broadening its scope to include climate change mitigation, spatial planning and enforcement would provide further opportunities to exchange experience and support regions where capacities are lower.

3. Environmental policy and performance evaluation mechanisms

3.1. Environmental monitoring and reporting

Since its creation in 1991, the State Environmental Monitoring (PMS) programme has been an effective unifying mechanism for collecting environmental information and for regularly evaluating progress in implementing the NEPs. The data collected have been also used by regional and local authorities to guide the application of policy instruments, such as EIAs, environmental permits and spatial development plans, and to guide investment, including the use of EU funds.

The PMS's development and management has been co-ordinated by the GIOS, in co-operation with the WIOSes. In addition, the GIOS co-ordinates data collection by other institutions. For example, the MoE has expanded its role as administrator of the Central Waste System, which contains data on waste generation and management; the National Water Management Authority has been in charge of the water cadastre since 2006; and the GDEP plays an increasingly important role as administrator of the Central Register of Nature Conservation Forms and the database on the Natura 2000 network. The National Centre for Emission Management, established in 2009, carries out national greenhouse gas emission inventories.

Several components of the PMS have been strengthened during the past decade. For example, assessment and monitoring of air quality have been continuously improved in line with EU requirements. In 2007, Poland enlarged air quality measurement to include heavy metals (As, Ni, Cd) and benzo(a)pyrene. In 2010, $PM_{2.5}$ measurement was introduced for air quality assessments and for calculating the national average exposure index as well as exposure indexes for cities with more than 100 000 inhabitants. With support from EU funds and European Economic Area and Norway grants, several regional inspectorates modernised their monitoring equipment and established new stations that improve the assessment system in areas of increased pressures where measurement has not been performed. Similarly, nature monitoring programmes have been strengthened by launching monitoring of the Natura 2000 special protection areas for birds, as well as monitoring of natural habitats and species, with particular focus on the Natura 2000 special areas of conservation. Since 2005, water quality assessment has been significantly adjusted and harmonised with WFD requirements. Coherent systems of monitoring and assessment of electromagnetic fields and noise levels in the environment were also developed.

The information generated in the PMS provides a solid basis for regular reporting on, and evaluation of, the state of the environment. Environmental statistical reports are published every year by the Central Statistical Office. Each edition includes international comparisons based mostly on standard indices and classifications used by international organisations, including the OECD and Eurostat. The 2014 edition will include, for the first time, the analytical part and data in Excel format. Every four years GIOS prepares an assessment report on the state of the environment. Analysis of individual environmental media follows the OECD pressure-state-response model, with corresponding indicators. The reports have been supported by interactive web applications and multimedia products (*www.gios.gov.pl/stansrodowiska*) also fed by the so-called "country mosaic report" prepared at the voivodship level. As a general rule, yearly or every two years the 16 regional divisions of IOS prepare assessment reports on the state of the environment in each region. All reports are available on their websites.

The progress reports on NEP implementation have been regularly presented to the Sejm. The most recent, on implementation of the 2009-12 NEP, completed in July 2014, was based on inputs including analysis of statistical and GIS data collected by institutions participating in the PMS, surveys of subnational administrations, in-depth interviews with key implementation agencies and case studies of good practice, especially related to investment programmes and their results.

The recent integration of environmental policy development with energy and other sectoral policies will require adjustment of the evaluation process. The System of Indicators for Monitoring and Programming of the Development Policy (STRATEG), created in 2013, is expected to support monitoring of the country's development. The system contains a wide range of national, regional and local indicators. The challenge is to integrate the evaluation procedures and sets of indicators related to the environment into the newly created system. Establishing a separate chapter on environmental protection in the annual reports on the implementation of the Mid-Term National Development Strategy could strengthen reporting on environmental policy implementation.

3.2. Supreme Audit Office

An important function in evaluating public administration performance is carried out by the Supreme Audit Office, which reports to the lower chamber of the Sejm. The NIK carries out *ex post* audits of the effectiveness and efficiency of government programmes, including the use of EU funds. It can also audit the activities of local government bodies as regards their legality, sound management, efficacy and integrity.

Over 2010-14, the NIK carried out 22 audits of national and regional programmes related to the environment. Several involved implementation of water, waste and forestry management programmes, but audits also covered, for example, implementation of development assistance policy in the environmental field and the MoE's treatment of public complaints and opinions. NIK reports have proved to be a very effective evaluation tool, especially since the results are widely publicised in the media. NIK judgments include evaluations of the way financial resources are managed and proposals for administrative or legal changes to improve performance and accountability (Box 2.2). When NIK auditors find criminal offences or negligence, they inform law enforcement bodies. The reports are discussed in the Sejm. Several recommendations are implemented during the reviews and others are usually implemented as soon as the results are published.

3.3. Environmental impact assessment

Poland's experience with EIA of projects dates back to the 1980s, but the legal provisions regulating the processes have been revised several times since then. The major reform was introduced with the adoption of the 2000 Act on the Provision of Information on the Environment and its Protection and on Environmental Impact Assessment, and in

Box 2.2. Audits of environmental programmes by the Supreme Audit Office

Identification and elimination of sites contaminated by expired plant protection products

Since the 1960s, several tonnes of plant protection products with expired validity dates had been stored in buried, unmarked concrete or brick structures. Since the 1990s, the IOS and local authorities have been taking stock of such repositories and their neutralisation. The 2006 National Waste Management Plan envisaged full elimination of all repositories by 2011. In 2012, the NIK evaluated progress in implementing the programme. Its assessment acknowledged that most toxic waste repositories listed in the inventories had been eliminated and that the process of neutralisation had been conducted properly, i.e. all safety procedures were adequately followed, including transport, treatment and final disposal. The review concluded that more than 90% of 211 repository sites were eliminated at a cost of at least PLN 175 million, with neutralisation in process at 20 out of 31 remaining dumps and no work started at 11. However, the audit also showed that in 147 cases the neutralised sites were not adequately monitored, i.e. no proper tests of groundwater in the immediate neighbourhood were carried out. The NIK concluded that no adequate measures were taken to ensure that all potential contaminated sites were identified, which could have serious consequences for the health of the population and ecosystems.

Review of application of sewage sludge as fertiliser

The 2014 NIK evaluation of the management of municipal sewage treatment plants concluded that up to 90% of controlled sewage treatment plants did not ensure appropriate tests of the quality of sewage sludge used as fertiliser. Over 13% of plants did no tests at all, and the quality of tests conducted by others did not guarantee proper protection against land pollution. Moreover, the audit showed that more than 40% of audited sewage treatment plants applied sludge in inappropriate places, e.g. in nature reserves, close to urban areas or close to water intake stations. Almost 73% of sewage treatment plants ran incomplete registers of sludge generation and transfer, not even providing all data required by law, for example on the contents of sludge solids, such as organic substances, heavy metals and parasites. The evaluation also questioned the reliability of regional authorities' verification of data authenticity. The NIK recommendations included requests to the environment minister and regional administrations to set up mechanisms that would ensure efficient sewage sludge management, including adequate tests of sludge and soil, provision of information by operators and proper functioning of regional databases.

Construction of onshore wind farms

In 2014, the NIK evaluated the construction of onshore wind farms in Poland. The evaluation of several projects concluded that local authorities made decisions concerning the location of wind farms without the necessary consultation with the public or ignored public protests. In nearly one-third of municipalities, wind power stations were located on land owned by city council members or local government employees, i.e. decision makers or persons who, on behalf of the municipality, participated in the decision-making process concerning the investment location. In 80% of municipalities studied, the issuing of wind farm permits depended on whether the investors financed the planning documentation or gave donations to the municipality. In some cases the permits were issued after the farm was constructed. The evaluation also found that Polish law did not specify the safe distance between wind farms and human settlements and did not define acceptable norms concerning other potential threats, such as infrasound or stroboscopic effects.

Box 2.2. **Audits of environmental programmes by the Supreme Audit Office** *(cont.)*

Considering the audit results, the NIK recommended defining ways to finance the municipalities' planning documentation related to the construction of wind power stations, developing a consistent methodology to measure noise generated by wind farms, effectively limiting possibilities of locating wind farms in environmentally protected areas, establishing the legal basis for permitting the use of wind farms and covering the use of wind turbines with technical inspections.

Source: www.nik.gov.pl/en.

2001 with the adoption of the comprehensive Environmental Protection Law, which anticipated the need to align with EU law on several environmental requirements, including EIA. The new laws presented a multistep approach: screening, scoping, EIA report preparation and review. They also broadened the provisions for public participation in the EIA process. The EIA procedures were adjusted to take account of the new administrative structure of the country. The most recent changes were introduced in 2008, with the adoption of the law on the release of information about the environment and its protection, and participation of the public in environmental protection and EIA (EIA Act), which clarified the procedures further.

Like the EU legislation, the Polish EIA regulations identify projects for which EIA is mandatory and those that may be subject to EIA after screening procedures, which determine the effects of projects on the basis of thresholds/criteria, or a case-by-case examination. The lists of projects were revised in 2010 to align with Annexes 1 and 2 in the EU EIA Directive. The selection of projects from the second group (after screening) is subject to decision by the competent administrative authority, after consultation with the appropriate RDEP and sanitary inspection. The regulations also established a third group of projects subject to EIA: those that could have significant effects on Natura 2000 sites. Such projects are subject to "Natura assessment" of environmental impact, which is carried out in addition to and independent of the EIA.

The institutional framework for EIA was significantly strengthened in 2008 when the GDEP and RDEPs were established (Section 2). Since then, decisions concerning selected inter-regional infrastructure projects (such as roads, railways, pipelines and similar projects from the Annex 1 list), are processed by the RDEPs. The RDEP also conduct the EIA of projects in Natura 2000 areas, as the second EIA phase required during the process of issuing a construction permit.[16] In cases of national-scale projects, such as the construction of a nuclear power facility and auxiliary investment, the EIA decision making lies with the GDEP. The GDEP and RDEPs provide assistance to other authorities responsible for EIA, such as municipalities, which continue to be in charge of issuing EIA decisions for most smaller projects within their jurisdiction; the heads of county offices (starostas) in the case of mergers, exchanges or divisions of land; and the director of a Regional Directorate of State Forests, which oversees projects related to conversion of public forest into agricultural land.

Developers are responsible for preparing the environmental report, which includes compiling data, overseeing research carried out at all stages of the assessment process, and preparing the scoping document, including the initial and main environmental impact statements. The developers also bear the cost of the environmental compensation, if required. The public and NGOs have the right to participate in the EIA process. Environmental NGOs have unique legal standing and a right of appeal to administrative courts without requiring consent from any other party to the EIA process. The competent authority is responsible for undertaking public consultation.

No standardised statistics are available concerning the number of EIA procedures carried out at the national or subnational level. Some informal evaluations show that the number of decisions carried out entirely by an RDEP remained between 80 and 100 a month in 2008-12 while the number of local EIAs in which an RDEP took part increased from around 200 a month in early 2009 to 1 800 a month in 2010-12. A database of EIA procedures is being developed, which will facilitate monitoring of EIAs and access to information regarding EIA procedures and decisions. The database should help improve the quality of EIAs and allow better co-operation between participating authorities.

The recent changes strengthened EIA procedures. The GDEP developed supporting documents that present standardised procedures and technical guidelines. Additional capacity at the regional level, along with training activities, accelerated the procedures. It is estimated that the time for issuing EIA decisions relating to infrastructure projects, especially roads and bridges, was reduced from 300 to 100 days. This progress allowed better absorption of EU funds. However, procedures are still subject to problems. Discontinuity between the preliminary design, which often contains overall analyses of alternatives, and the definitive design, developed in parallel with the EIA, hinders integrated appraisal of impact, mitigation, cost and alternatives. Other limitations include poor analysis of cumulative effects, organisational and expertise deficiencies of responsible authorities (especially at the local and regional levels) and the procedures' complexity. Monitoring of the impact of investment on the environment and *ex post* analysis are often missing. Many environmental statements, as well as non-technical summaries, tend to be voluminous, redundant and often written in complex and overly technical language, impairing communication of the results to the public and the responsible authority. Limited public participation and lack of trust among stakeholders contribute to frustration with EIA procedures by the administration, investors and the public. In several cases, stakeholder views were ignored, e.g. on road and renewable energy infrastructure projects (Boxes 2.2 and 2.3).

The GDEP is working on implementing a wide-ranging programme that will enable the creation of a unified, methodical EIA system for the administration responsible for the EIA procedures as well as project proponents and the public at large. The goal is also to raise the quality of documentation, including EIA forecasts and reports on environmental impact. Swift implementation of the programme will help streamline the investment process, improve absorption of EU funds through proper conduct of the procedure and improve monitoring of EIA in the country at large.

3.4. Strategic environmental assessment

SEA procedures were already part of municipal land use planning in the early 1990s. The procedures were formalised by the 1994 Spatial Planning Act, which required local plans to be subject to an evaluation of their environmental impact. The 2001 Environmental Protection Law, which broadened requirements for SEA to other plans and programmes, prepared the system for transposition of the SEA Directive (2001/42/EC).

Over 2000-08 a number of SEAs were undertaken. Although most continued to be applied at the local level, some high profile programmes, such as the Spatial Development Concept and the High Speed Rail Programme, were also subject to SEA. All national and regional operational programmes for the use of EU structural and cohesion funds have also been evaluated. Preparation of the SEAs has been guided by the provisions of the national legislation but also by dedicated guidance documents prepared at EU level, such as the Handbook on SEA for Cohesion Policy 2007-13 and the guide to Assessments of Plans and Projects Significantly Affecting Natura 2000 Sites. Handbooks on the EIA procedure and Natura 2000 aspects of spatial planning, published in 2009, also referred to SEA procedures.

The SEA Directive was transposed into Polish law through the 2008 law on access to information, public participation in decision making and EIA (EIA Act). It required SEA for many types of policies, including spatial plans[17] and sectoral planning documents,[18] which set out the framework for future implementation of projects likely to have a significant effect on the environment. SEA was also required for planning documents likely to have a significant effect on Natura 2000 areas.[19] Carrying out SEA is the responsibility of the authority in charge of preparing the documents subject to SEA. The law made the GDEP the competent body for delivery of opinions and consultation concerning SEA of documents prepared and amended by central government, while the RDEPs are responsible for other documents.

As in many other countries, the SEA procedures in Poland involve i) scoping; ii) environmental assessment, including preparation of an environmental report; iii) statutory and public consultations; and iv) preparation of an environmental statement (a written summary of the procedure). The plan and the environmental report have to undergo public consultation. Opinions on the plan and environmental report are sought from the authorities that participated in the scoping process (i.e. environmental – GDEP or RDEPs and sanitary). The environmental statements summarise how the authorities responsible for the preparation of project documents dealt with environmental considerations provided in the environmental report, opinions of competent authorities and within the public consultation process. Following approval, the authority is required to monitor significant environmental effects of implementation.

Over the years, SEA has evolved from merely fulfilling the formal requirement of environmental assessment to a practical tool which contributes to the integration of environmental considerations in the planning process. In the early years, environmental assessment of plans involved an already determined strategy without scope for influencing the strategic approach and without allowing identification of alternatives. Later a more comprehensive approach was developed, which was applied in one of the most successful and challenging SEAs ever carried out: for the 2004 National Development Plan.

There is evidence that SEA has helped improve the organisation of planning procedures and made policy making more transparent, for example through the requirements for public consultation and the preparation of environmental reports and environmental statements. However, the process has proved to be relatively lengthy, introducing additional iterations into planning as well as additional and wider consultation. The short time allowed for the SEA has often been detrimental to its quality. Assembling the right baseline information can prove difficult, as decisions have to be made on how much and what kind of information should be collated. This has often resulted in ill-targeted approaches and lengthy reports which were not effective decision-making and public consultation tools. Although the assessment of alternatives is a key part of SEA, many planners have difficulty generating reasonable alternatives, in particular for higher level plans. The iterative process of conducting SEA can result in plans being gradually modified as they are developed. In some cases it is particularly difficult to ensure that environmental recommendations not aligned with the prevailing political vision are included. As the SEA Directive does not indicate what constitutes a "reasonable alternative", there have been differing interpretations of "reasonableness" and, in some cases, no alternatives considered at all. The lack of local land use plans prevents the proper application of the SEA regarding local development plans, especially in the context of identifying nature protection areas.

4. Environmental permitting, enforcement and compliance assurance

4.1. Environmental permitting

Legal requirements for integrated environmental permits, in line with EU Directive 96/61/EC on integrated pollution prevention and control (IPPC), were introduced into Polish law in 2001, well before EU accession. In the following years an extensive support system was established that facilitated the introduction of integrated permits. It included establishing a BAT Centre in the MoE, creating technical working groups for IPPC sectors, elaborating sectoral guidelines and manuals and providing extensive training for administrators and industry. After a slow start, with only a small fraction of nearly 2 000 installations acquiring IPPC permits by 2006, the number issued increased, along with the number of installations subject to IPPC permitting. By 2010, 95% of a total 3 097 installations had received the permits: 2 577 existing and 388 new installations. Today, 99% of a total 3 269 installations are covered by the integrated system.[20] Also, many small installations with limited impact on the environment are subject to media-specific permits or notifications.

Depending on the type of activity, three tiers of public authorities issue environmental permits. For installations contained in List I activities (those with significant environmental impact according to the IPPC Directive) permits are issued by the marshal's office; for activities covered by List II it is the relevant starosta. Operations in areas restricted for purposes of defence and security are regulated by the relevant RDEP. In 2003-10, 65 large installations were subject to compliance programmes, which allowed them to gradually meet the requirements of integrated permitting. Integrated permits are issued for up to ten years. The competent authority reviews them at least every five years, more frequently if a change to the BAT allows a significant reduction in emissions without excessive cost or any changes in the legislation.

Since 2010, the integrated permitting system has been subject to significant revisions as part of the process of aligning national law with the EU Industrial Emission Directive (2010/75/EU). In July 2014, the Sejm adopted draft amendments to the 2001 Environmental Protection Law to reflect this directive. The amended law would expand permits' validity but also require the preparation of baseline reports on soil and groundwater contamination before an operation is begun or a permit is updated.[21] It would also introduce a definition of remediation that refers to cleanup obligations on the part of the operator. The revision sets out an overall maximum total annual emission volume for all installations covered. Some installations will be covered by a transitional national plan that will move the deadline for compliance to 2020.

The new legislation will require investment by various branches of industry to meet the revised emission levels. Warsaw University of Technology estimates the total cost of introducing the standards in the energy sector at EUR 535 million through 2016 and possibly over EUR 1 billion through 2025. However, the justification enclosed with the bill points out that the amendments would affect mostly those installations that were meeting only the minimum emission standards.

Although not part of the Industrial Emission Directive, further integration with EIA procedures should be considered in the reform of the permitting system. In several OECD countries, an integrated permit is granted as part of the EIA procedure and no separate procedure is required. This should allow reducing duplication in investigative and evaluation activities and reduce the administrative burden on investors.

4.2. Compliance monitoring and non-compliance response

Compliance monitoring and inspections of permit holding installations are carried out by the relevant WIOS in a unified way across the country following multiyear plans and detailed methodologies developed by the GIOS. The approach is aligned with the EU Recommendation on Minimum Criteria for Environmental Inspections. The GIOS and WIOSes co-operate closely with other authorities that undertake inspections, such as self-government bodies at subnational levels that check compliance with administrative decisions related to environmental protection, sanitary inspection (for drinking and bathing water), fire brigades, veterinary inspection, state labour inspection, trade inspection and construction supervision.

Since 2010, a new compliance monitoring and enforcement management system known as the "control system" has been in place to support activities of enforcement agencies. The system, developed as part of a long-standing partnership with the Norwegian Environment Protection Agency, contains a comprehensive set of rules and procedures for inspection processes. It covers annual and quarterly planning, drafting of inspection plans, carrying out of inspections, documentation, measurement, writing of protocols and issuing of follow-up orders. The control system is accompanied by an electronic support system which allows the generation of reports, protocols and inspection plans, and viewing of the status of follow-up orders on implementation.

Inspections are carried out in accordance with environmental regulations but also according to the 2004 Act on Freedom of Economic Activity, which set limits on the number of days that can be devoted to an inspection from any service (e.g. environment, labour, health and safety, fire). It also limits to one the number of organisations that can carry out inspections on a given day (unless an operator agrees or there is a threat to human life, health or the environment). All inspections also have to be announced, with between 7 and 30 days' notice. Planned inspections can include comprehensive audits as part of a broader enforcement campaign or specific problem-focused inspections. They can also include a desk study of self-monitoring reports. About 36% of all inspections are unannounced and carried out as a result of complaints.

The introduction of an explicit, well-defined, risk-based compliance assurance policy at the national level, and its application at the voivodship level, helped reduce both the administrative burden and environmental risks. The frequency of inspection depends on the type and size of installation, with the largest and most complex (Class 1) being inspected once a year, Class 4 once every four years and low risk installations (Class 5) only upon complaint. Provisions allow the GIOS to reduce inspection frequency if the operator has an EMAS or ISO 14001 certification and the installation was in full compliance at the last inspection. Information about each permitted installation is publicly available on the MoE website, including its permit, though inspection reports are not yet included. The WIOS also holds records of an installation's environmental monitoring.

The inventory of installations subject to compliance monitoring stood at 65 000 in 2012, up from 51 000 in 2003. In 2012, out of 30 000 compliance inspections, nearly 9 000 incidents of non-compliance were recorded. In about 95% of cases, formal breaches were recorded, but no significant environmental impact. However, in the remaining 447 cases, regulatory breaches were deemed likely to endanger or pollute the environment. Every WIOS has its own accredited laboratory which supports compliance monitoring activities.

The most common response to a violation is a written compliance order indicating corrective actions necessary and measures to monitor the relevant environmental impact. In 2012 the inspectors issued 7 035 such orders, while in 2003 the number was nearly 10 000 with fewer controls (17 000). Depending on the nature of the violation (e.g. degree of harm, intentional aspect), the inspector can directly impose a fine or take another administrative decision, e.g. suspending operations; or he/she can initiate criminal proceedings against the facility and/or responsible physical person. Different levels of fines apply to different types of infringement, calculated according to the regulations. They depend on the seriousness of the violation and are different for each environmental medium. A catalogue of fines for each infringement is available to the inspector in the field and the electronic control support system enables inspectors to check the status of follow-up orders. Administrative fines are transferred to environmental protection and water management funds at the relevant level according to a formula. Decisions of voivodship inspectors can be appealed to the GIOS. In 2012, the GIOS received 816 administrative appeals, mostly from operators. In 184 cases the decisions of the WIOS were cancelled or reconsidered.

Poland's environmental compliance assurance system has been strengthened through the decentralisation of compliance monitoring and inspections, but has also been made more efficient by streamlining of inspection procedures, reduction of administrative burdens and increased effectiveness of non-compliance responses. Decentralised inspections have certain advantages, as regional and local authorities can better monitor compliance in their jurisdictions. Better co-ordination of inspections among different agencies also increased the system's efficiency. The implementation of the new compliance monitoring and enforcement system supports inspection activities and helps increase their efficiency and effectiveness. Further efforts should be devoted to modernising laboratories and inspectors' monitoring equipment, and adjusting budgets to the growing responsibilities of the GIOS. Strengthening the relations between the GIOS and WIOSes could also improve the efficiency of the compliance and enforcement system. Additional work is needed to design performance indicators to characterise the effectiveness and efficiency of the activities. These efforts should be pursued, and a new performance management system developed, in the framework of results-oriented planning and budgeting. The development of an explicit and ambitious communication strategy and further development of the GIOS portal will help engage the public and the media in compliance promotion.

5. Promoting environmental democracy

Opening access to information, public participation in decision making and access to justice have formed one of the pillars of the country's economic and democratic transformation since 1989. The three elements became important instruments in defining, implementing and refining environmental policies. Their incorporation in the Act of 9 November 2000 on the Provision of Information on the Environment and its Protection and on Environmental Impact Assessment and in the 2001 Environmental Protection Law provided a strong basis for Poland to become one of the first countries to ratify, in February 2002, the UNECE Aarhus Convention. The most recent law on access to information on the environment and its protection, public participation in environmental protection and EIA (EIA Act), adopted in 2008, paved the way for the introduction of additional tools to strengthen environmental democracy.

5.1. *Access to environmental information*

Open access to environmental information is a constitutional right in Poland. The environmental law was among the first where this right was detailed before being introduced in general laws, such as the 2002 Law on Access to Public Information. The regulatory system is largely compliant with the Aarhus Convention and the EU directive on public access to environmental information (2003/4/EC).

Administrative entities are obliged to provide any information about the environment and its protection that is in their possession or intended for them, without requiring persons exercising this right to prove any legal interest. Information is supposed to be made available in the manner and form requested. If this is not possible, the administration holding the information is required to inform the applicant in writing, within 14 days of receiving the request, of the reasons for not making the information available. A refusal of a request for information has to be made in the form of an administrative decision, which can be appealed accordingly to provisions of the Code of Administrative Procedure. Fees for providing information on the environment and its protection are equivalent to costs incurred for the preparation of copies of documents.

The right to access to information by the public is matched by the efforts of public authorities to provide information. Draft environmental laws are accessible, together with all other legal acts, through the legislative platform of the RCL (*www.rcl.gov.pl*), which aims to ensure coherence and transparency of the legislative process. A dedicated environmental portal (*www.ekoportal.gov.pl*), administered by the MoE since 2006, has become the main vehicle for providing a wide range of information, including policy documents, information about the state of the environment, information about environmental requirements in investment processes and guidance on environment-related databases and registers. The Ekoportal gathers information shared by 1 500 administrative offices and receives on average 13 000 entries per month. In 2011-13, extensive training programmes were conducted for central administration officials on access to environmental information. A handbook for society and one for entrepreneurs, about rights and obligations related to environmental protection, were developed. The MoE carried out awareness raising campaigns, including recent efforts to facilitate the municipal waste management reform (Chapter 5).

Significant efforts have been made to present information on the state of the environment in ways that can encourage knowledge-based decision making and raise awareness on the part of the public. The GIOS publishes regular reports on the state of the environment. The reports are supported by an extensive set of indicators to show progress in implementing the NEP. The Central Statistical Office publishes detailed annual reports with environmental statistics and indicators. Increasingly, comprehensive information on environmental quality is provided at local level through municipal state of the environment reporting and in real time. Data sets gathered in the framework of state monitoring programmes are increasingly accessible as geospatial information through the GIOS web portal, for example the results of air, nature and water quality monitoring.

Despite such efforts, the practical application of the right to information still faces problems. According to analysis by the Supreme Chamber of Control, Polish law concerning access to environmental information is subject to differing interpretations, which affect the responsiveness of some offices. There are also irregularities in maintaining registers of publicly available documents, such as delays in making documents available, use of inappropriate forms or failure to provide access to all information, even if only part of the information is excluded. In some cases the authorities fail to appoint a person responsible for providing information about the environment.

5.2. *Public participation in environmental decision making*

There are several channels for citizens to participate in decision-making processes. The MoE provides draft acts, along with their justification and regulatory impact assessment, to interested entities, including public authorities, trade unions, business associations and NGOs, with requests for comments. Drafts are also subject to consultation with representatives of local governments, particularly with the local branch of the Joint Committee of the Central Government and Territorial Governments. After considering comments, the MoE prepares reports explaining the cases in which comments were not taken into account. Other forms of consultation are often used, such as public debates and seminars to which stakeholders are invited. NGO representatives regularly participate in the legislative work of Sejm subcommittees, and their initiatives have been included in legislation.

The laws on EIA, SEA, environmental permitting and land use planning also give the public the right to voice its opinion on projects and programmes before final decisions are made. Under this procedure, public authorities responsible for issuing an individual decision or for preparing a document (such as a plan, program or other strategic document) requiring public participation must notify the public about the launch of the procedure, the availability of relevant information for inspection through the system of publicly available records, and the possibility of submitting comments and recommendations. Any person, natural or legal, regardless of nationality, citizenship or domicile, has the right to submit comments or recommendations, and the authority is obliged to consider them. The authority must provide reasoning for its decisions and plans, and include information about public comments and recommendations and how they were used within the document or decision. Detailed information about these comments and final versions of documents as well as the decisions must be placed in a publicly accessible record, and the public has to be notified about it. The last decade witnessed several cases of these provisions being applied in practice (Section 3). Particular attention to public participation was paid in the process of approval of operational programmes for the use of the EU cohesion and structural funds. All of them were subject to SEA with broad public consultation.

Traditionally, environmental NGOs and pressure groups have been very active in Poland. NGOs have played an important role in raising questions about the potential environmental impact of significant road infrastructure projects, such as a proposed upgrade of the Via Baltica motorway (Box 2.3), as well as energy programmes and projects, especially relating to shale gas and coal exploitation and the development of conventional and renewable energy. Client Earth, Greenpeace, WWF and CEE Bankwatch co-operate with local pressure and interest groups and have jointly established a national network of environmental groups that has proved very effective. Environmental NGOs have a right to representation on the supervisory boards of the National Environmental Protection and Water Management Fund and the voivodship funds. They are also represented on advisory bodies such as the National Environmental Protection Council and the commission on genetically modified organisms.

Box 2.3. **Public participation in developing road infrastructure: The case of the Rospuda Valley**

The Rospuda is a small river in north-eastern Poland that flows through the north-western part of the large primeval forest wilderness area close to the town of Augustów. The Rospuda Valley is one of the most valuable wetland areas in Europe, with blanket, raised and temporary bogs. The valley has been a protected landscape area since 1989, is part of Natura 2000, is designated under the Directive on the Conservation of Wild Birds as a Special Bird Protection Area and is part of the Augustów Primeval Forest Sanctuary (since 2004). The Rospuda Valley is home to many rare plants, including wild orchids, and emblematic animal species, such as eagle, wolf and lynx.

In 2006 a modernisation of the Via Baltica transport corridor from the Czech Republic to Finland envisaged construction the Augustów bypass expressway, a 16 km section of roadway on concrete pillars across the valley and bogs. Residents of Augustów had demanded a bypass to ease lorry traffic to and from neighbouring Lithuania.

In December 2006 the European Commission opened infringement proceedings against the Polish government for consenting to the road project, which would severely damage important protected natural sites. Despite this action, local authorities allowed construction to start in February 2007, claiming all legal requirements had been met. However, the Polish ombudsman's office launched an appeal aimed at halting the work. The appeal was based on suspicion that alternative routes were not taken into consideration.

Against a background of intense campaigns of protests by environmental activists and counterprotests from the local community, the environment minister launched a multi-stakeholder dialogue to reach consensus on the bypass. The dialogue allowed the consideration of alternative approaches with a discussion on their costs and benefit. As a result in 2009 the plan to build the highway through the Rospuda Valley was abandoned, and the highway has been rerouted to completely avoid the wilderness area. An alternative design omitting the Rospuda Valley is expected be less expensive and only 2 km longer than the original route.

In some cases, however, the quality of consultations has not been up to the highest standards. The major flaws include inadequate provision of information during consultations or non-compliance with regulations concerning sufficient time to prepare for participation in the proceedings. For example, consultations are conducted at a very early stage in the drafting of development of policies or bills, and are not repeated even if consecutive drafts are prepared later. Some NGOs have criticised the time limit of 21 days to submit comments on EIA procedures. Institutions are reluctant to actively look for public involvement since this usually involves delays in decision making.

5.3. *Access to justice*

The Constitution provides safeguards for access to justice, including the right to compensation for any harm done by any action of an organ of public authority contrary to law, and the right to appeal in both administrative and judicial procedures. No specific procedures have been developed for challenging decisions or omissions of a public authority violating environmental legislation, and the public uses general channels for access to justice provided under administrative legislation.

Environmental organisations enjoy farther-reaching rights in certain proceedings related to the environment than other social organisations do in other proceedings. Namely, they may participate in proceedings with the rights of a party but without needing to prove that the public interest requires their participation. However, this right applies only to proceedings where public participation is required (e.g. regarding a decision that concludes an EIA procedure, or IPPC permits, but not on construction permits).

The Code of Administrative Procedure grants the right to appeal to the authority of second instance against administrative decisions. Environmental organisations have the right to complain to the administrative court about decisions made in proceedings requiring public participation, if justified by the statutory objectives of the organisation, even if it did not participate in a particular proceeding requiring public participation. Appeals are free of charge. The decision of the authority of second instance can be challenged in voivodship administrative court and decisions or judgements at voivodships level can be challenged in the Supreme Administrative Court. Filing an appeal against a decision of an authority of first instance automatically suspends its implementation. Filing a complaint to a court against a decision of an authority of second instance does not, but implementation of this decision may be suspended by the court upon a motion of the claimant, provide that he demonstrates that it is plausible that implementation of the decision would cause irreversible damage.

In cases where human rights are violated, citizens or their organisations may also file a motion to the ombudsman (Human Rights Defender). The ombudsman cannot issue a binding verdict in a given case (i.e. is not a court), but can participate in any administrative or court proceeding, bring a case before the relevant authority or court, or undertake other steps provided for by law. In practice, because of the ombudsman's position and prestige, such activities result in a case being settled in line with his/her motions. The reports on activity of the ombudsman published in 2009, 2010 and 2011 mentioned a total of only nine areas where non-compliance with environmental law was recorded and actions were undertaken to resolve it.

Costs of administrative and judicial-administrative proceedings are generally low and do not seem to constitute any obstacle to access to justice. However some organisations complain that the fees for bringing complaints to the voivodship administrative courts are excessively high. Even though persons without sufficient financial means can request an exemption from proceedings costs before civil or administrative courts, it is often not granted. This causes environmental organisations to forgo the opportunity to complain about administrative decisions of the administrative courts. Very few cases brought to civil courts concern damage to the environment as a common good. NGOs maintain that this is due to difficulties in proving the plaintiff's right to submit a case in protection of a common good.

There have been cases of public organisations and individuals opposing certain projects, or appealing administrative decisions granting permits, in order to seek financial gains from project promoters. This has led to a tendency to limit the scope of public participation and access to justice by narrowing the groups of persons considered parties in the proceedings; limiting the list of cases in which NGOs may participate with the rights of parties and consequently a right to appeal; introduction of a requirement to file a deposit while requiring the court to suspend a construction project; and limitation of the time frame for NGOs to submit notice of their participation in proceedings with the rights of a party.

Notes

1. The National Waste Management Plan 2006 (published in 2002) was updated by the 2010 plan (published in 2006) and the 2014 plan (published in 2010).
2. An action plan required by the EU Water Framework Directive.
3. The National Strategic Reference Framework 2007-13 was an agreement between Poland and the European Commission aiming to ensure that financing from EU funds was consistent with EU cohesion guidelines, and identified the link between EU priorities (drawn from the 2006 Community Strategic Guidelines for Cohesion) and national reforms.
4. In 2013, the Ministry of Regional Development was merged with the Ministry of Transport, Construction and Marine Economy to create the Ministry of Infrastructure and Development.
5. They are the Strategy for Innovative and Efficient Economy (Ministry of Economy), the Human Capital Development Strategy (Office of the Prime Minister), the Transport Development Strategy (Ministry of Transport, Construction and Marine Economy), the Efficient State Strategy (Ministry of Internal Affairs and Administration), the Social Capital Development Strategy (Ministry of Culture and National Heritage), the National Regional Development Strategy 2010-20 (Ministry of Regional Development), the National Security Strategy (Ministry of National Defence) and the Sustainable Development of Rural Areas and Agriculture Strategy (Ministry of Agriculture and Rural Development).
6. Under the new strategic framework, these plans will have to reflect the objectives of the ESE.
7. When scrutinising bills or amending legislation, the RCL considers the proposals' constitutionality, their conformity with general principles of law and their comprehensibility. Recent reforms have widened the RCL's responsibility to include drafting of all legislative documents, guided by the intent of the ministry concerned.
8. It develops the national water management programme; approves draft river basin management plans and plans for flood risk management and drought response; approves draft conditions for the use of waters in water regions; and keep a water cadastre for the country, taking the river basin districts into account. It also co-ordinates operations of seven regional water management boards.
9. It supervises activities of mine operators with respect to health, safety and fire protection, sustainable and environmentally sound deposit management, mining damage prevention, and mining plant construction and closure, including land reclamation and development of post-mining areas.
10. The agency supervises activities that could cause exposure to ionising radiation, regularly assesses the national radiation situation and undertakes measures in case of radiation emergency. Poland has no commercial nuclear power plants, but both scenarios in the nuclear energy policy adopted in January 2014 include a key role for nuclear power, and plans call for a first plant to be operational by 2024.
11. The voivodship inspectorates are part of a "unified administration" bringing together regional representation of various parts of government (e.g. police, veterinary inspection, fire brigade) under the leadership of the governor (voivod). The idea is to reduce administrative costs, improve co-ordination and avoid overlap. Under this system, the voivod's prerogatives include appointing the heads of these units, approving their structure and operating programmes, and creating or abolishing supporting units.
12. The GDEP also conducts tasks related to prevention and remediation of environmental damage, and supervises environmental information management and registration of organisations in the Eco-Management and Audit Scheme (EMAS). Its Department of Administrative Jurisdiction is an appeal body on matters concerning EIA related to Natura 2000, environmental damage, zoning and land use, and draft local land use plans.
13. Regional and local government revenue from national sources includes general revenue from property taxes, general transfers and subsidies from the central government budget and special-purpose grants from the central government budget. Regional and local government units also have a limited right to impose taxes and levies.

14. In 2014, its new members were appointed by the environment minister for a five year period.
15. These cover EIA, waste management, water supply and sanitation, air pollution management and energy, noise, integrated environmental permitting, and the New Financial Perspective 2014-20.
16. The RDEPs also assess impacts of projects not mentioned in Annexes 1 and 2 of the EU EIA Directive on Natura 2000 areas. In addition, they take part in all other EIA procedures (including Natura 2000 assessments) as an opinion-providing authority at the screening phase and as the approving authority in case of EIA.
17. Among them are the National Spatial Development Concept, studies of conditions and directions for the spatial development of a municipality, spatial development plans and regional development strategies.
18. The sectors involved are industry, energy, transport, telecommunications, water management, waste management, forestry, fishery and tourism.
19. This is the case for plans that are not directly related to protection of the Natura 2000 area or do not arise from protection requirements.
20. In 14 cases (0.4%), proceedings are pending in administrative courts on the issuance and/or suspension of permits.
21. The baseline report will be used to compare the site's initial status with its final status following the end of activities. Upon definitive cessation of activities, the final operator will have to once again assess soil and groundwater contamination with the relevant hazardous substances. The first drafts of the bill stated that all IPPC installations must prepare such a baseline report. The current version stipulates that a baseline report will have to be prepared only for those installations that meet both of the following conditions: i) the chemical substances and mixtures used, produced or emitted on the site cause a risk, and ii) there is a possibility of groundwater and soil pollution.

References

Bednarek (2012), *Strategiczna ocean oddziaływania na środowisko w planowaniu przestrzennym* [Strategic Environmental Assessment in Spatial Planning], Polskie Zrzeszenie Inżynierów i Techników Sanitarnych Oddział Wielkopolski na zalecenie Regionalnej Dyrekcji Ochrony Środowiska w Poznaniu, *http://mmm.rdos.gov.pl/doc/pozn/podrecznik_soos.pdf*.

Cent, J. et al. (2013), Emerging Multilevel Environmental Governance: A Case of Public Participation in Poland, *Journal for Nature Conservation*, Vol. 22, Issue 2, April, pp. 93-102, Elsevier, DOI: 10.1016/j.jnc.2013.09.005.

ClientEarth (2013), *Black Paper: Implementation of EU Climate and Energy Law in Poland*, ClientEarth Poland, Warsaw, *www.clientearth.org/reports/061113-climate-and-energy-black-paper.pdf*.

CoM (2008), *The State Environmental Policy for 2009-2012 and its 2016 Outlook*, Council of Ministers of the Republic of Poland, Warsaw, *www.mos.gov.pl/g2/big/2009_07/2826c539c3015384e50adac8fe920b0b.pdf*.

CoM (2002), *Polityka Ekologiczna Państwa na lata 2003-06 z uwzględnieniem perspektywy na lata 2007-10*, [State Environmental Policy 2003-06 and its 2010 outlook], Council of Ministers of the Republic of Poland, Warsaw, *www.mos.gov.pl/g2/big/2009_04/36383d1a880bbc0b65d0a1c501571e73.pdf*.

EBCD (2013), *"Self-regulation" vs. "Policing": Policy options for the New EU Framework on Environmental Inspections*, Report by the Secretariat of the Intergroup on "Climate Change, Biodiversity and Sustainable development", the European Parliament Intergroup on "Climate Change, Biodiversity and Sustainable Development", European Bureau for Conservation and Development, *www.ebcd.org/pdf/en/407-Full_Report_-_Environmental_Inspections.pdf*.

EC (2012), *Commission Staff Working Document: Poland*, accompanying the Report from the Commission to the European Parliament and the Council on the Implementation of the Water Framework Directive (2000/60/EC) River Basin Management Plans, COM(2012)670 Final, European Commission, Brussels, *http://ec.europa.eu/environment/water/water-framework/pdf/CWD-2012-379_EN-Vol3_PL.pdf*.

EEA (2011), *The 2011 Survey of Resource Efficiency Policies in EEA Member and Cooperating Countries: Poland, Country information on resource efficiency policies, instruments, objectives, targets and indicators, institutional setup and information needs*, European Environment Agency, Copenhagen, *www.eea.europa.eu/themes/economy/resource-efficiency/poland-2014-resource-efficiency-policies*.

ENTEC (2009), *Monitoring of Permitting Progress for Existing IPPC Installations*, Final report for the European Commission Directorate-General Environment, ENTEC UK in partnership with the Institute for

European Environmental Policy, *www.ieep.eu/assets/1308/EC_Monitoring_of_Permitting_Status_Final_Report_09076i3.pdf.*

GIOS (2014), *Stan Środowiska w Polsce: Raport 2014* [State of the Environment in Poland 2014], Chief Environmental Protection Inspectorate, Warsaw, unpublished draft.

GIOS (2012), *Program Państwowego Monitoringu Środowiska na lata 2013-15*, [State Environmental Monitoring Programme 2013-15], Chief Environmental Protection Inspectorate, Warsaw, *www.gios.gov.pl/zalaczniki/artykuly/PPMS2013-2015_str.int.pdf.*

GIOS (2009a), *Informacja o realizacji obowiązku posiadania pozwoleń zintegrowanych przez prowadzących instalacje według stanu na dzień 31 marca 2009*, [Information on the implementation of integrated permits by installations as of 31 March 2009], Chief Environmental Protection Inspectorate, Warsaw, *www.gios.gov.pl/zalaczniki/artykuly/informacja_IPPC_20090520.pdf.*

GIOS (2009b), *The State Environmental Monitoring Programme for the years 2010-2012*, Chief Environmental Protection Inspectorate, Warsaw, *www.gios.gov.pl//zalaczniki/artykuly/pms.pdf.*

GWP (2014), *The post-2015 Development Agenda: Poland. Stakeholder Perspectives on a Water Goal and its Implementation*, Global Water Partnership, Global Secretariat, Stockholm, *www.gwp.org/Global/About GWP/Publications/Reports/Country Consultation Reports/Country consultations 2014/Poland national consultation.pdf.*

IEEP et al. (2013), *Information collection and impact assessment of possible requirements for environmental inspections in the area of EU legislation on water, nature protection and trade in certain environmentally sensitive goods*, Final report for the European Commission, DG Environment, Institute for European Environmental Policy, Bio Intelligence Service and Ecologic Institute, Brussels and London, *http://ec.europa.eu/environment/legal/law/pdf/Final%20report%20inspections.pdf.*

IMPEL (2013), *IMPEL Review of Poland: Voluntary Scheme for Reporting and Offering Advice to Environmental Authorities*, The European Union Network for the Implementation and Enforcement of Environmental Law (IMPEL), European Commission, Brussels, *http://impel.eu/projects/iri-poland/.*

IMPEL (2012), *The implementation of the Environmental Impact Assessment on the basis of precise examples*, The European Union Network for the Implementation and Enforcement of Environmental Law (IMPEL), European Commission, Brussels, *http://ec.europa.eu/environment/eia/pdf/IMPEL-EIA-Report-final.pdf.*

Jendrośka, J. (2014), *Carbon Capture and Storage in Poland The Transposition of Directive 2009/31/EC into Polish Law*, University College London, Centre for Law and the Environment, Carbon Capture Legal Programme, *http://blogs.ucl.ac.uk/law-environment/files/2014/03/Poland-CCS-Report-Jerzy-Jendroska.pdf.*

Karpus, K. (2011), *Right to Access to Environmental Information in the Polish Environmental Protection Law*, Polish Yearbook of Environmental Law 2011, Wydawnictwo Naukowe Universytetu Mikołaja Kopernika, Toruń, *http://issuu.com/kpos/docs/polish_yearbook_of_environmental_2011/5?e=0.*

Laward (2011), *Environmental impact assessment in the investment process*, prepared by Lawards Sulej & Wójcik at the request of the Polish Information and Foreign Investment Agency S.A, Warsaw, *www.paiz.gov.pl/polish_law/environmental_impact_assessment.*

Milieu (2007), *Measures on Access to Justice in Environmental Matters (Article 9(3)) Country Report for Poland*, report prepared under contract to the European Commission, DG Environment, *http://ec.europa.eu/environment/aarhus/pdf/studies.zip.*

Ministry of the Environment (MoE) (2014), *Raport z Realizacji Polityki Ekologicznej Państwa w latach 2009-12 z Perspektywą do 2016 Roku* [Report on the Implementation of the State Environmental Policy 2009-12 and the 2016 Outlook], Ministry of the Environment, Warsaw, unpublished draft.

MoE (2013a), *National Implementation Report to the UNECE Aarhus Convention*, submitted in accordance with decisions I/8, II/10 and IV/4, 12 December 2013, Ministry of the Environment, Warsaw, *www.unece.org/fileadmin/DAM/env/pp/NIR_2014/NIR_2014_Poland_eng.doc.*

MoE (2013b), *Improving Environmental Monitoring and Inspection within the framework of Financial Mechanism of the European Economic Area 2009-2014*, Operational Programme Proposal by the Ministry of the Environment, Warsaw, *www.mos.gov.pl/g2/big/2012_03/6cc542f2502a9319c98bdb7f6e389d1b.pdf.*

MoG/MoE (2014), *Strategia Bezpieczeństwo Energetyczne i Środowisko; Perspektywa do 2020 r. (Energy Security and the Environment Strategy*, Ministry of the Economy, Ministry of the Environment, Warsaw.

Śleszyński, P. et al. (2014), "Analiza stanu i uwarunkowań prac planistycznych w gminach w 2012" roku [Report on the State and Conditions of Planning Works in Gminas in 2012], Institute of Geography and Spatial Organization for the Ministry of Infrastructure and Development, Warsaw, *www.mir.*

gov.pl/Budownictwo/Planowanie_lokalne_i_zagospodarowanie_przestrzenne/Informacje_przestrzenne/Planowanie_przestrzenne/Documents/analiza_2012.pdf.

Twardowska, K. (2013), *Strategiczne Oceny Oddziaływania na Środowisko*, [Strategic Environmental Assessment] General Environmental Protection Directorate, Warsaw, *www.wfosigw.gda.pl/biura/wfos/aktualnosci_download/936/3.pdf.*

Volkéry, A. et al. (2012) *Study on environmental complaint-handling and mediation mechanisms at national level,* Final report by the Institute for European Environmental Policy, Bio Intelligence Service and Ecologic Institute, Brussels and London, *http://ec.europa.eu/environment/aarhus/pdf/mediation_and_complaint-handling.pdf.*

West, C. (2011), *SEA Implementation and Practice: Making an Impact? A Consultant's Perspective,* paper presented on 21-23 September, Prague, *www.iaia.org/SpecialMeetings/prague11/proceedings/papers/FINAL PAPER SEA Application UK, Poland, Portugal.docx.*

Wołoszyn, W. (2004), "Evolution of environmental impact assessment in Poland: problems and prospects", *Impact Assessment and Project Appraisal*, 22:2, 109-119, DOI: 10.3152/147154604781765950.

PART I

Chapter 3

Towards green growth

This chapter examines the use of taxes and other pricing instruments to pursue environmental objectives, and progress in removing fiscal incentives that can encourage environmentally harmful activities. It reviews the role of Poland's environmental funds and EU support in environmentally related investment. It also examines incentives and barriers to stimulate investment in clean energy and sustainable transport. Finally, Poland's initiatives to promote eco-innovation and environmental goods and services are reviewed.

The statistical data for Israel are supplied by and under the responsibility of the relevant Israeli authorities. The use of such data by the OECD is without prejudice to the status of the Golan Heights, East Jerusalem and Israeli settlements in the West Bank under the terms of international law.

Assessment and recommendations

Poland does not have a specific green growth strategy, but sustainable development objectives are included in the National Development Strategy 2020 and in four medium-term, cross-cutting strategies. In 2011 work began on a National Programme for the Development of a Low-Emission Economy. It will aim to promote the transition to a low-emission economy by 2050. A draft document is expected to be completed in 2015.

Poland has participated in the EU Emissions Trading System (EU ETS) since its launch in 2005. The system covered about 50% of domestic greenhouse gas (GHG) emissions over 2008-12. As in most EU countries, emission permits were over-allocated, resulting in low allowance prices that did not provide sufficient incentives to invest in lower-carbon energy sources. This is likely to continue in the period to 2020, as Poland will remain somewhat shielded from the significant changes in the third phase of the EU ETS. Other barriers that limit the responsiveness of investment decisions to the carbon price include a high degree of state ownership and limited competition in electricity generation.

Since 2000, revenue from environmentally related taxes has increased, mostly due to higher taxes on transport fuels, the broadening of the energy tax base and rising levels of energy consumption. In 2012, a mineral extraction tax for copper ore was introduced. In 2012, revenue from environmentally related taxes reached 2.2% of GDP and 6.8% of total tax revenue, noticeably above the respective OECD averages of 1.6% and 5.2%. However, there is room to adjust the structure of these taxes to better reflect environmental externalities and thereby contribute to the goal of fiscal consolidation. For example, energy taxes are unevenly applied across energy sources and users, and do not provide a consistent carbon price. The excise duty on diesel is still below that of petrol even though diesel combustion emits more CO_2 and local pollutants per litre. Vehicle taxes account for a lower share of revenue from environmentally related taxes than in most OECD countries. Passenger vehicle tax rates are not based on environmental criteria, and this has contributed to a large increase in imports of polluting second-hand vehicles. The system of environmental fees and charges (some of which are classified as taxes according to OECD definitions) has not provided efficient price signals and, as planned by the government, should be reviewed.

Excise duties have been levied on coal since 2012, and on natural gas since 2013. However, a broad range of exemptions remains, notably for electricity generation, households and public administration. Agriculture benefits from a rebate on the tax on diesel. In addition, major water users are exempt from water abstraction fees (for aquaculture, irrigation and mining, and, subject to certain conditions, for power generation cooling and hydropower). These exemptions are costly to the public purse and reduce incentives to save energy and water and to switch to less polluting fuels. Commendably, the Ministry of Finance began to review tax expenditures in 2010. Regular, systematic reviews of tax expenditures and subsidies help improve their transparency and help identify those that may not be justified on economic, social or environmental grounds. Reform of taxes or subsidies should assess and minimise potential impacts of higher energy, water or waste prices on financially vulnerable households. Energy and water services represent a greater share of household expenditure than in most other OECD countries.

Poland has been, and until 2020 will remain, the largest beneficiary of EU cohesion and structural funds. The budget allocated to infrastructure and environment in 2007-13 – comprising EU and national matching funds – was the largest in EU history. While the lion's share of these funds was allocated to road transport, investment in environmental protection and water management nearly doubled over 2002-11. This helped increase the share of the population with access to water and waste services. Nevertheless, these sectors remain underfunded and it is unlikely that Poland will meet the 2015 deadline for implementing the EU Urban Waste Water Treatment Directive. In 2012, before the enactment of a new waste law, about 20% of the population still lacked access to municipal waste collection service, and landfilling accounted for 75% of municipal waste treatment, compared with an OECD average of 45%. User charges will have to play a more important role in financing operational and maintenance, and eventually the capital costs, of environmental infrastructure.

In addition to traditional environmental infrastructure, substantial investment is also needed to facilitate the transition to a resource-efficient, low-emission economy. In particular, the need to upgrade energy infrastructure is pressing, as nearly half the generating capacity is more than 30 years old, and transmission and distribution networks are ageing. This provides an opportunity to unwind the high degree of carbon lock-in in the current energy mix and should be based on a full assessment of costs, benefits and risks. The use of quotas and green certificates has increased the share of renewables in gross final energy consumption so that it is broadly in line with the 15% target for 2020. However, the incentives deployed favoured co-firing of biomass with coal in existing power plants, and resulted in biomass accounting for 60% of gross electricity generation from renewable sources in 2012. In addition to being unbalanced, this approach did not foster investment in more innovative technologies, and is not sustainable since old coal plants, which provide the bulk of co-firing, will have to retire after 2020 to comply with EU regulations. The cost-effectiveness of measures to promote renewables and related policies should be kept under careful review, as should their interaction with the EU ETS.

In 2012, Poland's energy intensity was more than 20% higher than the OECD Europe average. Thus there is significant potential to improve energy efficiency, particularly in housing and public buildings, and in district heating systems. A white certificate programme was eventually established and a variety of financing mechanisms are in place. However, some of these instruments have encountered difficulties in implementation and further efforts will be needed to meet the 2020 target for energy saving.

Poorly developed transport infrastructure has continued to be an important limiting factor for Poland's economic development. As a result, investment in transport infrastructure has risen significantly, from 0.7% of GDP in 2000 to 2.5% in 2011, well above the OECD average of 0.9%. In recent years, roads have accounted for 90% of transport infrastructure investment. However, to avoid further locking Poland into a carbon-intensive economy, measures to promote alternative, less carbon-intensive modes of transport should be explored, such as establishing incentives for rail infrastructure by increasing competition, enhancing private-sector involvement, reinforcing the sector regulator's independence and setting prices to recover the cost of operations, maintenance and, ultimately, investment.

A unique feature of environmentally related financing in Poland is the role of the environmental funds. The National Fund for Environmental Protection and Water Management and its 16 voivodship counterparts receive revenue from environmental fees and charges. They also manage EU funds and other financing from international sources, and help leverage a significant volume of investment by co-financing. The adoption of a strategic approach to programming has helped in the absorption of EU funds. However, there is scope to improve further the funds' performance, including by improving prioritisation and co-ordination, ensuring coherence and complementarity with EU funding programmes, increasing the share of repayable financing and more effectively leveraging private finance. The recent enactment of a law on public-private partnerships should help in the latter regard.

Eco-innovation has risen on the policy agenda and been integrated into strategic policies, largely driven by EU policies. Several initiatives have yielded positive results, such as GreenEvo, a programme that supports green technology exports. However, Poland still lacks an integrated framework that would foster synergy between environmental, energy and innovation policies. Eco-innovation faces the same barriers as innovation in general: insufficient research effort, weak industry-science links, difficult access to capital, uncertain return on investment and lack of economic and fiscal incentives. While there is some evidence that the environmental goods and services sector has grown in recent years, consideration should be given to the employment, skills and training implications of its further development. On the demand side, the extensive public sector has important potential for green public procurement. Despite successive actions plans, Polish performance in this area is weak compared to other EU countries, in part because there is no legal obligation to include environmental criteria in procurement decisions.

Recommendations

- Adopt the National Programme for the Development of a Low-Emission Economy; specify the measures needed to achieve its objectives, taking account of their cost-effectiveness, distributional impact and effect on competitiveness; outline a strategy for reducing the environmental impact of coal use, particularly for electricity production, while contributing to the global effort to limit the increase in atmospheric temperatures to no more than 2° C above pre-industrial levels.
- Review the system of environmentally related taxes and charges with a view to imposing an effective carbon tax on fuel used in the sectors not covered by the EU ETS; introducing taxes on passenger vehicles to internalise the environmental cost of vehicle use; simplifying and streamlining the system of charges on air and water pollution, water abstraction and waste landfilling so that externalities are appropriately priced; and providing targeted support for households adversely affected by higher energy, water or waste prices.
- Continue to regularly review and, when appropriate, reform tax expenditures and direct and indirect subsidies, based on their economic, environmental and social impacts.
- Strengthen measures to promote the transition to a resource-efficient, low-emission economy, including by supporting a more balanced renewables policy mix with less incentive for co-firing biomass with coal; continuing to strengthen the electricity transmission and distribution grid; reviewing and adjusting policy measures to achieve the energy saving target; and increasing incentives for rail infrastructure investment.

Recommendations *(cont.)*

- Regularly monitor the activities of environmental funds to ensure that they are in line with government priorities, provide value added in addressing environmental externalities and are cost-effective; strengthen their performance by improving prioritisation and co-ordination, ensuring complementarity with EU funds to assure their effective use, increasing the share of repayable financing and more effectively leveraging private finance.
- Develop and implement a comprehensive framework for promoting eco-innovation, including by increasing public support for R&D; strengthening incentives for the private sector, including by improved access to finance, especially for small and medium-sized enterprises; facilitating better co-operation among the public and private sectors and research institutions; speeding up the development of the environmental technology platform to identify areas of potential comparative advantage; introducing binding environmental requirements in public procurement procedures; and other measures to boost demand for environmental goods and services.

1. Introduction

Important reforms in the 1990s deeply transformed the structure of Poland's economy. Since the early 2000s, Poland has experienced impressive economic growth, allowing living standards to improve. The income gap with the OECD average narrowed, and income inequality and relative poverty decreased more than in most OECD countries. However, in gross domestic product (GDP) per capita Poland still ranks among the bottom five OECD countries, and economic disparities remain within and among regions. EU funds are an important driver of the economy. They have supported significant environmental investment resulting in improved access to environmental services. However, Poland is among the most resource- and carbon-intensive OECD countries. Enhancing the business environment and strengthening product market competition will be key to maintaining a high level of competitiveness and improving the innovativeness of the economy (OECD, 2014a).

Poland does not have a specific green growth strategy. Under the 2009 streamlined strategic framework, sustainable development objectives are part of the National Development Strategy 2020 and of four medium-term integrated strategies: Energy Security and the Environment; Innovative and Efficient Economy; Transport Development; and Sustainable Development of Rural Areas and Agriculture. These set priorities, including for activities to be funded under the 2014-20 EU financial perspective. Since 2008, most policy documents likely to have an impact on the environment (e.g. industry, energy, transport) have had to undergo strategic environmental assessment (SEA). However, integrating environmental concerns in energy, innovation and transport policies remains challenging.

Poland also has no specific national climate change policy beyond its EU targets. Although it achieved its Kyoto target, it may find it a challenge to meet its 2020 greenhouse gas (GHG) emission target in both EU ETS and non-EU ETS sectors, especially in the longer term as the EU has adopted more ambitious objectives (IEA, 2011). In 2011, Poland started elaborating a National Programme for the Development of a Low-Emission Economy, which would encourage the development and use of low-emission technology to promote growth and competitiveness. A draft document is expected to be completed in 2015.

In the longer term, significant change will be needed in Poland's power sector, which is still largely shielded from internalising the cost of carbon and other air pollutant emissions (OECD, 2012a). In planning future energy investment, it is unclear whether the full cost – economic, social and environmental – of options has been wholly accounted for. Besides shifting to a low-emission energy supply, transport policy and end-use efficiency will be important in lowering emissions over the next few decades (World Bank, 2011). Investment decisions will also need to address the need to adapt to climate change. The government adopted a National Adaptation Strategy in October 2013. It assessed climate change impacts and found these to be primarily negative, notably in terms of water resources, flooding and increasing temperatures. The strategy accordingly calls for "climate proofing" spatial planning and infrastructure decisions, notably in transport and energy. It also highlights the importance of training and information provision in the agriculture sector, and innovation policies and systems to target adaptation needs.

2. Greening the tax system

2.1. Overview

The ratio of tax to GDP has been below the OECD average since 2000. In 2011 it was 32.3%, while the OECD average was 34.1% (OECD, 2013a). Poland's level of public debt has gradually increased since 2000, reaching 57% of GDP in 2013 (OECD, 2014b). The fiscal deficit worsened slightly in 2013, due to the economic slowdown, to 4.3% of GDP.[1] Since 2004, fiscal objectives set out in EU convergence programmes have often been missed, and further tightening will be needed to meet the 2015 deficit target of 3% of GDP. Opportunities for fiscal consolidation lie in improving the efficiency of the tax system and raising additional revenue from environmentally related taxes while also reducing certain tax expenditures. Targeted transfers could alleviate potential regressive effects of these measures (OECD, 2014a).

After an upward trend in real terms between 2000 and 2008, revenue from environmentally related taxes declined until 2010 then grew again until 2012 (Figure 3.1). That year it accounted for 6.8% of total tax revenue and 2.2% of GDP, both above the OECD average, though broadly in line with the OECD Europe averages. Both shares decreased over 2007-11 before rebounding in 2012, reflecting the trend in taxation of transport fuels. More than in most other OECD countries, energy taxes account for most revenue from environmentally related taxes, while non-fuel taxes on transport (primarily vehicles) play a relatively minor role (Figure 3.1).

2.2. Taxes on energy products

Taxes on energy products contributed 86% of the revenue from environmentally related taxes in 2012, compared with 73% in OECD Europe (Figure 3.1). The share has remained broadly unchanged since 2005. Most energy excise revenue stems from taxes on petrol and diesel (88%), followed by electricity (8%), liquefied petroleum gas (LPG) (3%) and heavy fuel oil (1%). After exemptions provided by the EU Energy Taxation Directive (2003/96/EC) expired, excise taxes on coal were introduced in 2012 and on natural gas in 2013. However, a wide range of exemptions remains (Section 3; OECD, 2013b, 2013c).

Poland has made progress in limiting the tax burden on labour while increasing the implicit tax rate on energy (Figure 3.1). The tax burden on energy, measured as the ratio between energy tax revenue and final energy consumption, increased steadily to 2007 with increased transport fuel taxes (Figure 3.2). After staying relatively flat, it increased somewhat

Figure 3.1. **Environmentally related tax revenue**

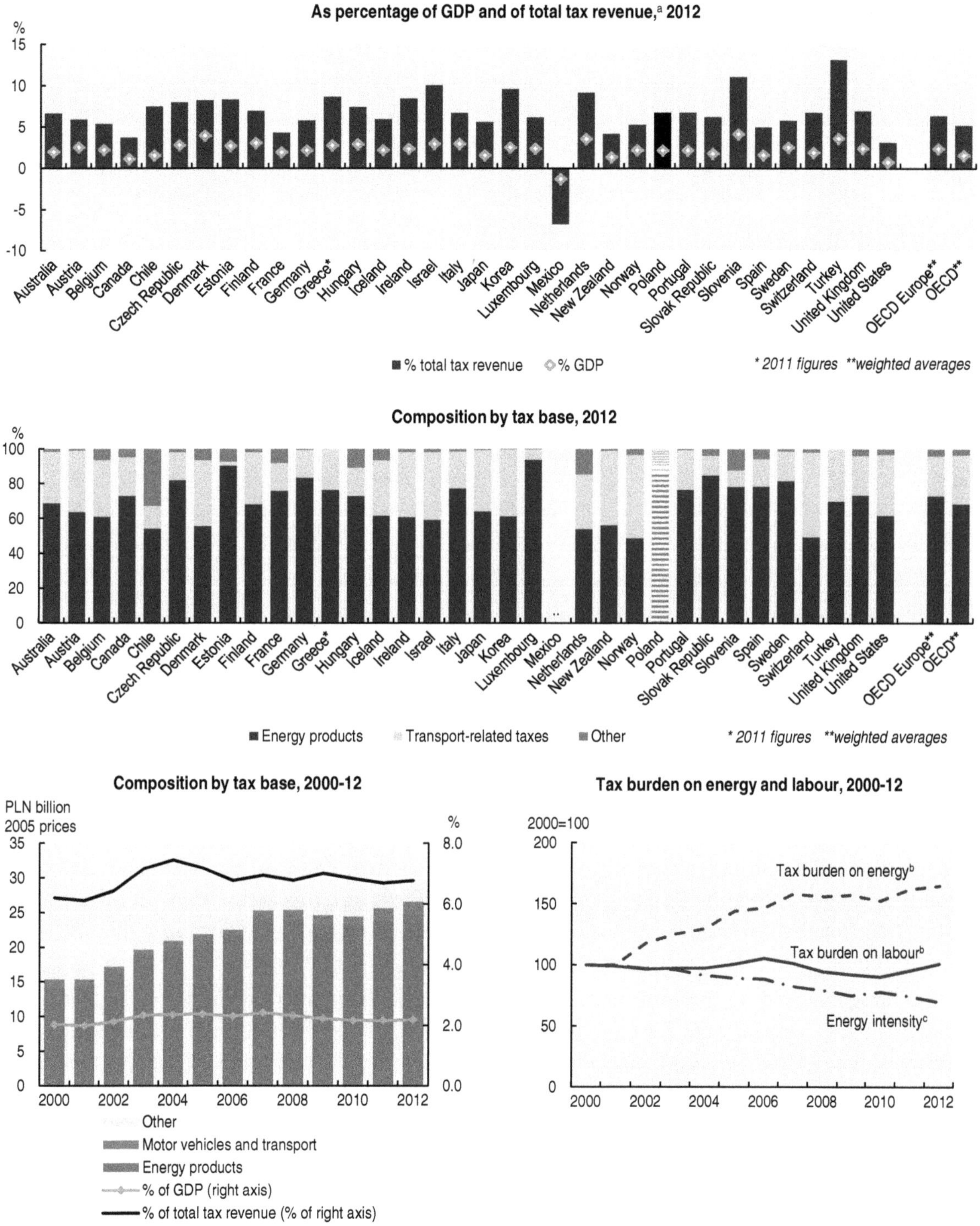

a) Mexico: the system used to stabilise end-use prices of motor fuels causes tax revenue to turn negative (i.e. become a subsidy) in years when the international oil price is high. Australia and Japan: 2011 data for ratios on total tax revenue.

b) Tax burden on labour: ratio between the revenue from taxes on labour income and social contributions and overall compensation of employees; tax burden on energy: ratio between the revenue from energy taxes and final energy consumption.

c) Total primary energy supply per unit of GDP.

Source: Eurostat (2014), *Government Finance Statistics* (database); Eurostat (2014), "Main Indicators", *Energy Statistics* (database); OECD (2014), *OECD Database on Instruments Used for Environmental Policy and Natural Resources Management;* OECD (2014), *OECD Economic Outlook No. 95* (database).

StatLink http://dx.doi.org/10.1787/888933197657

Figure 3.2. **Road fuel prices and taxes, 2000-13**

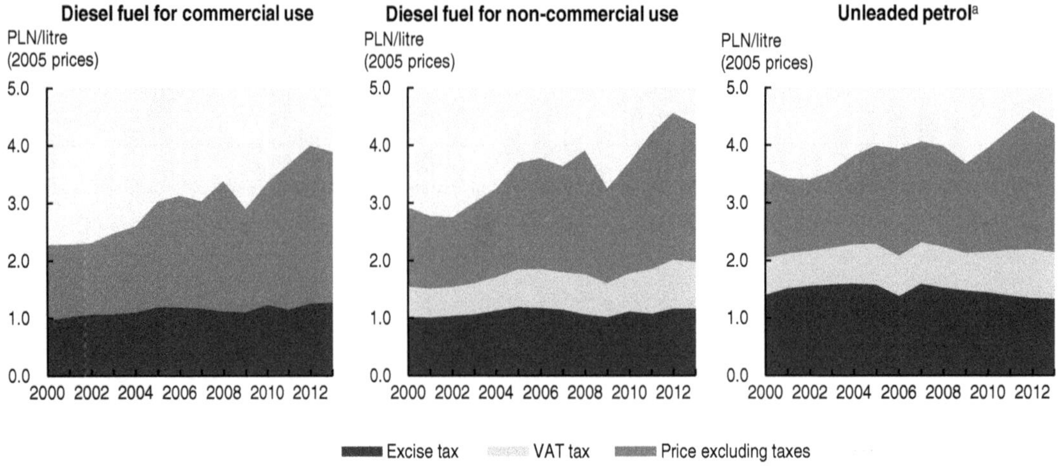

a) Unleaded premium (95 RON).
Source: IEA (2014), *IEA Energy Prices and Taxes Statistics* (database).

StatLink http://dx.doi.org/10.1787/888933197664

after 2010 due to the broadening of the energy tax base and increased diesel excise duty in 2012. However, the tax burden on labour has also increased since 2010.

As in other OECD countries, there is room to adjust the structure of energy taxation to better reflect environmental externalities, including those related to climate change and air pollution. When excise duties are expressed in terms of the carbon content of fuels and the various exemptions are taken into account, they vary significantly among fuels and users (OECD, 2013b). Diesel accounts for the majority of energy use in the transport sector but is taxed at a lower rate than petrol, despite the fact that its CO_2 emissions per litre are higher and its combustion emits more local pollutants. The share of diesel in the passenger car fleet rose from 15% in 2007 to 24% in 2011 (Anfac, 2013). Since 2007, the tax differential has narrowed: the nominal excise duty on diesel increased while those on petrol and LPG were unchanged. Given inflation, this means the rates for the latter two fuels fell (Figure 3.2). Yet the nominal rate on diesel was still 13% below that on petrol in 2013 and the differential is 27% if tax rates are expressed in terms of CO_2 emissions.

Although exceeding the minimum rates set in the Energy Taxation Directive (except on natural gas), excise rates for transport fuels are lower than in most other European countries (IEA, 2014). Transport fuel prices are also lower than in neighbouring countries (although not in terms of purchasing power parities). There is thus room to further increase the tax on diesel and to index the petrol and LPG tax for inflation, increasing the revenue and reducing the tax discrepancy. The transport fuel tax base was extended in 2011, when exemptions on excise duties for biofuels expired. Since consumption began in 2003, the use of biofuels has increased to reach 5.0% of transport fuels in 2012, above the OECD and OECD Europe averages of 3.6% and 4.5%, respectively (IEA, 2014).

Carbon prices implied by excise duties on transport fuels are well above those on fuels used in other economic sectors. The higher prices could be justified by the use of taxes on road fuels to internalise social costs specific to road transport, such as accidents, noise, congestion and local pollution, in addition to GHG emissions and road infrastructure costs (OECD, 2013b). Accounting for these externalities results in lower carbon prices implied by taxes on automotive fuels. However, the relative distortion in favour of diesel increases, as the local external costs of burning diesel are higher than for petrol (OECD, 2012a).

Outside the transport sector, oil product use is taxed at a higher rate for industrial processes than for heating. With exemptions in place, most fuels used for processes and heating remain virtually untaxed (OECD, 2013b). Efforts to better equalise implicit carbon price across different energy sources would lead to more cost-effective CO_2 abatement.

2.3. Carbon pricing through the EU Emissions Trading System

The EU ETS is the main instrument of climate policy. It covered about half of Poland's GHG emissions over 2008-12.[2] As in most other EU member states, Poland over-allocated allowances (each representing 1 tonne of CO_2 emissions) to installations covered by the ETS in the first phase, leading to surplus allowances and a collapse in the allowance price. During the second phase, Poland's overall cap required emissions to fall by 1% below their 2005 level. The average level of emissions fell below the allocated amount, except in 2008 (Figure 3.3). Emissions in EU ETS sectors are dominated by coal-fired power generation (EEA, 2013). The power sector emitted more than its allocated allowances in 2008, while verified emissions in industrial sectors have been below their allocated level thus far (EEA, 2014).

Figure 3.3. **Surplus and deficit in Poland's allocated allowances under the EU ETS, 2005-12**

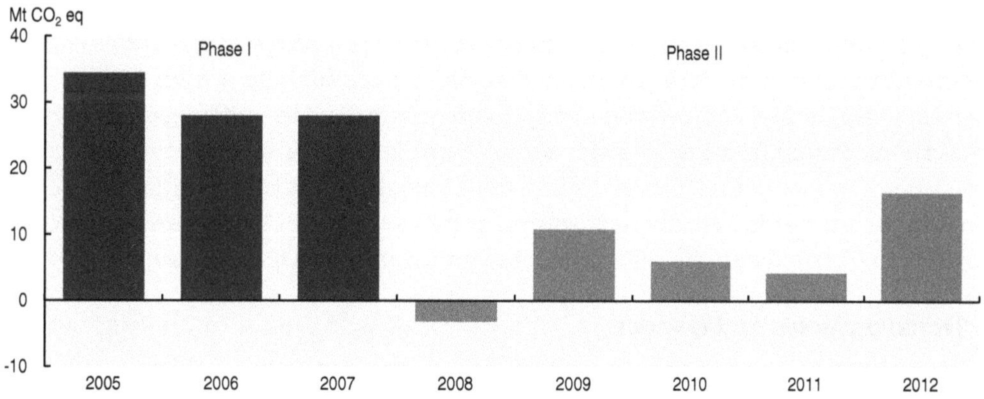

Note: Difference between allocated and verified emissions.
Source: EEA (2014), *EU ETS data viewer* (database).

StatLink http://dx.doi.org/10.1787/888933197673

Under the current phase of the EU ETS, Poland received a derogation allowing 405 million free allowances to certain installations in the electricity sector until 2020, conditional upon modernisation investment of equivalent value (Section 5.4).[3] Other industrial installations exposed to trade were granted free allocations based on their GHG emission performance against product benchmarks.[4] These sectors are receiving 423 million free allowances over 2013-20 (European Commission, 2013a). Analysis suggests that the rapid improvements in Polish industry's energy and carbon efficiency place most industry sectors within EU-wide emission performance benchmarks. The free allocation mechanism for industry sectors has tempered concerns about carbon leakage, and Polish industry has generally received free allocation at a level comparable to that of other EU countries (Sartor and Spencer, 2013).

The remaining allowances, about 703 million over 2013-20, are to be auctioned. Auctioning of allowances is a new source of government revenue, which could be used to further transition to lower-carbon energy sources, or lessen the social impact of transition. Under the revised EU ETS directive, half the revenue is meant to be used for action related to climate change. Decisions to freely allocate rather than auction allowances must consider the resulting reduction in government revenue, and the potential for using revenue in more economically productive ways. Overall, more than 65 million allowances were auctioned or sold in 2013, a major departure from the previous two phases. As of December 2013, auctions of Polish certificates had generated about EUR 244 million (EEX, 2013).[5]

From an environmental perspective, the EU ETS has maintained an upper limit on emissions from covered sectors through implementation of a hard cap. As in many EU countries, over-allocation, and collapsed and volatile allowance prices following the economic recession, as well as windfall profits for certain industries,[6] have meant that the CO_2 price signal has not been sufficient to significantly affect investment decisions regarding the electricity mix. This may change with the third trading period, which started in 2013, though an oversupply of allowances could result in a continued low carbon price.[7] Research suggests that the cost of allowances is generally passed on in wholesale electricity prices, whether or not the allowances are allocated freely (Reinaud, 2007; Laing et al., 2013). While this could theoretically also pass on the carbon price signal to final consumers, retail prices are affected by a range of market and policy factors, and evidence so far suggests that carbon prices under the EU ETS have not significantly affected retail electricity prices in the EU, including in Poland (European Commission, 2014a; Jouvet and Solier, 2013; Sijm et al., 2008). Other practical factors reduce the responsiveness of investment decisions to the carbon price signal. These include a high degree of state ownership, very limited competition in electricity generation, an underdeveloped organised wholesale electricity market and the vertical integration of electricity producers and distributors. The lack of an effective carbon price signal is particularly important in Poland, given investment needs over the next several decades as old coal-fired generation capacity will need to be retired and the rest considerably modernised (OECD, 2012a; IEA, 2011).

2.4. *Transport taxes and charges*

Since 2000, Poland's road vehicle stock has shown one of the fastest growth rates in the OECD and the transport sector is a growing source of GHG emissions (Chapter 1). Poland is one of the few European countries without explicit vehicle taxes linked to CO_2 emissions (OECD, 2012a). While theoretically less efficient than taxes on fuel or emissions from an environmental point of view, these taxes can nevertheless play a large role in affecting the level and composition of a national fleet (OECD, 2010a). The one-off tax levied on the sale or import of passenger vehicles is the largest source of revenue from vehicle taxation. In 2009, its rate was raised from 3.1% to 18.6% for cars with capacity greater than 2 000 cm^3. This has not reduced the share of such vehicles in the passenger car fleet, though the segment is rather small at 7%. Fees levied at the district level are also applied for vehicle registration and licensing. The lack of environmental consideration in car taxation has promoted large imports of older, second-hand vehicles. As there is no recurrent tax on car ownership in Poland, the share of non-fuel transport taxes in revenue from environmentally related taxes is much lower than in other OECD countries (Figure 3.1). Local governments levy a recurrent, weight-based tax on vehicles over 3.5 tonnes. It can be partly or completely refunded for vehicles engaged in combined transport shipments in

Poland (European Commission, 2013b). Local governments can also make exemptions to the tax, which could technically be used to encourage more environment-friendly vehicles. In practice, however, they have not been used for this purpose. Overall, revenue from vehicle taxes increased until 2008 and then declined as economic slowdown and post-2009 oil price recovery slowed the pace of car registrations.

Since 2011 an electronic road toll system for vehicles above 3.5 tonnes has been in place, with per kilometre rates differentiated according to Euro emission standards. The system has encouraged fleet renewal: by August 2013 the share of Euro V vehicles was 31%, compared with 23% in November 2011 (Kapsch, 2013, 2012). There are also tolls for all road users on specific sections of motorways and national roads that could be extended to the whole network.

The tax treatment of commuting expenses seems relatively neutral. Employee-paid commuting expenses are tax deductible using a flat rate, regardless of the form of transport used and distance travelled. Employer-paid expenses, including provision of parking spaces, are fully taxed regardless of the form of transport used. Personal use of company cars is considered a taxable benefit in kind, and the direct costs of vehicle use are a basis for taxation. However, how the tax is calculated is unclear and appears to vary, making it difficult to determine whether this taxable benefit is undervalued and therefore subsidising greater use of company cars for personal purposes (OECD, 2014c; KPMG, 2014).

2.5. *Other resource and pollution taxes and fees*

Poland has had a complex system of environmental fees and charges for over 20 years. Those that are unrequited payments (e.g. on air pollution and water effluents) are classified as taxes according to OECD definitions, although the Environment Protection Law calls them fees. Environmental fees and charges apply to a very broad range of pollutants (including CO_2 emissions for industrial sectors outside the EU ETS) at rates that are generally adjusted annually for inflation. The system is based on a "permit/charge/non-compliance fee model", combining an emission charge in conjunction with a permitting system. A base charge is applied to all emissions below the level stipulated in the permit required for the economic activity being conducted; a significantly higher penalty rate is applied to pollution above the permitted level (World Bank, 2005). Any economic activity requiring a permit is subject to reporting of emissions and payment of the charge if the value exceeds PLN 800 over a six-month period. Simplified calculation methods are provided for certain sources. Entities must report emissions even if they are not required to pay any charge.

The longest-running charges and fees are on air and water pollution, water abstraction and waste landfilling. Related revenue is earmarked for environmental protection and water management and is managed by environmental funds, counties and municipalities (Section 5.3). Total revenue has declined slightly in real terms over the past decade. While revenue from landfill charges increased with the sharp rise of charge levels, revenue from charges on air and water pollution and water abstraction declined as fee rates were stable while pollutant discharges and water use declined. Nevertheless, fee levels have not been high enough to provide an incentive to reduce pollution and use water efficiently (Hogg et al., 2014; Chapter 5). They could be raised to better reflect social and environmental externalities and, for example, help fund environmental investment.

In 2012, a tax on radioactive waste was established, levied per MWh of electricity generated by nuclear energy. Poland does not generate any nuclear power but plans to do so within the next decade; establishing this tax early on is a good way of signalling that costs associated with generation of nuclear waste need to be included in development plans.

In 2012, a mineral extraction tax for copper ore was introduced. Poland also changed the taxation regime for oil and gas extraction in 2014 to attract greater investment in this area and encourage exploration of unconventional shale gas (Terlecka and Leśniak, 2014; Chancellery, 2014; Ernst & Young, 2013). Although the set rates are relatively low by international comparison, they are projected to double the government's tax take from hydrocarbon extraction to 40% in 2020.[8] In addition, Poland imposes extraction fees. Materials incurring such fees include coal, oil, natural gas, soil, sand and gravel, and, since 2012, copper ore. Part (40%) of the related revenue is earmarked for the National Fund for Environmental Protection and Water Management to reduce the negative environmental effects of mining (mine closure and reclamation of degraded areas). Recent changes in legislation on hydrocarbons will reduce the share earmarked to the fund to 10% of revenue from extraction fees in 2016. However, revenue raised for the fund in 2016 is projected to be maintained at the 2012 level due to the increase in fee rates. Moreover, the fund will receive the total revenue from the extraction fee from offshore exploitation of hydrocarbons.

3. Removing environmentally perverse incentives

A broad range of exemptions from the payment of excise taxes constitute implicit environmentally harmful subsidies. They include exemptions from taxes on coal and natural gas, notably for electricity generation, households and public administrations, inputs into energy products, combined heat and power, agriculture, fishery and forestry, and heating by energy-intensive industries and industries covered by tradable permit schemes that have implemented environmental or energy efficiency improvements (OECD, 2013c; European Commission, 2013b).[9] These exemptions reduce incentives to save energy and switch to less polluting fuels. Exemptions are fully compliant with flexibility allowed for in the EU's Energy Taxation Directive, though they entail environmental and health challenges that would benefit from a more tailored approach. For example, coal use in inefficient domestic heating equipment is a significant source of urban air pollution, though this negative externality does not lead coal to be penalised in relation to less polluting fuels. Major water users are exempt from water abstraction fees, notably for aquaculture, irrigation, mining and, subject to certain conditions, cooling purposes in power generation and hydropower.

Other than these exemptions, two main types of subsidies for fossil fuels have been reported by the OECD (OECD, 2013c): direct support to the hard-coal industry and rebates on diesel fuel tax for farming. Subsidies to the coal industry have been framed by EU rules since Poland's accession, and state aid is no longer given for operating costs (OECD, 2013c). Many subsidies relate to historic liabilities such as the cost of closing mines, rehabilitating sites and supporting workforce transition. They have generally decreased since 2005, and have been eliminated for employment restructuring. Free provision of coal to miners is also being phased out with the introduction of cash equivalents. In addition, a one-off investment aid of PLN 400 million was provided in 2010 to cover initial fixed capital costs of accessing coal reserves in existing mines. Since 2008, the largest subsidy to coal has been compensation to electricity generators for the cancellation of long-term power purchase agreements. Annual amounts exceeded PLN 2 billion over 2009-11. Mining is also one of a few sectors that benefit from special old-age pension regimes, which are costly and limit sectoral and territorial labour mobility (OECD, 2014a).

In 2006, all EU member states were required to apply a minimum tax rate on diesel used in farming; since then, Poland has allowed farmers to apply for rebates on payment of the diesel excise duty up to a limit of 86 litres per hectare of utilised agricultural area. Budget outlays for the rebate have increased significantly in nominal terms, from PLN 114 million in 2006 to PLN 720 million in 2011 (OECD, 2013c). The exemption rate is determined annually by the Minister of Agriculture and Rural Development. Several other EU countries have such exemptions in place, though their rationale often remains unclear given the much more significant measures available to financially support the agricultural sector (such as the Common Agricultural Policy). Reform efforts in some countries have occurred in recent years, with the Czech Republic reducing the tax refund rate in phases starting in 2013. Similarly, in the Netherlands, pressure to reduce public deficits and the high administrative costs of having separate taxation rates on diesel used in agriculture and construction led to a unified tax rate from 2013, with some recycling of revenue back to the agricultural sector for environmental measures (Withana et al., 2012).

There is no comprehensive information on potentially environmentally harmful subsidies and tax expenditure. Since 2010, the Ministry of Finance has reviewed tax expenditure annually (Ministry of Finance, 2010). Poland could build on this exercise to establish a process for the review of environmentally harmful subsidies. Such a review would mean screening public support programmes against their potential environmental impact, the effect on public finances and, more generally, economic and social costs and benefits. This would improve the transparency of taxation and public expenditure and could be the basis for reforms of subsidies and special tax treatment that are not justified on economic, social or environmental grounds.

4. Towards green tax reform?

Poland will need to adopt additional measures to consolidate its fiscal position. Raising revenue from environmentally related taxes and cutting environmentally harmful tax expenditure could contribute to this effort, and achieve positive environmental and economic outcomes. The National Environmental Policy contemplated environmental fiscal reform but never followed up; the idea is also considered in the Strategy for Energy Security and the Environment but no implementation framework has been established (Council of Ministers, 2002, 2008). Vivid Economics (2012) found that increasing excise duty on diesel, progressively removing exemptions on residential coal and gas consumption and indexing energy tax rates to inflation could raise over EUR 5 billion annually by 2020, with a better or equivalent impact on economic activity and more CO_2 emission reduction than with other fiscal measures. Hogg et al. (2014) identified potential additional revenue equivalent to 1.45% of GDP in 2020, with environmental benefits estimated at 0.67% of GDP, mostly from reduced SO_X, NO_X and PM_{10} emissions from stationary sources and reductions in industrial use of natural gas and coal. The World Bank (2011) found that using revenue from environmental taxes or emission allowances to subsidise labour costs could lead to a more positive impact on employment than subsidising industries. Additional revenue could also be recycled to alleviate the impact of price increases on vulnerable people.

In 2012, spending on electricity, gas and other fuels (including transport fuels)[10] accounted for 13% of total Polish household expenditure, among the highest rates in the OECD. Water supply and sanitation services also represent a relatively high share of household spending, in particular for the poorest (OECD, 2010b). Recent OECD (2014d) analysis suggests that taxes on transport fuels have a progressive impact in Poland due to lower car use by poorer households, whereas those on electricity appear regressive. Although heating fuels are virtually untaxed in Poland, the effect of such taxes in other countries seems broadly neutral. Other factors, such as availability of public transport and district heating, can mitigate the adverse impact of energy taxes. These issues are not sufficiently analysed in Poland and could be further explored to minimise regressive effects.

Poland uses direct transfers to address affordability concerns. Municipalities grant an allowance to poor households to cover the difference between actual housing expenditure (including water and waste charges and energy) and a share of household income that depends on income level and dwelling size. About 3% of households received the allowance between 2010 and 2012. In 2013, such households became eligible for a lump sum energy benefit. These financially vulnerable customers can also file a request to their gas or electricity utilities for installation of a pre-paid metering system, the cost of which is to be borne by the supplier. As the Polish energy market is gradually being liberalised, such targeted direct transfers are a less distorting way of protecting vulnerable customers than maintaining artificially low tariffs.

5. Investing in the environment to promote green growth

5.1. *Expenditure on environmental protection*

According to the Central Statistical Office, between 2006[11] and 2011 total public[12] and business[13] environmental expenditure[14] increased from 1.6% of GDP to 1.9%. This relatively high and growing percentage reflects the effort to meet EU environmental requirements. Public expenditure, mainly at subnational levels, remained slightly higher than that of business (Figure 3.4). As in most other OECD countries, wastewater and waste management absorbed the largest share at, respectively, 58% and 28% of total public expenditure, on average. Investment accounted for about two-thirds of public environmental expenditure on wastewater management but only 14% on waste management, mainly for operating expenditure of municipally owned utilities. Private specialised producers of environmental services accounted for about one-third of businesses' environmental expenditure. The bulk of their spending related to operating expenses of waste services. The electricity, gas and water supply subsector made up a further third of business environmental expenditure. The share of this sector in total business investment in air protection grew from 52% in 2006 to 81% in 2011 due to the need to modernise and replace ageing coal-fired power plants to comply with EU requirements on air and climate protection.

5.2. *Investment in environmental protection and water management*

Between 2002 and 2011, total investment in environmental protection nearly doubled. The growth was particularly striking after 2007 with the increased allocation of structural and cohesion funds to wastewater management (Figure 3.5). In 2011, the public sector accounted for about 80% of total investment in wastewater management and more than half of total investment in waste management. In 2012, with the exception of noise and vibration abatement and R&D, all environmental protection activities were affected by the overall decline in investment resulting from the economic slowdown, fiscal consolidation measures and the ending of the 2007-13 EU financial cycle. However, investment should pick up again in 2014-15 with disbursement of EU funds.

Since 2002, the near doubling of investment in wastewater management has helped increase the share of population connected to sewage treatment plants, which grew by

Figure 3.4. **Expenditure on environmental protection**

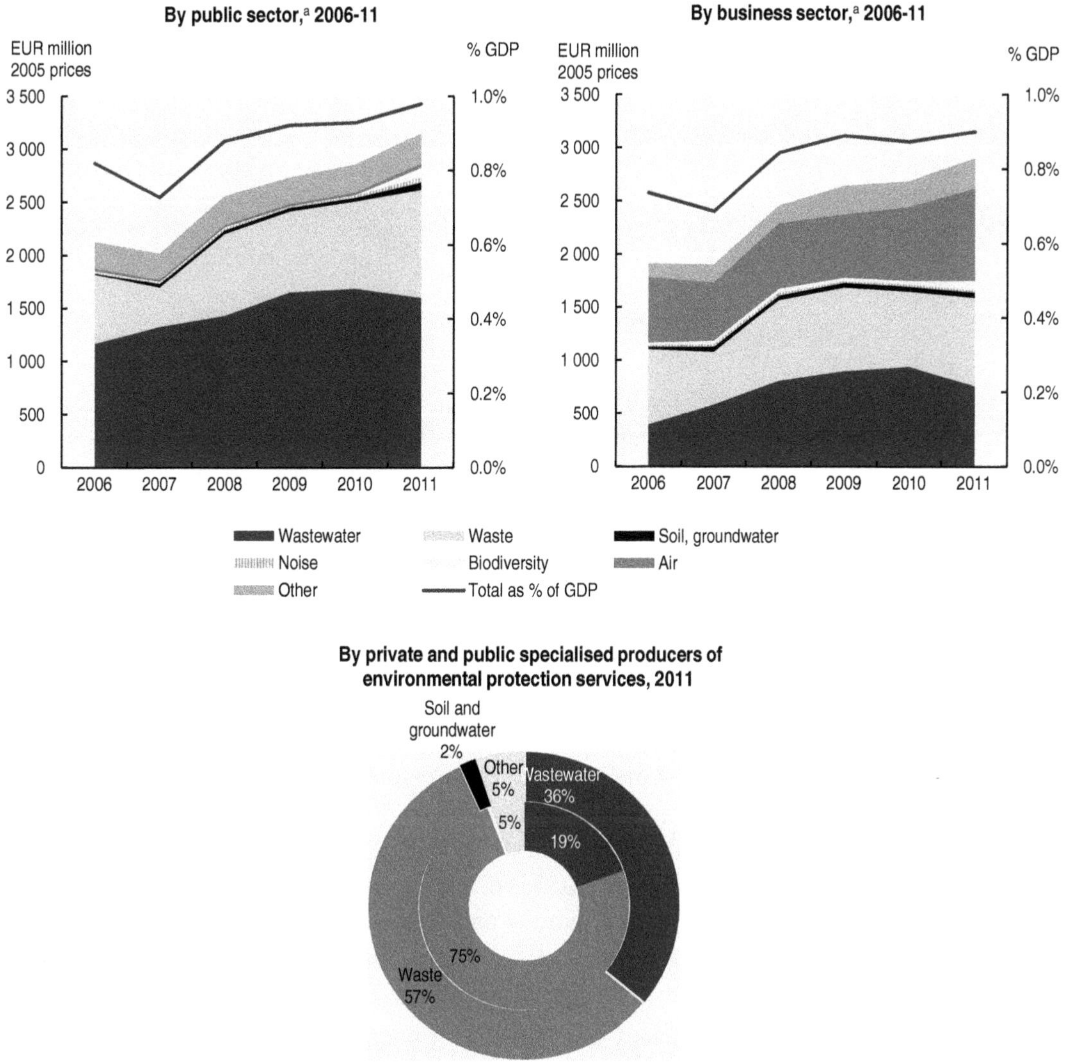

Inner circle: Private specialised producers: 1.1 EUR billion
Outer circle: Public specialised producers: 2.0 EUR billion

Note: Data refer to investment and internal current expenditure (excluding payments to specialised producers of environmental protection services) less receipts from by-products (e.g. material recovered as a result of waste treatment). Includes expenditure on i) pollution abatement and control covering air protection, waste and wastewater management, protection and remediation of soil and groundwater, and other environmental protection activities (R&D, administration, education); and ii) biodiversity and landscape protection. Excludes expenditure on water supply.
a) Including specialised producers of environmental protection services.
Source: OECD (2014), *OECD Environment Statistics* (database).

StatLink http://dx.doi.org/10.1787/888933197685

12 percentage points to 69% in 2012. Although this rate is below the OECD average of 77%, Poland exceeded the goals of 90% of urban population and 30% of rural population connection rates, set in the 2007 National Cohesion Strategy (Ministry of Regional Development, 2007). However, interim targets of the Urban Waste Water Treatment Directive were not achieved and Poland is unlikely to meet the 2015 deadline for implementing the directive due to planning deficiencies and a financing gap (European Commission, 2013c, 2012b; MoE, 2013). The national municipal wastewater treatment programme, adopted in

Figure 3.5. **Investment in environmental protection and water resource management, 2002-12**

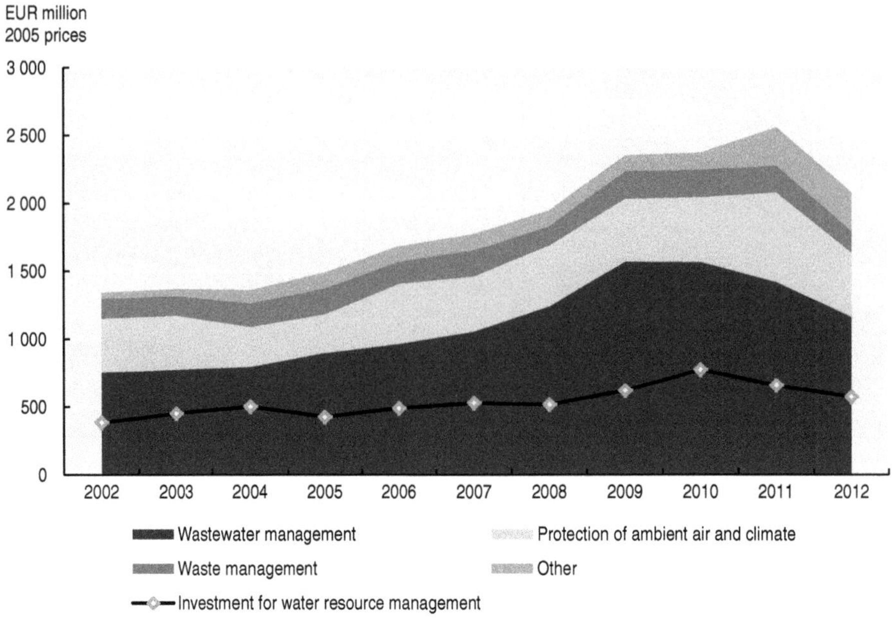

Source: CSO (2013), *Environment 2013.*

StatLink http://dx.doi.org/10.1787/888933197698

2003 to fulfil the directive requirements, is being revised for the fourth time and should address these bottlenecks. According to the draft revision, PLN 29.4 billion (EUR 7 billion) in investment will be required to implement the directive, which would mean maintaining the 2012 investment level until 2015. This new estimate is 22% below the previous figure following a reassessment of sewerage needs. EU funds are expected to meet 47% of the funding need and government (central and local) finance 38%.

Investment in water management rose at a slower pace than investment in wastewater management over 2002-11. Although the share of population with access to water supply reached 88% in 2012, there are wide variations between regions and between rural and urban areas (Chapter 1). Revenue from charges on water abstraction and effluent discharges decreased over the decade and remains insufficient to cover the cost of water and sanitation services. Removing exemptions on water abstraction charges for mining, energy, aquaculture and irrigation would help bridge this gap. In addition, the water industry is very fragmented and dominated by municipally owned utilities. Establishing an independent water and sanitation service regulator could improve efficiency by imposing productivity targets using international benchmarking and yardstick regulation, and could promote economies of scale (OECD, 2014a).

Despite a 35% increase in investment over 2002-11, waste infrastructure remains unsatisfactory. In 2012, about 20% of the population still lacked access to municipal waste collection services, and landfilling accounted for 75% of municipal waste treatment, compared with an OECD average of 45% (Chapter 1). It is estimated that over EUR 6 billion in investment is needed for municipal waste management between 2014 and 2020, an annual average investment about four times the level in 2012 (Chapter 5).

5.3. Financing investment in environmental protection and water supply

EU funds

Since 2004, Poland has benefitted from large inflows of EU funds, which have helped finance investment and contributed to economic growth. With EUR 68 billion[15] allocated over 2007-13 and EUR 77 billion (structural[16] and cohesion funds) over 2014-20, Poland is the largest beneficiary of EU cohesion policy, receiving about one-fifth of total EU funds (Figure 3.6) (European Commission, 2014b).

Figure 3.6. **EU structural and cohesion funds, 2007-13 and 2014-20**

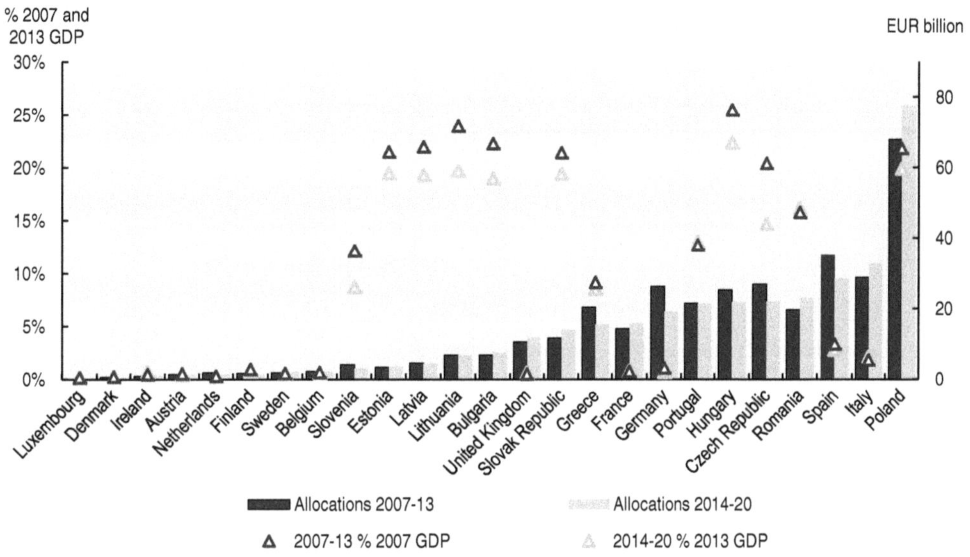

Note: Only recipients from both periods are shown.

Source: European Commission (2014), "Summary of the Partnership Agreement for Poland, 2014-2020"; European Commission (2013), *Analysis of the Budgetary Implementation of the Structural and Cohesion Funds in 2012.*

StatLink http://dx.doi.org/10.1787/888933197708

The Operational Programme Infrastructure and Environment (OPIE) 2007-13 was the biggest operational programme in EU history at nearly EUR 38 billion (Figure 3.7).[17] Of this, EU funds provided EUR 28 billion and national matching funds the remainder (Ministry of Regional Development, 2007). Transport infrastructure was the top priority with 69% of funding, followed by environment (including water resource management) at 16% and energy-related projects at 8%.[18] In the next phase (2014-20), OPIE amounts to EUR 32 billion, with EUR 28 billion once again coming from EU funds. Transport continues to receive the lion's share of funding. Environmental protection represents 14% of allocations and the low-emission economy 6%. Thus the focus on climate-related support is greater than in the previous programming period (Ministry of Infrastructure and Development, 2014a; European Commission, 2014b). These themes are also part of regional operational programmes, which were allocated 41% of EU funding over 2014-20 compared with 25% in 2007-13, underlining the need for effective vertical co-ordination of public investment.

Poland's overall absorption of EU funds accelerated significantly after financial management and control procedures were simplified in 2010. By the end of 2013, projects worth EUR 64 billion in grants had been contracted by operational programme beneficiaries, representing 93% of EU allocations (Ministry of Infrastructure and Development, 2013).

Figure 3.7. **Operational Programme Infrastructure and Environment, by priority**

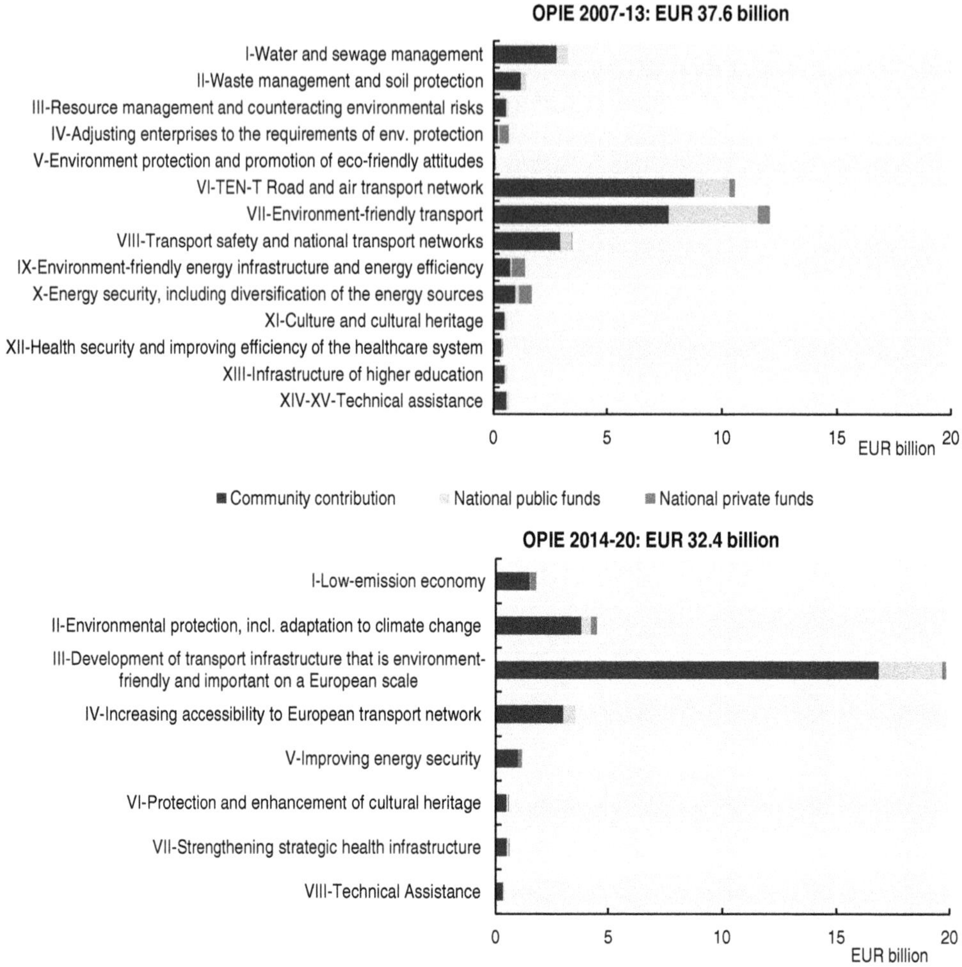

Source: Ministry of Infrastructure and Development (2014), Draft Operational Programme Infrastructure and Environment 2014-2020, 8 January 2014; Ministry of Regional Development (2007), *Operational Programme Infrastructure and Environment, The National Strategic Reference Framework 2007-2013.*

StatLink http://dx.doi.org/10.1787/888933197712

Poland was also successful in absorbing EU funds to build environmental infrastructure. Under OPIE 2007-13, 92% of EU funding on environment[19] had been contracted by the end of 2013 (Ministry of Infrastructure and Development, 2014b). However, progress on disbursement should be better linked to results. Evaluation studies have shown that outcomes of some environmental projects (e.g. sewage treatment, solid waste management, natural disaster prevention) have been undermined by geographic dispersion, and recommended a clearer delimitation of functional areas served by infrastructure (European Commission, 2012a). Since 2009, the share of EU support in financing investment in environmental protection and water management has exceeded that of national environmental funds (Figure 3.8).

Environmental funds

As implementing bodies of environmental priorities in OPIE 2007-13, the National Fund for Environmental Protection and Water Management (NFEPWM) and the 16 Voivodship

Figure 3.8. **Financing investment in environmental protection and water resource management, 2002-12**

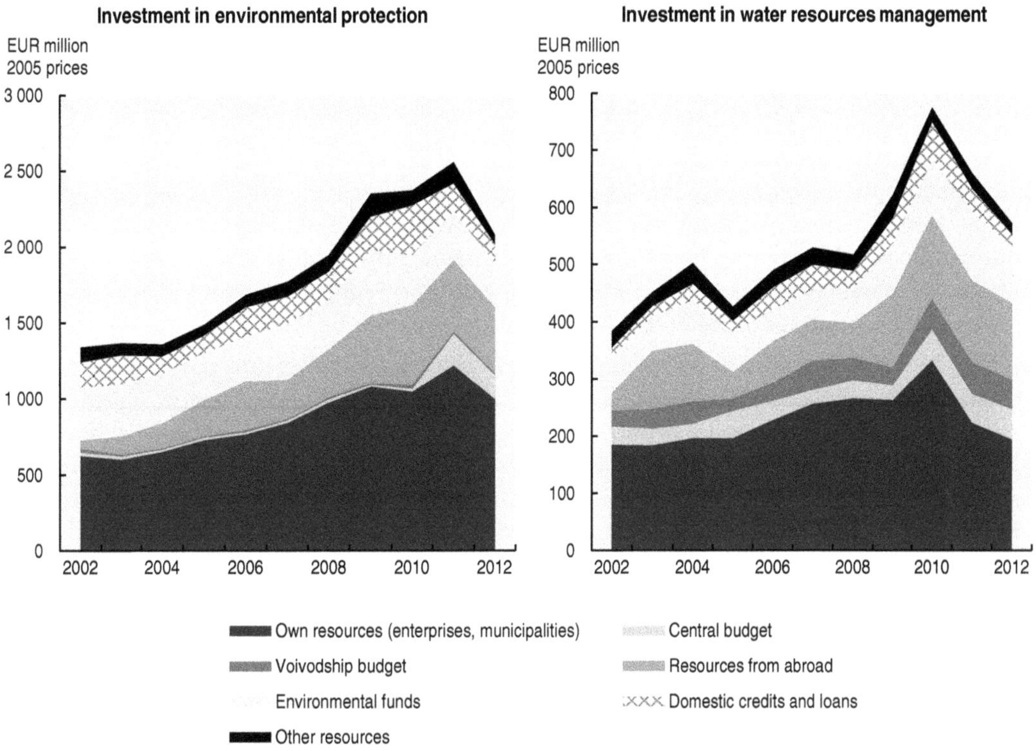

Source: CSO (2014), "Environmental Protection", *Local Data Bank* (database).

StatLink http://dx.doi.org/10.1787/888933197729

Funds for Environmental Protection and Water Management (VFEPWMs) have played important roles in absorption rates. Environmental funds have been key institutions for financing environmental projects in Poland, giving preferential loans and grants to municipalities, public utility companies, business and households. Since 2010, county and municipal (powiat and gmina) funds have been closed. Municipalities have been receiving about 30% and counties 10% of revenue collected from environmental charges[20] and fees, provided that they support environmental protection. Also in 2010, the repayment period ended for the Polish EcoFund, funded by international debt-for-environment swaps (Box 3.1). The NFEPWM and VFEPWMs are now the main instruments for financing environmental expenditure programmes. They draw their resources domestically, co-finance projects and manage EU funds[21] and other revenue from international sources, in particular European Economic Area and Norway grants.[22] Between 2004 and 2014, out of EUR 1.1 billion allocated to Poland under these grants, EUR 320 million was devoted to projects on environment and climate change.

Domestically, environmental funds receive part of the proceeds of environmental charges and fees: 21% to the NFEPWM and 39% to the VFEPWMs. Over 2009-13, environmental charges and fines contributed as much as loan repayment to NFEPWM revenue (Figure 3.9). Fees on imports of used vehicles and substitution fees and penalties from the green certificates system have been other significant sources of NFEPWM income. While the former are likely to decrease as Poland complies with the requirements of the end-of-life

Box 3.1. **The Polish EcoFund**

The EcoFund was an independent, non-profit foundation established by the Ministry of Finance in 1992. It was created when six creditor countries (members of the "Paris Club") agreed to waive repayment of part of Poland's public debt if the funds were used for environmental protection, a so-called debt-for-environment swap.

As a result, the EcoFund had a stable and predictable source of revenue: funds previously set aside for debt repayment. Over the debt repayment period to 2010 the fund disbursed about PLN 2.5 billion. Although the sum was relatively small, its impact was significant due to a powerful leveraging effect on other financial sources. The EcoFund's close attention to achieving high benefit/cost ratios offered reassurance that it avoided the inefficiency sometimes associated with earmarked programmes.

The Polish EcoFund was renowned for well-designed expenditure programmes and rigorous management procedures based on the following criteria: a strict framework of clearly defined environmental priorities and project eligibility criteria; clear requirements for, and strictly professional relations with, applicants; clearly defined appraisal and selection criteria emphasising environmental benefits and cost-effectiveness; and careful monitoring of projects to ensure proper use of funds and achievement of environmental effects. These procedures led to objective, transparent and accountable decision making. As a result, it was an effective catalyst for initiating needed environmental investment in Poland, and its approach and working methods provide a useful reference for other public environmental funds.

Source: OECD (2007), "Making Environmental Spending Count", *Policy Brief*; OECD (2003), *OECD Environmental Performance Reviews: Poland*; The System of Financing Environmental Protection in Poland, CoP 19, Warsaw.

vehicles directive, the latter dropped significantly in 2013 as prices of green certificates fell (Section 5.4, Chapter 5).

Increased EU inflows have helped strengthen the institutional capacity of environmental funds. The NFEPWM's staff grew from 270 people in 2003 to 530 in 2013 (NFEPWM, 2004, 2013). It gained experience in implementing different forms of financing environmental protection[23] involving banks and the private sector. However, the methods for allocating funds and the selection criteria for projects have not always been clear to potential beneficiaries (IEA, 2011). Since 2009, the NFEPWM has taken a more transparent and results-oriented approach of four-year funding cycles. It developed a strategy reflecting its priority programmes, the rules for co-financing projects and selection criteria (NFEPWM, 2012a). A joint strategy with the VFEPWMs was also developed to improve co-ordination (NFEPWM, 2012b). Over 2009-12, the NFEPWM kept operating costs stable and improved processing time of applications. Its best practices were rewarded both domestically[24] and in Europe. However, it fell short of its objective to leverage private finance, partly due to the overlap between its programmes and EU funds. It also failed to achieve its target on funding renewable energy sources, due to delays in adopting the new law (Section 5.4). Project planning and evaluation were hampered by the large number of priority programmes, limited use of cost-effectiveness criteria and differences across VFEPWMs in assessing environmental needs and reporting environmental outcomes (NFEPWM, 2012a, 2012b). The 2013-16 strategies[25] recommended reducing the number of priorities and increasing the share of repayable financing in relation to non-repayable from own sources. Given the uncertainty of EU funding levels after 2020, there is a need to

Figure 3.9. **The National Fund for Environmental Protection and Water Management**

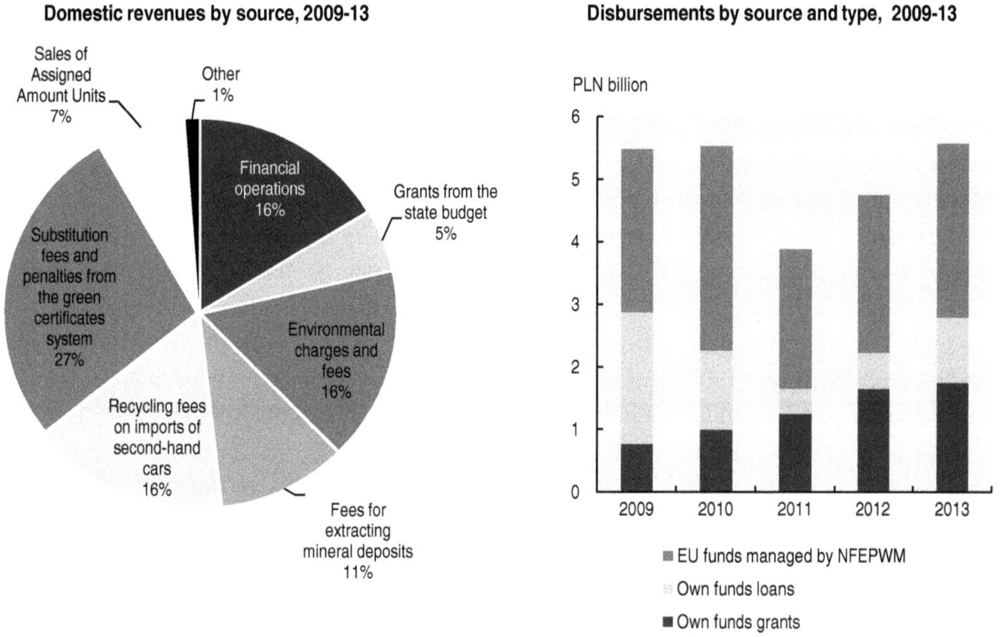

Source: NFEPWM (2012), *Action Strategy of the National Fund for Environmental Protection and Water Management for 2013-2016 with a View to 2020;* NFEPWM, *Annual Reports.*

StatLink http://dx.doi.org/10.1787/888933197731

raise environmental charges and develop incentives to mobilise private finance for environmental infrastructure.

Private participation

EU funds and loans and subsidies from environmental funds do not cover water and sanitation services' full investment cost. Municipalities co-finance investments with their own resources, most often in the form of bank loans and increasingly via municipal bonds (OECD, 2009). In recent years, there has been progress in intermunicipal co-operation to provide infrastructure for water treatment and waste management, often involving joint applications for EU funds or other external finance (OECD, 2013d). The main driver of this trend has been EU conditionality in multilevel funding arrangements.[26] However, the fragmentation of the water and sanitation sector, the dominance of municipally owned utilities and the tendency of municipalities to set below-cost tariffs to protect local monopolies have deterred further private involvement (OECD, 2014a). Poland aims to increase private sector participation in water and waste infrastructure under the recently amended public-private partnership law. By the end of 2013, 12 water and sewerage projects and 9 waste projects had been announced, though few had been signed.

5.4. Investment in "clean energy" and sustainable transport

Although Poland achieved its Kyoto target, meeting its 2020 GHG emission target in both EU ETS and non-EU ETS sectors may pose a challenge, which could be even more acute in the longer term as the EU has adopted more ambitious objectives (IEA, 2011; European Commission, 2014c). Heavy reliance on coal means Poland has the third most carbon-intensive electricity system in the OECD. The need to upgrade energy infrastructure is pressing, as nearly half of generating capacity is more than 30 years old, and transmission and distribution networks are also ageing. The IEA has estimated[27] that this would involve EUR 195 billion in investment over 2010-30. This challenge is also an opportunity to move away from carbon lock-in (IEA, 2011).

The 2009 Energy Policy of Poland to 2030 (now being revised) aimed at mitigating the power sector's environmental impact by improving energy efficiency and diversifying the energy mix towards gas, nuclear power and renewables. It also outlined strategies for carbon capture and storage and for compliance with the EU ETS directive. Under the latter, Poland was granted a derogation to provide free allowances to its power sector worth about EUR 7.4 billion[28] over 2013-19, conditional upon investment of equivalent value to modernise electricity generation and diversify the energy mix (European Commission, 2014d). Accordingly, Poland presented a national investment plan of 347 projects with a total value exceeding PLN 119 billion (EUR 28 billion). It largely supports hard-coal plants (upgrades and new plants), followed by gas and nuclear, with some biomass and one hydropower plant (ClientEarth, 2012). Nevertheless, the European Commission judged that these investments would allow Poland to diversify its electricity production sources and help in reaching Europe's 2020 objectives by reducing GHG emissions (European Commission, 2014d).

Energy efficiency

Poland's 2011 Energy Efficiency Action Plan (EEAP) provided a final energy savings target of 11% by 2016 compared to the 2001-05 average. Under new EU legislation (2012/27/EU), Poland's 2014 EEAP set an indicative target for 2020 of stabilising primary energy consumption at about the 2010 level (Chapter 1). This will require strengthening energy efficiency policies in all sectors. In 2013, Poland's energy intensity was 19% higher than the OECD Europe average. There is significant potential to improve energy efficiency, particularly in housing and public buildings, but also in district heating systems. Public support and the "white certificate" system are the main EEAP instruments to achieve the 2020 target.

Since 1998, the Thermo-modernisation Fund, overseen by the Ministry of Infrastructure and Development and managed by the state-owned Bank Gospodarstwa Krajowego, has been the key instrument for thermal improvement investment in existing buildings. It has provided subsidised loans mainly to building owners and local government to renovate apartment buildings. The fund targets "best practice" renovations, focusing on projects that would not be attractive under normal lending conditions. Between 2004 and 2013, its subsidies totalled PLN 1.5 billion, but dependence on transfers from the central government budget has led to large variations in funding: for example, no money was received in 2010 (BGK, 2014). The programme has helped develop energy audit services (Ciszewska, 2014). However, besides a lack of sufficient and stable funding, it has been hampered by complexity and the perception of risk, which has put off some commercial banks and potential investors (Rekiel, 2014).

The NFEPWM has increasingly supported investment in energy efficiency and renewables through numerous programmes that are not always easy to track. Over 2011-13, it disbursed about PLN 1 billion under a green investment programme using, in particular, the proceeds from sales of surplus assigned amount units from the Kyoto commitment period 2008-12,[29] PLN 780 million from OPIE priority IX and PLN 535 million in a programme for projects on renewables and high-efficiency co-generation (NFEPWM, 2013). The NFEPWM expects the amount to more than double over 2013-16, notably through a quadrupling of loans (NFEPWM, 2012a).

An innovative financing facility for energy efficiency investments targeting small and medium-sized enterprises (SMEs) was established in 2011 by the European Bank for Reconstruction and Development (EBRD) in collaboration with various banks. This facility, the Polish Sustainable Energy Financing Facility (PolSEFF), had provided over EUR 170 million in loans by the end of 2013 and paid out EUR 17 million in incentives following completion of investments (PolSEFF, 2014). In 2013 under PolSEFF II the EBRD made an additional credit line of EUR 200 million available, supplemented by EUR 25 million for grants provided by the NFEPWM.

Planned since the 2007 EEAP, the "white certificate" system for energy savings was finally implemented in 2013.[30] It was expected to achieve more than one-third of the savings outlined in the 2011 Energy Efficiency Action Plan. However, results of the first tender were lower than expected: only 1.4% of the obligation was met using white certificates, the rest being met by payment of the substitution fee (Ciszewska, 2014). Unless projects in the next auction rounds result in significant savings, Poland may struggle to meet its 2020 target. A similar tradable certificate system has been used since 2007 to support high-efficiency combined heat and power/cogeneration. However, it has not led to significant new investment due to regulatory uncertainty (IEA, 2011).

Renewable energy sources

Since 2005, mandatory quotas for power companies and a green certificate system have encouraged the use of renewable energy sources. The share of renewable sources in gross final energy consumption rose from 7.2% in 2005 to 11.0% in 2012 and Poland seems on track to meet its 2020 target of 15% (Ministry of Economy, 2010, 2014). However, renewables accounted for only 10% of electricity generation in 2013, half the OECD average (Chapter 1). Although quotas and green certificates have been successful in developing wind capacity, the system did not spur investment in new types of technologies because it encouraged the development of co-firing biomass with coal in existing power plants as a way to comply with the obligation without much investment. Too many green certificates were issued for biomass co-firing, which weakened their price and made them unattractive to investors in newer technology. As a result, the renewable energy mix is quite unbalanced, with biomass accounting for 60% of gross electricity generation from renewable sources in 2012 (Ministry of Economy, 2014). Should Poland reach its 2020 renewables target with co-firing, this achievement will be short-lived, as old coal plants, which provide the bulk of co-firing, will have to retire after 2020 to comply with EU regulation (OECD, 2012a).

Since 2011, the government has envisaged various options to reform the support system. This has created uncertainty for investors and slowed the pace of investment. In 2012, it proposed linking the price of green certificates to the cost of technology and introducing a feed-in tariff for small renewables projects. The current proposal (July 2014) introduces renewables auctions instead of green certificates. Existing projects can choose to benefit from the previous (still in force) system of green certificates for up to 15 years, or join the auctions. The government will reserve 25% of the auctions for small producers. Large biomass (> 50 MW) and hydropower (> 5 MW) installations will be excluded. The value of green certificates will be halved for plants that co-fire biomass with other fuels (coal, lignite, waste, gas, oil, etc.). The government estimates that the new system will lower the cost, which is passed on to end-users via a surcharge on the electricity price, by more than 40% by 2020.[31] The new law will take effect in 2016.

The NFEPWM also works in partnership with six banks to provide subsidised loans for investment in solar water heaters, offered to individuals, investors and housing associations. With a budget of PLN 450 million over 2010-14, the programme also supports market development, as the heaters are made in Poland. Uptake of solar water heaters had already begun before the programme launch in 2010, on purely economic grounds (IEA, 2011). The programme has had a positive impact on sales: by mid-2014, co-financing had been provided for over 65 000 installations.

Old transmission and distribution grids have been another key obstacle to renewables development. Transmission interconnections add flexibility and can be a cost-effective way to address variability, besides facilitating exports and improving supply security (IEA, 2011). Legal and technical barriers to obtaining permits for grid connection and connection fees have also complicated the development of distributed and small-scale generation. Amendments to the Energy Law in 2013 removed administrative barriers to the development of micro-installations, including waiving grid connection fees, and allowed them to sell electricity back to the grid. The Renewable Energy Institute has estimated that in the decade up to 2012, some PLN 6-7 billion was invested in on-grid and off-grid heat and power microgeneration by private individuals (IEO, 2013).

Sustainable transport

Since 2000, with support from EU funds, the volume of investment in inland transport infrastructure has more than quintupled. The GDP share of transport investment rose from 0.7% in 2000 to 2.5% in 2011, well above the OECD average (0.9%). As in other transition economies, Poland has been investing more heavily in roads, which have accounted for 90% of transport infrastructure investment in recent years. However, poorly developed transport infrastructure continues to be one of the most limiting factors for development (OECD, 2011). Despite significant investment, the density of motorways remains among the lowest in the EU and the rail network is substantially underinvested. Together with growing motorisation rates and an ageing car fleet, this has resulted in high levels of congestion and air pollution. Road transport accounts for 95% of total inland passenger transport and 75% of freight.[32] Growing GHG emissions from transport may prevent Poland from achieving its 2020 emission target in non-EU ETS sectors (European Commission, 2014c).

Until recently, little progress had been made in addressing the environmental impact of transport. OPIE 2007-13 was the main channel to promote sustainable transport. More than EUR 5 billion of EU funds was allocated to modernise and expand railway infrastructure, develop intelligent transport systems and promote intermodal transport (Ministry of Regional Development, 2007). However, absorption of EU funds for upgrading rail infrastructure has been hampered by inefficient management of the state-owned incumbent operator and prioritisation of road transport by the authorities[33] (OECD, 2014a; European Commission, 2014c). The non-competitive and inefficient tariff system has not provided sufficient revenue to meet the operating costs of the rail service despite high access charges. OECD economic surveys have recommended strengthening incentives for investment in rail infrastructure by increasing competition, enhancing private-sector involvement, reinforcing the sector regulator's independence and setting up a pricing system allowing for operating cost recovery (OECD, 2012a). Although significant progress has been made in freight, third-party access by non-government providers remains an issue (OECD, 2014a).

In recent years, Poland has taken measures to improve the absorption of EU funds in rail infrastructure. For example, railway investment was prioritised in the 2011 Multi-Annual Programme of Railway Investments to 2013 of the Transport Development Strategy (which looks forward to 2030) (Council of Ministers, 2014a). However, the funding allocated to the programme was repeatedly scaled down and implementation of infrastructure projects remains challenging (Council of Ministers, 2012, 2013, 2014a).

6. Promoting environmental technology and eco-innovation

6.1. General innovation capacity

Between 2007 and 2012, Poland's gross domestic expenditure on R&D rose from 0.57% of GDP to 0.90%, driven by significant increases in the national research budget and EU funding[34] (OECD, 2014e; European Commission, 2013d). Despite this effort, Poland's innovation performance is one of the poorest in the OECD, where the average R&D intensity stands at 2.4% of GDP. There is a long way to go to reach the national target of 1.7% of GDP by 2020.

Polish firms, particularly SMEs, spend very little on R&D and innovation – about 0.3% of GDP, compared with 1.6% for the OECD as a whole. Business spending is mostly allocated to technology absorption (European Commission, 2014d). As a result, triadic patents per capita and per GDP score among the lowest in the OECD. Polish companies report high costs and poor access to finance as the main barriers to innovation investment (European Commission, 2013e). At the same time, low labour costs and the quality of R&D personnel make Poland attractive for R&D activities of large companies from other EU countries (European Commission, 2013d). Funding from abroad increased from 2% of business R&D expenditure in 2000 to 8% in 2012 (compared with 6% in the OECD), also reflecting the importance of EU funds in the Polish innovation system. A small proportion of public research is funded by industry (32%, versus 60% in the OECD), indicating weak industry-science links, a legacy of the state-planned economy (OECD, 2012b; OECD, 2014e). Despite a strong tradition in basic science, Poland's public R&D expenditure and scientific output are relatively low. This is explained, in part, by fragmented sources of research funding, lack of competition and weak incentives for research excellence (OECD, 2012b).

To address these challenges, the government reformed the science system in 2010 and the higher education system in 2011. This spurred significant changes, including a move towards more competitive funding, the creation of agencies for applied research (the National Centre for Research and Development[35]) and basic research (the National Science Centre) and efforts to tackle fragmentation (2011 National Research Programme) through concentration of funding on the best performing institutions. These changes were dovetailed with the evolution of the governance structure by the establishment of two advisory bodies: the Committee for Science Policy and the Committee for Evaluation of Scientific Institutions (European Commission, 2013d). In the framework of the Europe 2020 Strategy, the Council of Ministers adopted the Strategy for Innovative and Efficient Economy in 2013. Its implementing programme, the 2014-20 Enterprise Development Programme, includes measures to support business innovation and sets priorities for granting EU funds (Council of Ministers, 2014b). Funds allocated to this programme are estimated at PLN 25.5 billion (EUR 6.1 billion) in addition to the EUR 8.61 billion EU contribution to support innovativeness and competitiveness (Operational Programme Smart Growth) for 2014-20. Including regional operational programmes, about EUR 10 billion in EU funding has been earmarked for innovation for 2014-20.

6.2. Eco-innovation performance

Eco-innovation mirrors Poland's general innovation performance. In 2012,[36] environment accounted for 6% of the government R&D budget, a relatively high proportion thanks to EU support, which has to be seen in the context of a very low overall budget. Funds allocated to energy R&D programmes were even more limited (2% of the total R&D budget), with most projects focusing on cleaner fossil fuels while energy efficiency and renewables received less support (IEA, 2011). Insufficient research effort is reflected by a very limited, though growing, number of patent applications in these fields (Figure 3.10).

Figure 3.10. **Patents in environment- and climate-related technologies**

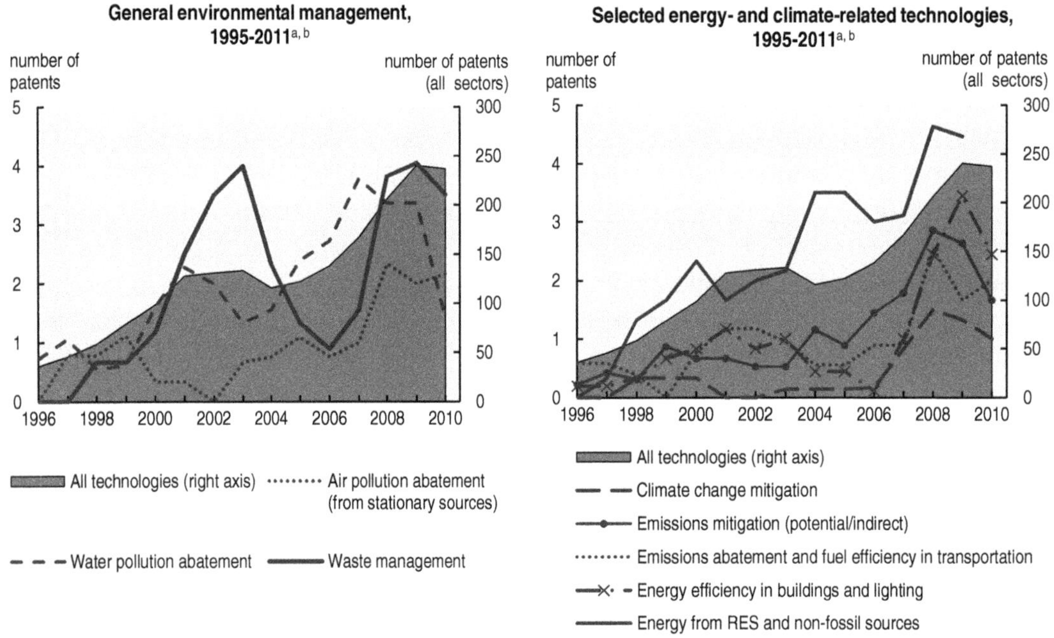

a) Patent applications are based on the priority date and the inventor's country of residence, and use fractional counts on filings under the Patent Co-operation Treaty at international phase (European Patent Office designations).
b) Three-year moving average data.
Source: OECD (2014), *OECD Patent Statistics* (database).

StatLink http://dx.doi.org/10.1787/888933197745

Despite this relatively poor performance, a number of good initiatives should be highlighted. The GreenEvo programme, for example, has been successful in supporting exports of green technology (Box 3.2). Since 2011, the GEKON programme, jointly implemented by the NFEPWM (PLN 200 million allocated), and the National Centre for Research and Development (about PLN 300 million allocated) has stimulated co-operation between science and industry on environmental technology (MoE, 2014). EU funds have helped establish eco-innovation-oriented clusters such as the Silesian Environmental Technology Cluster, the Baltic Eco-energy Cluster and the Clean Energy Cluster of the province of

Małopolska and Podkarpackie. Poland is among the seven countries participating in the EU Environmental Technology Verification Programme. It provides for third-party verification of technology performance, thereby reducing risk for investors and purchasers and increasing market access for innovative environmental technology. In 2013, the Polish Institute of Technology and Life Sciences in Poznań received accreditation to verify biomass products and biomass-based energy technology. The Institute of Environmental Protection in Warsaw is preparing for the accreditation procedure in the area of materials, resources and recycling, including waste management technologies (Miedzinski, 2014).

Box 3.2. **GreenEvo: Promoting Polish eco-innovation abroad**

The GreenEvo "green technology accelerator", a programme of the Ministry of the Environment, aims at promoting environmental technology exports from Polish SMEs. It was set up after Poland hosted the United Nations Framework Convention on Climate Change summit in Poznań (2008), to facilitate international transfer of technology.

To join GreenEvo, companies must be selected by a jury chaired by the environment minister. Although no direct funding is provided, the GreenEvo label gives companies access to a range of government support services: training, market analyses, trade missions, networking and matchmaking. In 2013, the programme had a portfolio of 40 companies offering solutions in the areas of air quality, biodiversity protection, energy efficiency, renewable energy, waste management, and water and wastewater management. The same year, exports of GreenEvo Winners increased by more than 50%, their turnover grew on average by 36%, and 40% of them created new jobs. GreenEvo was awarded the European Award for Best Practice 2014 by the European Society for Quality Research.

Source: http://greenevo.gov.pl/en/.

6.3. The eco-innovation policy framework

Eco-innovation has emerged in the policy agenda with EU integration. In line with the 2004 EU Environmental Technology Action Plan (superseded by the EU Eco-innovation Action Plan in 2011), the government adopted an implementation road map in 2006 to promote environmental technology. Although the road map and its 2007 implementing programme were first steps to introduce the concept of environmental technology and start building a research network, they had only moderate political impact and were not updated as originally foreseen (WIFO, 2009).

Later, in line with the Europe 2020 strategy, eco-innovation was increasingly integrated into major strategic documents (Miedzinski, 2014). Environment and energy were identified as strategic areas in the 2011 National Research Programme. The 2012-20 National Development Strategy notes eco-innovation as a possible area of specialisation. Since the 2013 Strategy for Innovative and Efficient Economy outlines eco-innovation as a driver for increasing knowledge, skills and abilities, it is one of the horizontal objectives of the 2014 Enterprise Development Programme, which directs EU support until 2020 (Council of Ministers, 2014b). Environment-related issues figure prominently in the related Smart Specialisation Strategy seeking to tap into Polish innovation potential and build on its assets and strengths, an *ex-ante* condition for access to EU funds. Out of the 18 sectors identified, 9 relate to eco-innovation, including healthy food, waste reduction, sustainable transport, energy-efficient construction and water efficiency technology, as well as material substitution. This emphasis has a high potential to develop a more comprehensive strategic policy approach and to concentrate public funds on the most promising eco-innovative solutions (Miedzinski, 2014).

However, further work is needed to specify target sectors and refine the system of monitoring national smart specialisations. The environmental technology platform (meant to mobilise resources and connect stakeholders for the development of technologies), which was expected to be completed in 2012, has yet to be established. The estimated allocation of funds to increase resource efficiency represents only 4% of funding by the Enterprise Development Programme. Poland still lacks an integrated approach to eco-innovation policy. By adopting the National Programme for a Low-Emission Economy, which seeks the development and use of low emission technology to promote growth and competitiveness, the government would provide a clear policy signal and foster synergies between environmental, energy and innovation policies. Given that coal is expected to be Poland's primary energy source in the medium term, greater focus could be given on innovation related to carbon capture and storage (CCS). If CCS is not commercially available over the next 15 years, real tensions will emerge between economic and climate policies, leading to both economic and environmental costs.

Eco-innovation faces the common barriers to general innovation in Poland: insufficient research effort, weak industry-science links, difficult access to capital, relatively high cost environmental technology, lack of market demand, uncertain return on investment and lack of economic and fiscal incentives (Miedzinski, 2014). More than in other OECD countries, green public procurement could be used to boost demand for eco-innovation. Despite recent privatisation plans, the level of Polish public ownership is one of the highest in the OECD (OECD, 2014a). Public procurement amounts to about 20% of GDP, among the largest shares in the OECD. National action plans for green public procurement were adopted in 2007, 2010 and 2013, and the share of public contracts involving environmental criteria increased from 4% in 2006 to 12% in 2012. Poland's objective is to reach 20% by 2016. However, awarding of public contracts has relied too heavily on the criterion of lowest price (OECD, 2014a), and the level of green public procurement is low compared to other EU countries (European Commission, 2012c). There has been no legal obligation but only recommendations to include environmental criteria in procurement decisions.

Eco-innovation does not constitute a driving force for new business opportunities in Poland. It still tends to be perceived as consisting of end-of-pipe, environmental protection technology rather than cross-cutting innovation. The transition to a low-carbon economy is perceived as a threat in companies and SMEs. Implementation of stringent environmental regulations is seen solely as a cost and not as an opportunity to build an innovative and competitive economy. Insufficient knowledge on potential economic benefits of eco-innovation leads entrepreneurs to invest in cheap technology and meet minimum legislative requirements (EIO, 2012).

7. Promoting environment-related markets and employment

There is no statistical follow-up on the environmental goods and services (EGS) sector,[37] reflecting a lack of policy focus on the potential contribution of environmental policies to economic growth. However, in the context of the development of European Environmental Economic Accounts, the Central Statistical Office conducted a pilot survey in 2008 which estimated EGS sector output at 6% of GDP and employment at 329 000 jobs.

Despite methodological issues, there is some evidence that the sector has grown in recent years, in line with increased investment in provision of environmental services. Eurostat recently estimated that between 2007 and 2011, EGS output in Poland increased from 3.8% to 5.0% of GDP while related employment increased by 24% (European Commission, 2014f). National statistics show that output of the water, sanitation and waste management industries[38] increased by 31% over 2005-12 and employment in related activities grew by 7% over 2011-13 (CSO, 2013).

In 2012, in the context of a contracting European market, the Polish renewables sector expanded, generating turnover worth EUR 4.31 billion (1.1% of GDP) and contributing to 33 835 direct and indirect jobs (Observ'ER, 2013). Reflecting the development of biomass co-firing in coal electricity plants, turnover in the biomass sector grew from EUR 1.85 billion to EUR 1.99 billion and employment increased from 19 050 to 20 500 people between 2011 and 2012. Support measures also helped boost the wind and solar thermal industries. In 2012, related markets were worth EUR 1.26 billion for wind and EUR 241 million for solar heat and employed 2 815 and 2 540 people, respectively. The same year, Poland became the third largest EU market for solar thermal systems. Growth was driven by the sharp hike in the price of gas from Russia and the success of the subsidy programme financed by the NFEPWM (Observ'ER, 2013).

The agricultural sector has great potential to create green jobs in rural areas as demand for high-quality food in Poland and the EU grows. Since 2003, the agricultural area devoted to organic farming has increased more than tenfold, reaching 4.6% of the total agricultural area in 2012, not far from the EU average of 5.7% (Chapter 1).

Developing monitoring and analysis of the economic and social impact of environment-related policies would help raise awareness of the potential for job creation and economic growth, and address the perceived threat from the EU energy and climate package. Various studies have shown the economic, environmental, health and social benefits of climate change mitigation policy in the long run. For example, the World Bank (2011) found that Poland could reduce its GHG emissions by about one-third by 2030 (relative to 1990) with little cost to incomes and employment. A recent study (Bukowski, 2013) found that low-emission modernisation (a package of measures on energy efficiency, modernisation of the energy sector and diversification of the energy mix) would increase GDP by 0.5% by 2030 and 1% by 2050 compared with the business-as-usual scenario. Over 2015-50, the effect on employment would be neutral, with green jobs replacing others. In 2013, a climate modelling unit was established by the ministers of finance, economy and environment, with World Bank support. Its first report suggested that the European Commission proposal for the 2030 climate and energy policy may underestimate the associated economic costs, and it highlighted particular high costs for Poland and other new EU member states (Center for Climate Policy Analysis, 2014).

Notes

1. In 2014, pension changes reversed part of the 1999 reform and created a one-off budget surplus in 2014.
2. Installations covered by the EU ETS are required to limit emissions in line with a set cap. Installations are awarded allowances, each representing a tonne of emissions in CO_2 equivalent, and actual emissions must fall within the amount allocated; any shortfall must be made up by purchasing emission allowances, or international carbon credits within certain quantitative limits. The EU Emissions Trading Directive (2003/87/EC) required each participating country to assign an amount of allowances to companies operating under the ETS, using national allocation plans for

the 2005-07 pilot phase as well as the next phase in 2008-12. For the current phase, 2013-20, the amount of allowances to be allocated freely is being reduced and the amount to be auctioned increased, meaning more installations will need to pay to obtain allowances. In addition, the 2020 emission cap has been set at EU level, 21% below the 2005 national level. All allowances to the power sector are to be auctioned; the level of free allocation to manufacturing industries is set at 80% in 2013, and will drop to 30% in 2020.

3. The derogation applies to countries where, in 2006, more than 30% of electricity was produced from a single fossil fuel and GDP per capita at market price was 50% or lower than the EU average. Installations that were in operation or for which the investment process was physically initiated by 31 December 2008 can receive free allocations.
4. Generally set at the average GHG emission performance of the 10% best performing installations in the EU producing a given product.
5. Poland also has access to a reserve of allowances set aside to be auctioned by EU countries with lower than average income. Its share is 325 million allowances. In addition, it will benefit from 2% of EU-wide auction revenue distributed to countries to reward emission reductions predating the EU ETS, estimated at an additional 45 million allowances (Sandbag, 2014).
6. Because the price of allowances is passed through to consumers via price increases, even when the allowance is provided free of charge, several electricity producers across Europe benefited from substantial windfall profits in the first two trading periods of the EU ETS. See Ellerman et al. (2010) and an overview of estimates in Laing et al. (2013).
7. A temporary solution to the approximately 2 billion surplus allowances was agreed in February 2014, with the auctioning of 900 million allowances postponed until 2019. This provides only a temporary boost to carbon prices, since allowances are being removed from the market between 2014 and 2018, but the overall impact is more uncertain as allowances will be re-injected from 2019.
8. The new taxes will be collected from 2020.
9. In practice, excise tax applies only to steam coal and coking coal for industry (IEA, 2014).
10. Estimated at 60% of expenditure for operation of personal transport equipment.
11. The methodology for estimating environmental expenditure has changed since the 2003 Environmental Performance Review of Poland, so related figures are not comparable.
12. Including public specialised producers of environmental protection services.
13. Including private specialised producers of environmental protection services.
14. Investment and internal current expenditure (excluding payments to specialised producers of environmental protection services) less receipts from by-products (e.g. material recovered as a result of waste treatment). Includes expenditure on i) pollution abatement and control covering air protection, waste and wastewater management, protection and remediation of soil and groundwater, and other environmental protection activities (R&D, administration, education); and ii) biodiversity and landscape protection. Excludes expenditure on water supply.
15. The initial allocation of EUR 67.3 billion was raised to EUR 67.9 billion in 2010.
16. European Regional Development Fund and European Social Fund.
17. OPIE 2007-13 was revised several times. In the version adopted in January 2014, EU allocations totalled EUR 28.3 billion, compared with EUR 27.9 billion in the 2007 version.
18. Including 5% for improving energy security.
19. Priorities I-V.
20. Charges related to air and water pollution, water abstraction and landfilling.
21. The NFEPWM manages projects above EUR 25 million; the VFEPWMs manage smaller projects.
22. The European Economic Area and Norway grants represent the contribution of Iceland, Liechtenstein and Norway to reducing economic and social disparities and to strengthening bilateral relations with 16 EU countries in central and southern Europe.
23. Revolving funds, preferential loans, interest rate subsidies, partial repayment of bank loan capital, fund sharing with commercial banks.
24. The subsidy programme on solar panels received the best practice certificate in the European Public Sector Award in 2011. In 2012, the Ministry of Regional Development honoured the NFEPWM in the competition "Best Practices for Management of Strategic Development in Poland".

25. The Strategy of the NFEPWM and the Joint Strategy of the NFEPWM and the VFEPWM for 2013-16 are expected to be updated with the adoption of national legislation regarding EU funds for 2014-20.

26. Allocation of EU funding is conditional upon compliance with EU environmental legislation. In some cases, conditionality is set by domestic managing authorities and can include positive incentives: project assessment criteria under Wielkopolska's ROP, for instance, are designed to encourage intermunicipal investment in infrastructure such as water filtration or waste management facilities.

27. IEA reference scenario. A second scenario assuming additional mitigation measures to put global GHG emissions on a stabilisation path of 450 parts per million of CO_2 equivalent would require cumulative additional investment of EUR 113 billion in 2010-30.

28. At 2010 prices.

29. About PLN 780 million (EUR 190 million) was generated from sales of unused assigned amount units over 2009-12.

30. The white certificate system requires that electricity, gas and heat providers present certificates, each of which represents energy savings of 1 tonne of oil equivalent (toe), for 3% of their total sales in a given year. They must submit these to the Energy Regulatory Office or pay a substitution fee of PLN 1 000/toe per missing certificate, accruing to the NFEPWM. Certificates are generated through energy saving projects, selected through a tender procedure overseen by the Ministry of Economy. Each project must lead to minimum savings of 10 toe per year.

31. The cost of the current system was estimated at PLN 17.8 billion over 2006-12.

32. Based on values expressed in passenger-km and tonne-km.

33. The government investigated the possibility of reallocating funds to road construction, even though only 25% of the OPIE 2007-13 transport programme was initially allocated to rail (versus 58% for road), but the European Commission did not allow it (OECD, 2014a).

34. Out of EUR 67 billion of structural funds allocated to Poland over the 2007-13 programming period, around EUR 15 billion (23% of the total) relates to R&D, information and communication technology, business environment and SMEs.

35. The implementing agency of the Minister of Science and Higher Education.

36. There is no consistent time series available on the government budget on R&D by objective.

37. Following the OECD/Eurostat definition, the ESG sector includes production of technologies, goods and services whose main goal is to prevent or minimise pollution and minimise the use of natural resources.

38. NACE section E (water supply, sewerage, waste management and remediation activities).

References

Anfac (2013), European Motor Vehicle Parc 2011, Asociación Española de Fabricantes de Automóviles y Camiones, Madrid, *www.acea.be/uploads/statistic_documents/2013_ANFAC_Report.pdf.*

BGK (2014), "Dane liczbowe Funduszu Termomodernizacji i Remontów" [Figures: Thermo-modernisation Fund], (Bank Gospodarstwa Krajowego) [State Development Bank], Warsaw.

Bukowski, M. (2013), *Low-emission Poland 2050*, Warsaw Institute for Economic Studies, Warsaw.

Chancellery (2014), "Government has Adopted Shale Gas Acts", News 11 March, The Chancellery of the Prime Minister, Warsaw.

Center for Climate Policy Analysis (2014), *Economic effects of the proposed 2030 climate and energy policy framework on Poland and other EU regions: Results based on the PLACE global CGE model*, Center for Climate Policy Analysis, Warsaw.

Ciszewska, A. (2014), personal communication.

ClientEarth (2012), "Summary Briefing of Analysis of Polish National Investment Plan for Article 10c) ETS Directive application for transitional free allowances", ClientEarth Poland, Warsaw.

Council of Ministers (2014a), *National Reform Programme Europe 2020, update 2014-2015*, Adopted by the Council of Ministers on 22 April, Warsaw, *http://ec.europa.eu/europe2020/pdf/csr2014/nrp2014_poland_en.pdf.*

Council of Ministers (2014b), Enterprises Development Programme until 2020, Warsaw, *www.mg.gov.pl/files/upload/17484/PRP_wersja_przyjęta_przez_RM_08042014.pdf.*

Council of Ministers (2013), *National Reform Programme Europe 2020, update 2013-2014*, Adopted by the Council of Ministers on 30 April, Warsaw, *http://ec.europa.eu/europe2020/pdf/nd/nrp2013_poland_en.pdf.*

Council of Ministers (2012), *National Reform Programme Europe 2020, update 2012-2013*, adopted by the Council of Ministers on 25 April, Warsaw, *http://ec.europa.eu/europe2020/pdf/nd/nrp2012_poland_en.pdf.*

Council of Ministers (2008), *The National Environmental Policy for 2009-2012 and its 2016 Outlook*, Council of Ministers, Warsaw, *www.mos.gov.pl/g2/big/2009_07/2826c539c3015384e50adac8fe920b0b.pdf.*

Council of Ministers (2002), The National Environmental Policy for 2003-2006 and its 2010 Outlook, Council of Ministers, Warsaw, *www.ecolex.org/server2.php/libcat/docs/LI/MON-083598.pdf.*

CSO (2013), *Statistical Yearbook of Industry-Poland 2013*, Central Statistical Office, Warsaw.

EEA (2014), *EU Emissions Trading System (ETS) Data Viewer*, updated 28 May, European Environment Agency, Copenhagen.

EEA (2013), *Trends and Projections in Europe 2013: Tracking progress towards Europe's climate and energy targets until 2020*, Publications Office of the European Union, Luxembourg.

EEX (2013), *Auctions by the transitional common auction platform*, December, European Energy Exchange, Leipzig.

EIO (2012), *Eco-Innovation Observatory, Country Profile 2012: Poland, www.eco-innovation.eu/images/stories/Reports/Poland_2012.pdf.*

Ellerman, A.D., F. Convery and C. de Perthuis (eds) (2010), *Pricing Carbon: The European Union Emissions Trading Scheme*, Cambridge University Press, Cambridge, UK.

Ernst & Young (2013), *Global Oil and Gas Tax Guide 2013*, Ernst & Young Global Limited, UK.

European Commission (2014a), *Energy Prices and Costs Report*, Commission Staff Working Document accompanying COM(2014) 21 final and SWD(2014) 19 final, SWD(2014)20 final/2, European Commission, Brussels.

European Commission (2014b), Press release, European Commission adopts "Partnership Agreement" with Poland on using EU Structural and Investment Funds for growth and jobs in 2014-2020, European Commission, Brussels, *http://europa.eu/rapid/press-release_IP-14-596_en.pdf.*

European Commission (2014c), Commission Staff Working Document, Assessment of the 2014 national reform programme and convergence programme for Poland, SWD(2014) 422 final, European Commission, Brussels.

European Commission (2014d), "State aid SA.34674 (2013/N) – Poland Derogation of Article 10c of Directive 2003/87/EC on emission trading – free allowances to power generators", C(2013) 6648 final, European Commission, Brussels.

European Commission (2014e), Eco-Innovation Observatory, Eco-Innovation Scoreboard 2013, *www.eco-innovation.eu/index.php?option=com_content&view=article&id=481&Itemid=69.*

European Commission (2014f), Practical guide towards compiling Environmental Goods and Services Sector (EGSS) statistics, European Commission, Luxembourg, *https://circabc.europa.eu/d/a/workspace/SpacesStore/5488fa2a-014b-46ec-8c9e-2993ea9076fd/Practical%20guide%20towards%20compiling%20EGSS%20statistics.pdf%7C.*

European Commission (2013a), *Questions and Answers on the Commission's Decision on National Implementation Measures (NIMs)*, updated 22 October, DG Climate Action, European Commission, Brussels.

European Commission (2013b), *Taxes in Europe Database v.2*, Taxation and Customs Union, European Commission, Brussels.

European Commission, (2013c), Report from the Commission to the European Parliament, the Council, the European Economic and Social Committee and the Committee of the Regions, Seventh Report on the Implementation of the Urban Waste Water Treatment Directive (91/271/EEC), {SWD(2013) 298 final}, COM(2013) 574 final, European Commission, Brussels.

European Commission (2013d), *Research and Innovation performance in Poland, country Profile 2013*, European Commission, Luxembourg, *http://ec.europa.eu/research/innovation-union/pdf/state-of-the-union/2012/countries/poland_2013.pdf.*

European Commission (2013e), *2013 EU Survey on Industrial R&D Investment Trends*, European Commission, Luxembourg.

European Commission (2012a), *Expert evaluation network delivering policy analysis on the performance of Cohesion policy 2007-2013, Year 2 – 2012, Task 2: Country Report on Achievements of Cohesion policy Poland*, European Commission, Brussels, *http://ec.europa.eu/regional_policy/sources/docgener/evaluation/pdf/eval2007/expert_innovation/2012_een_task2_pl.pdf*.

European Commission, (2012b), *Technical assessment of the implementation of Council Directive concerning Urban Waste Water Treatment (91/271/EEC)*, Situation as of 31 December 2009 or 31 December 2010, Annex V as of 9 October, European Commission, Brussels. *http://ec.europa.eu/environment/water/water-urbanwaste/implementation/pdf/Annex%20V_20121009.pdf (p.112)*.

European Commission (2012c), *The Uptake of Green Public Procurement in the EU27*, prepared by the Centre for European Policy Studies and the College of Europe for the European Commission, Brussels.

Hogg, D. et al. (2014), *Study on Environmental Fiscal Reform Potential in 12 EU Member States*, Final Report to DG Environment of the European Commission, No. 07.0307/ETU/2013/SI2.664058/ENV.D.2, Aarhus University, Aarhus and Eunomia Research and Consulting, Bristol, UK.

International Energy Agency (IEA) (2014), *Energy Prices and Taxes, 2nd Quarter 2014*, IEA/OECD, OECD Publishing, Paris.

IEA (2014), *Energy Balances of OECD countries*, IEA/OECD, OECD Publishing, Paris.

IEA (2011), *Energy Policies of IEA Countries: Poland 2011 Review*, IEA/OECD, OECD Publishing, Paris.

Institute for Renewable Energy (*Instytut Energetyki Odnawialnej*) (IEO) (2013), *The Development Plan for Microgeneration for Poland Based on Renewable Energy Sources until 2020: A Synthesis*, Institute for Renewable Energy in collaboration with members and partners of the Association of Employers of the Renewable Energy Forum (ZP FEO), IEO, Warsaw.

Jouvet, P-A and B. Solier (2013), "An Overview of CO_2 Cost Pass-through to Electricity Prices in Europe", *Energy Policy*, Vol. 61, Elsevier, Amsterdam, pp. 1370-1376.

Kapsch (2013), "Kapsch: Electronic Toll Collection System Operating Successfully in Poland for Two Years", Press Release August 6, Kapsch TrafficCom, Vienna.

Kapsch (2012), "Poland Showing Excellent Results after a Year with Toll System", Press Release July 10, Kapsch TrafficCom, Vienna.

KPMG (2014), "Income Tax: Taxation of International Executives – Poland", KPMG Research, Taxation of International Executives, Regulatory Update, 20 February, KPMG Tax M Michna Sp.K, Warsaw.

Laing, T. et al. (2013), "Assessing the Effectiveness of the EU Emissions Trading System", *Centre for Climate Change Economics and Policy Working Paper No. 126, Grantham Research Institute on Climate Change and Environment Working Paper No. 106*, Centre for Climate Change Economics and Policy and Grantham Research Institute on Climate Change and Environment, University of Leeds, Leeds and London School of Economics and Political Science, London.

Miedzinski, M. (2014), *Eco-Innovation Observatory, Country Profile 2013: Poland*, *www.eco-innovation.eu/images/stories/Reports/EIO_Country_Brief_2013_Poland.pdf*.

Ministry of Economy (2014), *Interim Report on progress in the promotion and use of energy from renewable sources in Poland in 2011-2012*, Ministry of Economy, Warsaw.

Ministry of Economy (2010), *National Renewable Energy Action Plan*, Warsaw.

MoE (2014), *Report on the implementation of the National Environmental Policy for the years 2009–2012 with an outlook to the year 2016*, Ministry of the Environment, Warsaw, *www.mos.gov.pl/g2/big/2014_07/6dd2de63756634cf4a4518471331e596.pdf*.

MoE/National Water Management Authority (2013), *Roboczy projekt*, IV Aktualizacja, Krajowego programu oczyszczania ścieków komunalnych- IV AKPOŚK, [Working Draft, Fourth Update, National Programme for Municipal Waste Water Treatment], Ministry of the Environment, Warsaw.

Ministry of Finance (2010), *Tax Expenditures in Poland*, Ministry of Finance, Warsaw.

Ministry of Infrastructure and Development (2014a), *draft Operational Programme Infrastructure and Environment 2014-2020*, 8 January 2014, Ministry of Infrastructure and Development, Warsaw.

Ministry of Infrastructure and Development, (2014b), *2013 Annual Report on the implementation of the Operational Programme Infrastructure and Environment*, as approved by the Programme Monitoring

Committee Resolution No. 3/2014 of 3 June, Ministry of Infrastructure and Development, Warsaw, *www.pois.gov.pl/AnalizyRaportyPodsumowania/Documents/Sprawozdanie_POIS_2013_05062014.zip*.

Ministry of Infrastructure and Development (2013), 30-12-2013 *,Postępy w realizacji Narodowej Strategii Spójności 2007-2013 – stan na 29 grudnia 2013 r.*, Ministry of Infrastructure and Development, Warsaw, *www.funduszeeuropejskie.gov.pl/AnalizyRaportyPodsumowania/poziom/Strony/postepy_nss_29122013_30122013.aspx*.

NFEPWM (2013), *2013 Annual Report*, National Fund for Environmental Protection and Water Management, Warsaw.

NFEPWM (2012a), *Action Strategy of the National Fund for Environmental Protection and Water Management for 2013-2016 with a view to 2020*, National Fund for Environmental Protection and Water Management, Warsaw.

NFEPWM (2012b), *Joint Action Strategy of the National Fund and the Voivodship Funds for Environmental Protection and Water Management for 2013-2016 with a perspective to 2020*, National Fund for Environmental Protection and Water Management, Warsaw.

NFEPWM (2004), *2003 Annual Report*, National Fund for Environmental Protection and Water Management, Warsaw.

Observ'ER (2013), *The State of Renewable Energy in Europe*, Edition 2013, 13th EurObserv'ER, Paris.

OECD (2014a), *OECD Economic Surveys: Poland 2014*, OECD Publishing, Paris, *http://dx.doi.org/10.1787/eco_surveys-pol-2014-en*.

OECD (2014b), *OECD Economic Outlook*, Vol. 2014/1, OECD Publishing, Paris, *http://dx.doi.org/10.1787/eco_outlook-v2014-1-en*.

OECD (2014c), *Personal Tax Treatment of Company Cars and Commuting Expenses: Estimating the Fiscal and Environmental Costs*, OECD Taxation Working Papers Series, OECD Publishing, Paris, *http://dx.doi.org/10.1787/5jz14cg1s7vl-en*.

OECD (2014d), "The distributional effects of energy taxes: preliminary report", Internal OECD document, Joint Meetings of Tax and Environment Experts, June, OECD Publishing, Paris.

OECD (2014e), *Main Science and Technology Indicators Volume 2013 Issue 2*, OECD Publishing, Paris, *http://dx.doi.org/10.1787/msti-v2013-2-en*.

OECD (2013a), *Revenue Statistics 2013*, OECD Publishing, Paris, *http://dx.doi.org/10.1787/rev_stats-2013-en-fr*.

OECD (2013b), *Taxing Energy Use: A Graphical Analysis*, OECD Publishing, Paris, *http://dx.doi.org/10.1787/9789264183933-en*.

OECD (2013c), *Inventory of Estimated Budgetary Support and Tax Expenditures for Fossil Fuels 2013*, OECD Publishing, Paris, *http://dx.doi.org/10.1787/9789264187610-en*.

OECD (2013d), *Poland: Implementing Strategic-State Capability*, OECD Public Governance Reviews, OECD Publishing, Paris, *http://dx.doi.org/10.1787/9789264201811-en*.

OECD (2012a), *OECD Economic Surveys: Poland 2012*, OECD Publishing, Paris, *http://dx.doi.org/10.1787/eco_surveys-pol-2012-en*.

OECD (2012b), *OECD Science, Technology and Industry Outlook 2012*, OECD Publishing, Paris, *http://dx.doi.org/10.1787/sti_outlook-2012-en*.

OECD (2011), *OECD Urban Policy Reviews: Poland*, OECD Publishing, Paris, *http://dx.doi.org/10.1787/9789264097834-en*.

OECD (2010a), *Taxation, Innovation and the Environment*, OECD Publishing, Paris, *http://dx.doi.org/10.1787/9789264087637-en*.

OECD (2010b), *Pricing Water Resources and Water and Sanitation Services*, OECD Studies on Water, OECD Publishing, Paris, *http://dx.doi.org/10.1787/9789264083608-en*.

OECD (2009), *Dealing with post-decentralisation implications in the water sector*, OECD Publishing, Paris.

OECD (2007), "Making Environmental Spending Count", *Policy Brief*, Paris, *www.oecd.org/env/outreach/39376495.pdf*.

OECD (2003), *OECD Environmental Performance Reviews: Poland*, Paris, *http://dx.doi.org/10.1787/9789264100961-en*.

PolSEFF (2014), "Statistics – PolSEFF Results", PolSEFF, Warsaw, *www.polseff.org/en/statistics.html*.

Reinaud, J (2007), "CO_2 Allowance and Electricity Price Interaction: Impact on Industry's Electricity Purchasing Strategies in Europe", *IEA Information Paper*, International Energy Agency, OECD Publishing, Paris.

Rekiel, M. (2014), "Thermo-modernization Program in Poland", presentation made at the 2nd Workshop on Energy Efficiency in Buildings, 15-16 May, Energy Community Secretariat, Vienna.

Sandbag (2014), *Sharing the Load: Poland's Coming of Age on Climate Policy*, Sandbag Climate Campaign, London.

Sartor, O. and T. Spencer (2013), "An Empirical Assessment of the Risk of Carbon Leakage in Poland", *Working Paper* No. 08/13, Institut du développement durable et des relations internationales, Paris.

Sijm, J.P.M. et al. (2008), "The Impact of the EU ETS on Electricity Prices", *Final Report to DG Environment of the European Commission*, Energy Research Centre of the Netherlands, Petten.

Terlecka K. and K. Leśniak (2014), "Poland: Shale Gas – Recent Developments", 19 March, Schönherr Attorneys at Law, Warsaw.

Vivid Economics (2012), *Carbon Taxation and Fiscal Consolidation: the Potential of Carbon Pricing to Reduce Europe's Fiscal Deficits*, report prepared for the European Climate Foundation and Green Budget Europe, Vivid Economics, London.

WIFO (2009), "ENV-MAP Project Task 2, Assessment of ETAP Roadmaps with Regard to their Eco-innovation Potential", report commissioned by the Environment Directorate of the OECD, Austrian Institute of Economic Research, Vienna, *http://ec.europa.eu/environment/ecoap/pdfs/env-map_projektt2_finalreport_countryprofiles_final.pdf*.

Withana, S. et al. (2012), *Study Supporting the Phasing Out of Environmentally Harmful Subsidies: Annexes to Final Report*, a report by the Institute for European Environmental Policy (IEEP), Institute for Environmental Studies – Vrije Universiteit, Ecologic Institute and Vision on Technology for the European Commission – DG Environment, IEEP, Brussels.

World Bank (2011), *Transition to a Low-Emissions Economy in Poland*, Poverty Reduction and Economic Management Unit, Europe and Central Asia Region, World Bank, Washington DC.

World Bank (2005), *Environmental Fiscal Reform: What Should be Done and how to Achieve it*, World Bank, Washington DC.

PART II

Progress towards selected environmental objectives

PART II

Chapter 4

Forestry and biodiversity

Forests in Poland are an important source of income and valuable repositories of biodiversity. This chapter examines Poland's institutional and policy framework for integrating forestry and biodiversity policies and the key role played by State Forests in managing public forests. It analyses the instruments adopted, progress achieved and further efforts needed for the conservation and sustainable use of forests and forest biodiversity. It also examines how biodiversity and forestry objectives have been mainstreamed into other key policy areas, such as agriculture and land-use planning, and provides recommendations for a more co-ordinated and coherent policy framework.

Assessment and recommendations

Forests in Poland are both an important source of income and valuable repositories of biodiversity. Thus there are good reasons to make forest and biodiversity policies coherent and consistent. In 2012, the forest sector accounted for 2% of GDP, employed over 300 000 people and had an annual turnover of nearly USD 25 billion. About two-thirds of the flora and fauna found in Poland are associated with forest environments. The Białowieża Forest is the only primeval forest remaining in Europe. Some 20% of species threatened in the EU – including 40% of EU Red List mammals – are present in Poland, underlining the significance of Poland's biodiversity policy at the European level.

While effective legal and policy frameworks have been developed for both forestry and biodiversity, the two sets of policy objectives are not fully aligned. The development of the National Biodiversity Strategy and Action Plan 2014-20 provides an opportunity to promote better policy integration. Adjustments may also need to be made to the National Forest Policy (NFP). Both sets of laws and policies also need to take account of Poland's ambitious commitment under Natura 2000, whereby forest habitat protection increased to cover 38% of forests held by State Forests – Lasy Państwowe (LP).

The management of public forests (80% of total forests) and biodiversity has benefitted from a high-quality, stable institutional framework. LP was established in 1924. It is now an independent agency under the Ministry of the Environment (MoE). Its main activities are organised in forest districts and its primary objective is to manage its forests on a self-financing basis. The forest districts have integrated nature protection in their management practices since the inter-war period. As a result, populations of many protected forest mammals have increased, and Polish forests host more game animals than those in most other EU countries. The 1991 Forest Act required forest districts to report on their achievements through forest district nature protection programmes, as a companion report to the forest management plan. This is unique in Europe, and perhaps the world, and has enabled the LP to maintain an inventory of all forms of nature protection on the 7 million ha of forest it administers. The inventory contains all the elements to create a knowledge base to support forest management and allow monitoring of forest biological diversity at the national level.

The LP shares responsibility for the management of Natura 2000 sites in national forests with the General Directorate for Environmental Protection (GDEP). Both institutions are supervised by the MoE. Despite some efforts to co-ordinate the activities of the two bodies within the MoE, there is ambiguity about their respective roles and responsibilities. To facilitate co-ordination, shared responsibilities should be implemented jointly, to the extent possible, at national, regional and local level. Given the large share of LP forests in Natura 2000 sites, the LP should adapt its rules and practices to better protect biodiversity; the GDEP could help it in this regard. Co-operation in this area would be enhanced by development of a comprehensive assessment of the economic value of ecosystem services provided by forests.

The LP has implemented measures that have helped conserve biodiversity while increasing the volume of standing wood and the potential timber harvest. Measures that have contributed to this achievement include an increase in forest cover; a better age and species structure of forested trees; a higher percentage of stands older than 80 years; increased natural regeneration; and a reduction in clear-cutting. Nearly all public forests are certified under internationally recognised programmes. Impressive efforts have also been made to raise awareness and disseminate knowledge on sustainable forestry practices. In 2013, the LP was awarded the UNESCO Prize for Environmental Preservation in recognition of its outstanding contribution in the fields of research, education and awareness raising.

Despite these achievements, there remain important challenges to better integration of conservation and sustainable use of biodiversity into forestry practices. Polish forests are still characterised by species imbalance, partly as a result of poor soil conditions. Pine still accounts for 60% of trees. The ratio of natural regeneration to planting has increased but remains one of the lowest in Europe. Despite progress in recent years, Poland has less deadwood in its forests than most other EU countries. Some forest types, notably alluvial forests, have not been adequately protected, resulting in reduced populations of some protected forest birds, such as black grouse. While Poland has a national scheme to certify the origin of its own forest seeds, it is not a member of the OECD Scheme for the Certification of Forest Reproductive Material.

It is estimated that about 7% of forest area is designated primarily for conservation of biological diversity. Almost half of forest habitat protection is through laws designating national parks and nature reserves; most of the other half involves forests that the LP has designated as having a nature protective function. However, most "protective forests" are in mountainous areas and were designated for protection of soil or water; habitat protection accounts for about 4% of their area. Implementation of Natura 2000 implies a massive expansion of management effort in the protected forest area, yet as of September 2014, management plans for about 15% of the network area had been approved. Moreover, there is evidence that most of the Natura 2000 forest habitats are not in good condition.

Effective management of Natura 2000 sites will require substantially more financial resources; one estimate suggests that the 2014-20 programme will require 12 times the amount allocated in 2007-13. The bulk of this will have to come from the central budget, the national environmental fund and EU sources. But new mechanisms should also be examined, such as wider use of access charges and the development of payment for ecosystem services (PES), which until now has not received much attention. A new tax regime applied to the LP will further constrain the limited opportunities from this source. Private foresters have opportunities to access financing for afforestation within the framework of the Common Agricultural Policy. An assessment should be prepared of measures applied in agriculture, forestry and other sectors that may adversely affect biodiversity, with a view to reforming them. For example, the current practice of issuing construction permits in the absence of a land use plan contributes to encroachment in forests and should be reformed.

Recommendations

- Ensure that the Action Plan for the National Biodiversity Strategy 2014-20 and forest policy objectives are consistent with Natura 2000 targets and coherent; consider what adjustments to the NFP might be needed.
- Complete the designation of protected forests within Natura 2000; provide guidance and support for the preparation of related management plans, including guidance on the basic types of standards that such sites should meet; and clarify how existing and new sources of finance could be mobilised to support the management of these sites.
- Ensure consistent and effective implementation of Natura 2000 management plans and forest management plans through joint activities of the LP and GDEP at national, regional and local level; clarify the roles and responsibilities of the LP and GDEP in the management, monitoring and evaluation of Natura 2000; strengthen the creation of ecological corridors in forests outside the Natura 2000 network.
- Amend the Spatial Planning Act to make the development of local land use plans obligatory and consistent with relevant Natura 2000 provisions; provide support to enable municipalities to prepare local land use plans that integrate consideration of the conservation and sustainable use of biodiversity.
- Mobilise private foresters to help achieve sustainable forestry objectives by strengthening dialogue with forest owners' associations and developing partnerships, for example for joint forest management and the sale of forest products.
- Building on forest districts' nature protection inventories and other sources, prepare comprehensive assessments of Poland's forest biodiversity and the economic value of ecosystem services provided by forests; assess opportunities for developing PES in both public and private forests.
- Consider adhering to the OECD Scheme for the Certification of Forest Reproductive Material with a view to sharing best practices related to management of forest genetic diversity.

1. Integrating forestry and biodiversity

1.1. *The forest sector*

The forest area of Poland has grown steadily since the Second World War. Forests cover 9 million ha, or 29% of the territory, on a par with the OECD average. The body known as State Forests – Lasy Państwowe (LP) administers public forests, which currently account for 77% of all forests, by area (Table 4.1). The LP is also in charge of implementing the National Forest Cover Augmentation Programme, which aims at increasing the forest cover to 30% of the territory by 2020 and 33% by 2050. The latter target may prove difficult to achieve, though, given the increasing difficulty of freeing up land for afforestation in a changed economic context since Poland joined the European Union in 2004.

An important issue that remains to be resolved is restitution of forested land to people whose property was confiscated during the post-war socialist period. Both the extent of claims and levels of compensation require clarification. An agreement could affect not only forest ownership but also income taxation of the forest sector (Section 3.1).

In 2012, the forest sector[1] accounted for 2% of GDP, employed over 300 000 people and had annual turnover of nearly USD 25 billion. It is thus a significant economic sector. Until the early 1990s most Polish wood production went to markets in Central and Eastern Europe, including the former USSR.

Table 4.1. **Poland's forest area**

	1995	2000	2010	2012	Change 2000-12	Share in 2012
	'000 ha				%	
Total	**8 756**	**8 865**	**9 121**	**9 164**	**3**	**100**
Treasury-owned	*7 186*	*7 262*	*7 351*	*7 355*	*1*	*80.3*
of which:						
Administered by the LP	6 868	6 953	7 072	7 079	2	*77.2*
National parks	162	181	184	185	2	*2.0*
Other	156	128	95	91	-29	*1.0*
Commune-owned	*76*	*79*	*84*	*84*	*6*	*0.9*
Privately owned	*1 494*	*1 524*	*1 686*	*1 725*	*13*	*18.8*
of which:						
Individual owners	1 397	1 428	1 587	1 623	14	*17.7*
Land co-operatives	68	69	67	67	-3	*0.7*
Agricultural co-operatives	14	9	6	5	-44	*0.1*
Other	15	18	26	29	61	*0.3*

Source: CSO (2013).

Since EU accession, the industry has witnessed a significant increase in production and trade and a reorientation of trade towards EU countries, particularly Germany, Sweden, France, Italy, the Benelux countries and Finland.

Most of the wood industry was privatised in the early 1990s. This brought in foreign capital, notably from Germany (a major trading partner in the furniture industry), Sweden and France, and allowed modernisation of production systems.

1.2. *Importance of forests for conservation and sustainable use of biodiversity*

More than 30 000 species (two-thirds of the flora and fauna species found in Poland) are associated with forest environments (Fronczak, 2013). These include 60% of vertebrates, over 80% of fungi and most mosses, ferns, horsetail varieties and club mosses. Large groups of flowering plants and insects live in, or are in some way associated with, forest ecosystems. Moreover, the Białowieża Primeval Forest is the only primeval forest remaining in Europe, and thus its protection is especially important.

Overall, taking all habitat categories together, the share of known species under threat[2] is lower in Poland than in many other OECD countries. The shares of threatened species are 12% for mammals, 8% for birds and 11% for vascular plants. Among the 34 OECD countries, Poland ranks seventh best for mammals, third best for birds and fourteenth best for vascular plants (OECD, 2013).

However, some 20% of EU threatened species[3] – including 40% of EU Red List mammals – are present in Poland, which has an important responsibility for protecting those within its territory (IUCN, 2013). EU Red List species in Poland are found mostly in forests, grasslands and wetlands. These ecosystems require particular attention to preserve habitats of sensitive species.

2. Legal and policy framework

2.1. *Forestry*

Poland's post-communist government adopted the Forest Act in 1991 with the goal of achieving sustainable forest management that respects ecological balances. The act (as amended in 1997) defines sustainable, multifunctional forest management as "activity aiming at shaping the structure of forests and their utilisation at the pace and in the manner which ensures their biological diversity, high productivity, potential for regeneration and the ability to fulfil, now and in the future, their protective, economic and social functions at a local, national and global level, without harming other ecosystems".

The aim of Polish forestry policy is to safeguard the permanence of forests and their protective, economic and social functions. In particular, the 1997 National Forest Policy provides for i) increasing forest resources, ii) improving their state and providing comprehensive protection, and iii) promoting multifunctional forest management according to criteria formulated by the Helsinki process.[4] The National Forest Policy (NFP) sets key forest policy objectives, some with quantitative targets and timetables. Overall, Poland is on track to meet the mid- to long-term forest policy objectives set in the NFP and has achieved some targets ahead of time (Table 4.2).

Table 4.2. **Key forest policy objectives**

Aims and priorities	Quantitative targets 2020	Quantitative targets 2050	Performance (as of end 2013)
Increasing Poland's forest resources			
Forest cover	30%	33%	29.3%
Improved state of forests			
Share of broadleaved species		33%	30%
Share of multispecies tree stands		48%	..
Broadleaved understorey in pine stands		1 Mha[a]	..
Share of stands more than 80 years old		25%	25%
Multifunctional forest management			
Attainment of "relative harmony"between the three functions			
Ecological functions			
Increased water flow regulation properties of forests			31 Mm3[a, b]
Carbon sequestration	4.5 Mt[a]	9 Mt[a]	36 Mt[a, c]
Improvement in local climates			..
"Biological shaping" of forest edges			..
Linking of forest areas by ecological corridors			..
Full assessment of the natural resources of forests			CRs[d]
Productive functions			
% increase of timber resources in forests	15%	20%	38%
Annual timber harvest potential from managed forests	24 Mm3[a]		36 Mm3[a]
Annual timber harvest potential from monoculture stands[e]		1.5 Mm3[a]	1 Mm3[a]
Establishment of associations of private forest owners			13[f]
Social functions			
Broadening of society's knowledge on forests			13 PFCs[g]

a) Mt = million tonnes; Mha = million hectares; Mm^3 = million cubic metres.
b) Refers to water retained by small-scale water retention infrastructure.
c) Carbon sequestration assessment method has changed significantly since Poland started reporting to UNFCCC (in 2008); 2012 data from the National Inventory Report to UNFCCC of 27 May 2014.
d) CRs = companion reports to forest districts' forest management plans.
e) Pine plantations under the National Programme for the Augmentation of Forest Cover (1995).
f) 13 regional associations and the Polish Union of Private Forest Owners Associations.
g) PFCs = promotional forest complexes + 50 forest education centres, 250 forest exhibitions, 517 teaching shelters, 957 educational trails, 1 756 education points and 2 235 other facilities.
Source: NFP (1997); MoE (data on performance).

2.2. Conservation and sustainable use of biodiversity in forests

The 2004 Nature Conservation Act (as amended in 2008) specifies the aims, principles and forms of nature and landscape conservation. It contains provisions on protection, management and control of fauna and flora in national parks and nature reserves, with rules for their exploitation. It also implements the EU Birds and Habitats Directives (2009/147/EC, 92/43/EEC). However, buffer zones adjacent to protected areas should be better defined in the act.

The aim of Polish nature conservation policy is to "preserve nature as a whole". The National Biodiversity Strategy 2007-13 (NBS) includes the unquantified goal of increasing the area and number of protected areas, based on Natura 2000. The 2010 biodiversity target, to "significantly reduce the rate of biodiversity loss", agreed by parties to the Convention on Biological Diversity (CBD) in 2002, has not been met. The Natura 2000 network would enable compliance with the new CBD target of expanding the global protected area network to at least 17% of the terrestrial area by 2020 (so-called Aïchi Biodiversity Target 11).[5]

Another law that is important for the integration of forestry and biodiversity policies is the 2003 Spatial Planning Act regulating local land use planning. However, only 28% of land is covered by binding local land use plans and many individual construction permits are issued on a case-by-case basis (OECD, 2011). To prevent encroachment on protected areas, including national parks, protected area administrations carry the burden of proof: they must show that development would have detrimental environmental effects. This is not easy to do and the national parks administration often lacks the capacity to make the case. Effective protection of forests and biodiversity requires a comprehensive approach based on binding local land use plans that also include Natura 2000 provisions when appropriate, rather than an ad hoc approach based on construction permits. This change would entail major revision of the act. In the interim, the act could be amended to limit its application to areas where there are as yet no local land use plans.

2.3. Consistency and coherence of forestry and biodiversity policies

The National Biodiversity Action Programme 2007-13 is coherent with NFP objectives and even adds to them (e.g. maintaining riparian forests, protecting forest wetlands). Such alignment of policy objectives should be continued in future planning periods. More needs to be done, however, to align forest and nature policies and other policies affecting land use. In particular, farm production support indicates a fundamental imbalance between forestry and agriculture.

While the programme's proposed forestry-related activities are steps in the direction of improving forest biodiversity, no targets or measures are proposed to implement them. Development of the NBS 2014-20 and its action plan provides an opportunity to promote greater coherence between biodiversity and forestry objectives, especially if the NFP is updated concomitantly. In particular, new targets to enhance nature protection in forests should be set as part of the overriding objective of establishing and maintaining the Natura 2000 network. This includes nature protection on Natura 2000 sites of public and private forests, as well as in forests that are outside the network but contribute to its effective functioning (e.g. ecological corridors, edge habitats). More needs to be done to align legislation, particularly through major revision of the Spatial Planning Act and updating of the Nature Conservation and Forest acts. Amendment of the Spatial Planning Act should aim to correct the land use imbalance between forestry, nature and agriculture by making local land use plans binding and including Natura 2000 provisions in them.

3. Institutional arrangements

The MoE oversees both forest and nature policies. Co-ordination is overseen by the undersecretary of state/chief nature conservator and the Department of Forestry and Nature Conservation. The MoE also supervises the LP and national parks, which have their own administrations. It hosts the General Directorate for Environmental Protection (GDEP), which shares responsibility for management of Natura 2000 sites in national forests with the LP. To ensure that this co-operation is mutually beneficial, clarification of rules and responsibilities is urgently needed.

3.1. *State Forests (LP)*

The long existence of the LP has supported the development of a robust scientific basis to underpin sustainable forest management. The area administered by the LP has steadily increased. It now amounts to more than three-quarters of the total forest area, and the LP is the largest manager of public forest in the European Union. A supervised unit department under the MoE,[6] it works to maintain the extent and quality of forests owned by the national Treasury. That is its core activity: it oversees timber harvest, silviculture (tree tending, stock renewal and afforestation) and protection against stress factors such as forest fires and insects.

The LP comprises the Directorate-General of State Forests (DGSF), 17 Regional Directorates of State Forests (RDSFs), 9 forest protection teams and 11 regional inspectorates. The basic organisational units of the LP are forest districts, which employ more than 90% of the LP's 25 000 staff. Each district is led by a forest district manager, who has autonomy in managing forests according to the forest management plan and who is responsible for their condition. There are 430 forest districts, with average area of 17 500 ha.

Article 50 of the Forest Act specifies that "the LP shall engage in activity on the basis of financial self-sufficiency, thereby covering the costs of activity from own revenue". This means timber sales must finance the "basic forest management tasks" (e.g. silviculture, forest protection) that the LP carries out.

Other tasks, such as increasing forest cover, responding to emergencies including ecological disasters, enhancing nature protection and forest education, may receive funds from the central budget under article 54 of the act. More precisely, the LP may be granted public financial support for the following tasks commissioned by the government:

- buying land for afforestation, reforestation or nature preservation
- implementing the National Forest Cover Augmentation Programme
- renewing forests affected by air pollution, arson, storms, pests and disease
- taking inventory of forests' condition
- preparing and implementing protection plans for LP nature reserves and supervising areas within the Natura 2000 network
- creating and running promotional forest complexes
- preparing afforestation plans for private landowners and checking their completion
- implementing programmes co-financed by foreign sources.

As part of efforts to reduce public budget deficits, the government recently decided to levy a 2% fee on LP revenue from timber sales, from 2016. This concludes a series of proposals over the last decade to reduce income tax disparities between forestry, agriculture and other sectors (Box 4.1). When the Forest Act was passed in 1991, it included no taxation of timber sales income, the aim being to facilitate the LP's transition to a market economy. At the end of the post-war socialist period, in 1989, the LP employed 125 000 staff and faced a dramatic fall in domestic demand and export markets for wood. Only in the mid-2000s did its financial situation start to improve (Figure 4.1), after a significant structural adjustment (e.g. the staff was cut down to 25 000 people). Most former LP employees have established their own forest companies, thereby helping to create a competitive market for forestry services.

Box 4.1. **Reforming income taxation of forestry and agriculture**

Several reforms have been proposed in the past decade to reduce income tax disparities between forestry, agriculture and other sectors. Revenue from all forestry activity and most agricultural activity is still tax exempt. Only 2-5% of farmers (e.g. those involved in greenhouse farming, poultry production and large-scale pig farming) are liable for income tax under the 1984 Agricultural Tax Act.

In 2004, a 5% tax on income of some state-owned enterprises, including the LP, was proposed. The proceeds would have allowed the government to meet compensation demands from people whose property was confiscated during the post-war socialist period. The proposal was eventually abandoned because agreement on a formula for levels of compensation could not be reached.

In 2008 another bill was put forward, which proposed creating a special fund to compensate former landowners for property lost during the socialist period. The sum of claims for compensation was estimated at PLN 570 million/year over 15 years. The bill was not passed.

Source: OECD (2005); Parlińska (2008).

Figure 4.1. **Financial results of State Forests, 2001-12**

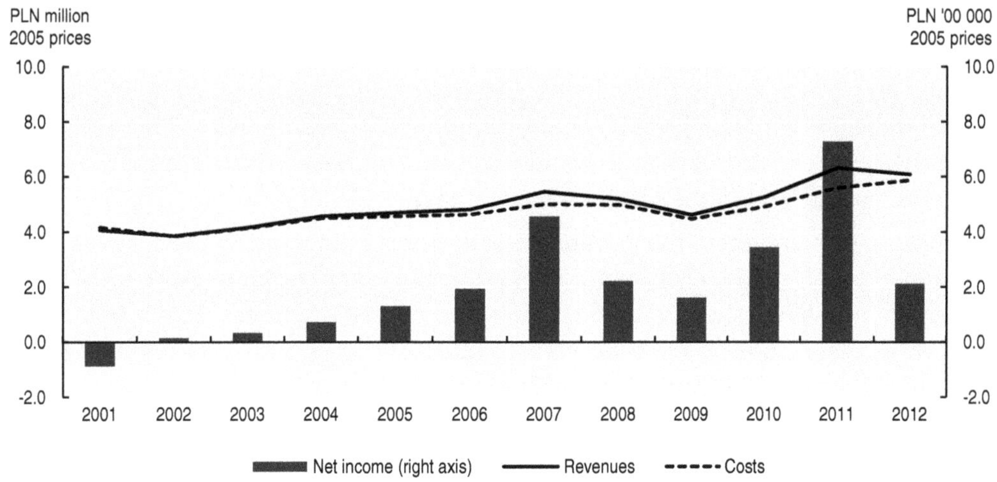

Source: Country submission.

StatLink http://dx.doi.org/10.1787/888933197756

At current sales levels and timber prices, a 2% fee on revenue from timber sales amounts to around PLN 130 million (The Voice of the Forest, 2014). This will be in addition to the forestry tax paid by the LP on property, worth PLN 130-170 million a year (CSO, 2013).

With a view to reducing the public budget deficit, it was decided that the LP should contribute to the central budget a lump sum of PLN 1.6 billion in 2014 and 2015. Payment of the lump sum should not affect the LP's operating ("basic") activities, which are essential to maintain the forest cover and forest quality, but it will affect LP investment.

In 2014, the LP intended to cut investment on forest road construction to obtain PLN 1 billion of the required PLN 1.6 billion. It is less clear how the remaining cuts of PLN 600 million in 2015 would be made. From 2016, the effect on LP investment of the 2% fee has yet to be assessed. LP's revenue depends on the demand for, and price of, wood: on average, LP timber prices rose from PLN 137/m^3 in 2009 to PLN 183/m^3 in 2012 (CSO, 2013). LP revenue grew by 17% between 2008 and 2012, reaching PLN 7 billion in 2012 and allowing investment to nearly double over the period, to PLN 1 billion in 2012 (CSO, 2013). In 2013, equity over fixed assets was still about PLN 1 billion (The Voice of the Forest, 2014).

3.2. *Private forests*

Little information is available on the economic, environmental and social functions of private forests. Unlike other Central European countries, Poland has a significant amount of private forest land (1.5 million ha or 18% of the forest area). Only large forest estates were nationalised during the socialist period, while small private properties – resulting from the dismantling of some large forest estates in the 1920s – were maintained. However, these small private forest holdings face multiple challenges. One is fragmentation, with an average size of less than 1 ha. Another is the extent of derelict plots, due to difficulty in obtaining harvesting permits. The standing volume is significantly lower than in LP forests (107 m^3/ha against 194 m^3/ha), reflecting an imbalanced age structure (more than 60% of the stands are less than 40 years old).

Efforts to sustainably manage private forests have been far more limited than in public forests. Even though the 1991 Forest Act applies to all forests and requires the LP to provide extension and advisory services to private forest owners, private owners appear to lack incentives for sustainable forest management. In particular, restrictions of forest harvesting on private land combined with the absence of forest management plans have led to an increase in illegal ("wild") cuts on many private properties. This trend is not without risk to forest biodiversity, especially as some of these private stands host unique ecosystems, particularly in the south and north-east.

Structural adjustment of the private forest sector is hampered by the scattered nature of forest stands. Grouping forest owners together can create economies of scale in forest management and allow them to better respond to demand for forest goods and services. Forest owner associations have been created, along with an umbrella organisation, the Polish Union of Private Forest Owner Associations.

3.3. *Ministry of the Environment*

The MoE Department of Forestry and Nature Conservation primarily oversees:

- forestry, nature conservation, forest and forest land protection, hunting, environmental impact assessment (EIA)
- preparation for EU co-financing of nature conservation and forestry under the European Agricultural Fund for Rural Development (Section 4.2) and the Operational Programme Infrastructure and Environment

- the GDEP, the LP, the Forest Research Institute, the Forest Reproductive Material Office, the Polish Hunting Association and national parks.

A central public authority under the MoE,[7] the GDEP is the ministry's nature conservation arm and is in charge of EIA. The GDEP was established by the 2008 act on accessing information about the environment and its protection, the participation of the public in environmental protection, and environmental impact assessment (known as the EIA Act). The main activities of the GDEP are:

- managing nature reserves, Natura 2000 sites and species protection through 16 Regional Directorates for Environmental Protection (RDEPs)
- undertaking EIA and strategic impact assessment (SEA)
- keeping a central register of nature protection areas
- acting as a clearing house.

Poland is actively involved in and highly committed to international co-operation in forestry. It prepared and hosted the fifth Ministerial Conference on the Protection of Forests in Europe (Forest Europe) in Warsaw in 2007.[8] The conference resulted in two Warsaw Resolutions: "Forests, Wood and Energy" and "Forests and Water". During Poland's holding of the EU Presidency in the second half of 2011, the MoE and the LP convened several meetings of EU forest directors as well as meetings on sustainable forest management in the context of climate change. The MoE has always supported negotiations on a legally binding agreement on forests in Europe. In 2013 it hosted the fourth session of the Intergovernmental Negotiating Committee for a Legally Binding Agreement on Forests in Europe.

Poland has held the vice-presidency of the United Nations Economic Commission for Europe's Committee on Forests and Forest Industry bureau since 2012. The MoE and the LP regularly report to the Forest Resource Assessment programme of the Food and Agriculture Organization of the United Nations (FAO), as well as the UNECE/FAO/Forest Europe Report on the State of Europe's Forests. The MoE and the LP hosted a workshop in September 2014 as Poland's contribution to the UNECE/FAO action plan on forests in a green economy. The MoE is an active participant in the United Nations Forum on Forests, held every two years at UN Headquarters in New York.

3.4. *National parks*

The national parks have their own administration, formerly run by the Polish Board of National Parks and since 2004 by the MoE. Its role is to ensure the long-term survival of Poland's most valuable and threatened species and habitats, and to protect the historical and cultural heritage within park boundaries.

Public financial support of national parks has increased in recent years, but only as a transitional measure. The outlook could darken if a forthcoming change to the parks' legal status – aiming to reduce reliance on public funds – is not accompanied by significant efforts by the parks to diversify funding. For example, visitors to national parks could be charged an access fee. Another option could involve municipalities whose citizens benefit from national parks providing support. Warsaw municipality, for example, could compensate Kampinos National Park for providing free access to Warsaw residents. A comprehensive national survey of adults revealed that forest recreation is highly valued in Poland, suggesting that there may be a willingness to pay (Bartczak et al., 2008). Forest recreation trip frequency and per trip values are higher in Poland than the average for EU countries, even though incomes are lower. On the other hand, there is often opposition when proposals are made to start charging for an "acquired right" such as free access to national parks. This suggests that the introduction of access charges should be accompanied by a well-designed information campaign.

Until the end of 2010, the central budget covered only 10-12% of national parks' financial requirements, with about 20% coming from the National Fund for Environmental Protection and Water Management. Though reliance on EU funds was increasing, the parks relied heavily on non-budgetary financing. Their income derived essentially from LP transfers from timber sales and access fees collected by so-called auxiliary enterprises operating in parks (Pater, 2011). Half of auxiliary enterprise profit was transferred to the central budget and the rest could be used to finance park management.

Pursuant to the 2009 Public Finance Act, which took effect in 2011, auxiliary enterprises have been liquidated as they could no longer perform tasks of public budget units or collect revenue on their own account. As a result, since 2011 the parks have been transferring all of the enterprises' revenue to the central budget. In 2011, some 70% of the parks' total operating costs – around PLN 200 million – were paid by the central budget (Pater, 2011). For major parks, the aim is for the central budget to cover all operating costs (Box 4.2). In 2012, the LP provided the national parks with PLN 8 million out of its profit of PLN 260 million.

Box 4.2. **Kampinos National Park**

Kampinos National Park, located in the immediate vicinity of Warsaw, is the only European park to border on a capital city and one of only two such sites in the world. One-third of its annual budget of around PLN 30 million comes from the central budget (for administrative costs), one-third from the National Fund for Environmental Protection and Water Management (for nature protection) and the rest from entrance fees, as well as EU support and the Forest Fund (Section 4.3). Warsaw residents are granted free access to the park while non-residents have to pay an access fee.

Source: Kampinos National Park administration.

National parks are central budget units: their expenses can be covered by the central budget, and their revenue must accrue to it. Due to the liquidation of the auxiliary enterprises, the Nature Conservation Act is being revised to give the parks legal status, which would allow them to retain revenue and seek EU funding, thereby reducing the need for funding from the central budget.

3.5. *Institutional mechanisms to foster integration of forestry and biodiversity policies*

The large share of Natura 2000 sites in LP forests (Section 4.2) has obliged foresters to change their forest management rules and take additional responsibility for the condition of protected sites. For example, areas in the network are subject to additional land use constraints, and EIA requirements were introduced in 2008 for afforestation on Natura 2000 sites.

The EIA Act replaced the relevant provisions regarding the EIA previously included in the 2001 Environmental Protection Law. It introduced more explicit EIA provisions for development on Natura 2000 sites. Consent (an "environmental decision") can only be given on certain conditions: the absence of alternative solutions, imperative reasons of overriding public interest, or compensatory measures ensuring coherence of Natura 2000.

Pursuant to the Nature Conservation Act (articles 33 and 34), all projects likely to have a significant effect on Natura 2000 sites are subject to EIA. Lists of such projects are set out in a 2010 EIA ordinance. Depending on the size, complexity and location of the project, environmental decisions are issued by the relevant RDEP, the GDEP, county governors, LP regional directorates for projects involving reclassification of Treasury-owned forests as agricultural land, or the local governor.

The Nature Conservation Act was amended in 2013 to ensure consistent implementation of Natura 2000 and forest management plans. The plans must be prepared concomitantly. For example, in the Białowieża Forest, the Natura 2000 plan, management plans for three forest districts and the management plan for Białowieża National Park were prepared simultaneously. Less than 10% of districts have their ten-year forest management plans renewed every year, so such combined planning efforts will have to take place gradually. Meanwhile, where forest management plans do not include specific provisions for nature protection on Natura 2000 sites, Natura 2000 plans apply.

The work of inventorying forest biodiversity undertaken by the LP forest districts since the 1990s has been truly remarkable (Section 4.4). It led, in particular, to the publication of companion reports to the forest districts' management plans. All the elements are there to create a knowledge base at the national level on biological diversity in LP forests.

4. Policy instruments

Instruments to enhance nature protection in Polish forests have included forestry practices, regulatory approaches, finance and other economic instruments, as well as information measures. This section assesses how these various instruments can help meet biodiversity objectives and the results achieved.

4.1. Sustainable forestry practices

Forest cover and afforestation

The forest area has continuously increased since the end of the Second World War. Forest now covers 29% of the land area, a proportion roughly on a par with the OECD average (OECD, 2013) and on track to meet the 2020 forest cover target of 30% in the NFP (Table 4.2). By the end of 2012, the forest area amounted to 9.2 million ha, a 3% increase since 2000 (Table 4.1). In Central and Eastern Europe, only Russia and Ukraine exceed this, and Poland has the 14th largest forest area in the OECD.

The National Forest Cover Augmentation Programme sets forest cover targets of 30% by 2020 and 33% by 2050. With support from the European Investment Bank, afforestation accelerated after 1995, doubling from around 10 000 ha per year in the early 1990s to some 20 000 ha per year to the mid-2000s. During the period from 1995 to 2004, the LP and private farmers were each responsible for half of the afforestation achieved. Since 2004, with EU accession, the Rural Development Plan (RDP) has included payments for farmland afforestation (Section 4.3), so that farmers now account for most afforestation.

Most RDP afforestation financing (80%) comes from EU co-financing of the European Agriculture Guidance and Guarantee Fund and the European Agricultural Fund for Rural Development, with Poland's own resources making up the rest. Payments provide not only for tree planting but also for their maintenance, along with payments for income forgone when converting farmland into forest land. Training courses and technical support provided by the Ministry of Agriculture and Rural Development, the Agency for Restructuring and Modernisation of Agriculture and the LP have helped private land owners prepare and implement afforestation plans.

After good initial uptake in 2004-06,[9] the attractiveness of the EU afforestation payment diminished (Figure 4.2). This is essentially because since 2007, meadows and pastures have been excluded from afforestation to prevent degradation of valuable grassland habitats. Furthermore, the RDP has not provided support to land located within the Natura 2000 network, unless the planned afforestation is deemed compatible with the protection plans of the areas. In 2007-13, to be eligible afforestation projects had to cover at least 0.5 ha and be a minimum of 20 metres wide, unless the land bordered a forest (Król, 2013). This requirement was relaxed for 2014-20: it is now at least 0.1 ha regardless of whether land borders a forest.

Figure 4.2. **Afforestation of agricultural land, 1945-2012**

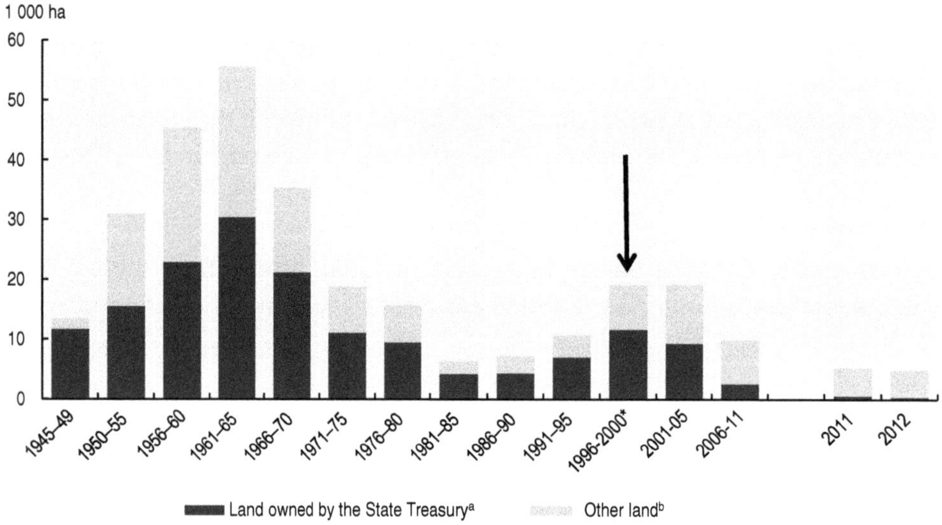

Note: Farmland not suited to agricultural production and wasteland; annual average for the periods 1945-49 to 2006-11.
* 1995 marks the start of the National Forest Cover Augmentation Programme.
a) Includes land administered by the State Forests (LP) and, to a much lesser extent, national parks.
b) Includes privately owned land and, to a much lesser extent, land owned by gminas.
Source: CSO (2013), *Environment 2013.*

StatLink http://dx.doi.org/10.1787/888933197762

Exposure of Polish agriculture to the market economy in the early 1990s initially led to a rapid increase in fallow land, especially after Poland shifted from central planning to market-driven prices for farm outputs and inputs. Highly subsidised collective and state-owned farms, which had accounted for about 20% of farmland, were restructured and many privatised, so that much marginal land was abandoned, especially in the north and west, making it potentially available for afforestation. It is estimated that fallow land increased nationwide from 1% of arable land in 1990 to 18% in 2002 (Kozak, 2010).

It has become much more difficult to find land for afforestation since EU accession, as a significant amount of farmland has been returned to agricultural production. This is due largely to the introduction of direct payments per unit of farmland in 2004 (Section 4.3), which in turn increased farmland prices: they rose from PLN 15 000/ha in 2009 to PLN 18 000/ha in 2013 (APA, 2014).

Land available for afforestation will be further reduced by the creation of habitat protection zones under Natura 2000 (Section 4.2). So far afforestation has taken place on land of poor agricultural quality, with no assessment of its nature value in terms of biodiversity. Hence, the policy relevance of the long-term NFP target is questionable. The economic context has changed significantly since it was set, and it is increasingly difficult to find land for afforestation. Poland may thus find it difficult to meet the 2050 target. More generally, any forest cover target should take account of nature protection objectives (based on Natura 2000, among other things).

Forest age structure

Structural diversity in forests creates a wide range of habitats (Forestry Commission, 2011). Forest management has considerably improved the age structure of Polish forests in the post-war period. Age classes are now more balanced,[10] and stands older than 80 years have doubled since 1945 to 2 million ha, allowing Poland to meet the 2050 NFP target early (Figure 4.3, Table 4.2).

Figure 4.3. **Structure of Polish forests, 2012**

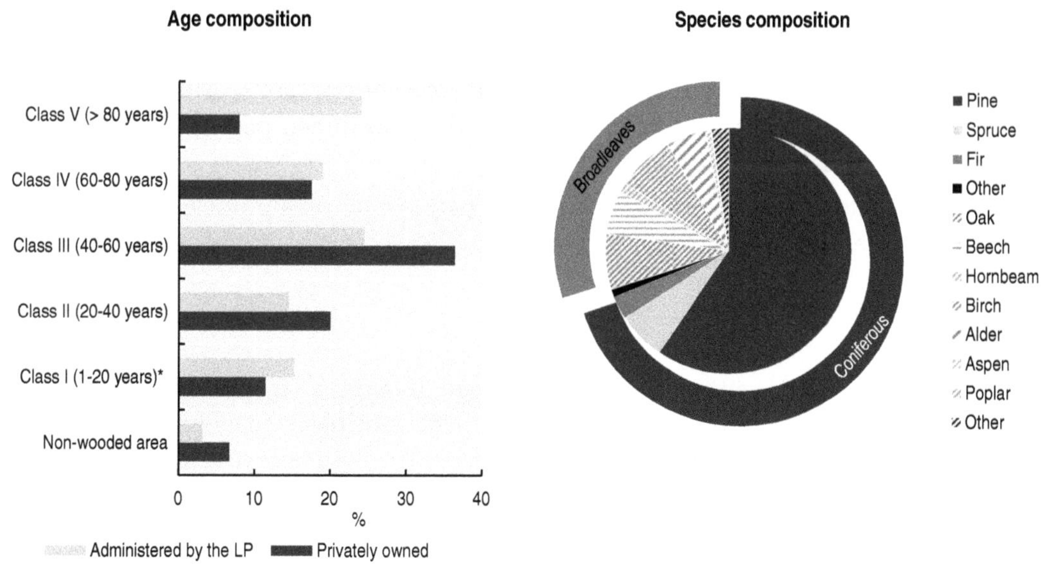

* Including restocking area.
Source: CSO (2013), *Environment 2013*.

StatLink http://dx.doi.org/10.1787/888933197772

Improvement of the age structure has been most notable in the forests administered since 1924 by the LP. Stands older than 100 years now account for 12% of the forest area administered by the LP, up from 8% in 2003.[11]

Tree species structure

Diversity of tree species is generally beneficial for biodiversity (Forestry Commission, 2011). The species structure of Polish forests has significantly improved. The share of stands with prevalence of broadleaved species is 30%, up from 13% in 1945, and Poland is on track to meet the 33% NFP target by 2050 (Table 4.2). Pine stands decreased from 75% of all stands in 1945 to 60% in 2012 (Figure 4.3). The species structure is fairly similar for LP and private forest, with slightly more broadleaves in private forest.

Major tree dieback episodes have provided opportunities to convert monocultures into mixed forests. For example, renewal efforts in the Beskid Mountains in the Carpathians have converted spruce-only stands into mixed forests with prevalence of fir and beech. In the Middle Sudetes, larch and many broadleaved species (e.g. beech, birch, alder, mountain ash) were used for forest renewal in the Jizera Mountains, allowing these species as well as native spruce to be returned to the Sudeten forests.

However, Polish forests are still characterised by species imbalance, partly reflecting soil conditions. Scots pine remains dominant. Some 85% of Polish forests are in lowland areas, which often are natural habitats for broadleaves,[12] so there is still room for improvement on the share of broadleaves.

Natural regeneration

Native woodlands, and especially ancient woodlands, have a very high biodiversity value or potential, and support a large proportion of priority species – those species that are rare and at risk of extinction, threatened or have special requirements (Forestry Commission, 2011). Natural regeneration of native tree species is therefore of high benefit to biodiversity. Natural regeneration (as opposed to regeneration via tree planting) has increased from 3-4% of forest renewal in the 1970s-1990s to around 10-12% since 2000. But the share remains one of the lowest in Europe (Forest Europe, 2013). This partly reflects poor soil conditions in the area of around 50% of Polish forest, possibly restricting the potential for successful natural regeneration.

The LP decided to allow natural regrowth in part of the Piska primeval forest (aka the Szast Forest) after it was devastated by a storm in 2002. This is a unique experiment on an EU scale.

Forest deadwood

Until the late 20th century, across all Europe, deadwood in managed forests was removed because it was thought that forests had to be "sanitised" to be healthy. Over time this led to the widespread impoverishment of woodland biodiversity. It has since been acknowledged that a wide range of plant and animal species depend on dead or dying wood for habitat (e.g. European otter) or as a food source (e.g. beetles).

Generally speaking, the greater the volume of deadwood, the greater the value of a forest for biodiversity. For example, in the United Kingdom up to a fifth of woodland species depend on dead or dying wood for all or part of their life cycle (Humphrey and Bailey, 2012). The amount of deadwood in forests is now increasingly used as a key international indicator of forest ecosystem biodiversity.

Poland has less deadwood in its forests than most other EU countries. With 5.7 m^3/ha of standing and lying deadwood, Poland ranks fourth lowest among the 20 EU countries for which data are available (Forest Europe, UNECE, FAO 2013). The volume of deadwood is much higher (35 m^3/ha) in forests of national parks.

Current evidence for EU forests suggests that, in the long term, deadwood (not including stumps, usually retained after felling) should average roughly 20 m^3/ha (Humphrey and Bailey, 2012). This does not mean deadwood must be uniformly distributed; efforts to create, maintain and manage deadwood habitats should be directed where they are most needed, in areas of high ecological value.

Progress has been made in reducing deadwood removal related to sanitary thinning. Sanitary thinning primarily consists of removing trees damaged by factors such as wind damage, pests, pollution and severe weather. In some areas it is used as an opportunity to remove old, naturally decaying trees so as to enhance forest productivity. This is the case in Poland, where sanitary thinning has included both damaged trees and deadwood. Nevertheless, except in 2007,[13] deadwood removal from sanitary thinning as a share of merchantable timber has been halved since 2000 and was down to 15% in 2012.

Selection-cutting

Another indicator of forest biodiversity relates to timber harvest management. Selection-cutting (as opposed to clear-cutting) is often thought to be more beneficial for biodiversity, though there is still a lack of knowledge about how forestry without clear-cuts affects biodiversity. Selection-cutting, which means felling only some trees at each harvest, allows the forest to remain uneven-aged and averts the need to replant. Since it does not disrupt forest continuity the way clear-cutting does, selection-cutting is expected to allow for the survival of the most species. In Germany and Switzerland, selection-cutting is common and clear-cutting generally forbidden, while North America and Sweden are moving to this position (Lundel, 2013). In Poland, clear-cuts as a share of timber removal were halved to 18% between 1990 and 2012 (CSO, 2013). The area of clear-cuts decreased from more than 40 000 ha/year in 1980 to around 25 000 ha/year over the last decade (Figure 4.4).

Figure 4.4. **Areas of clear-cutting, 1980-2012**

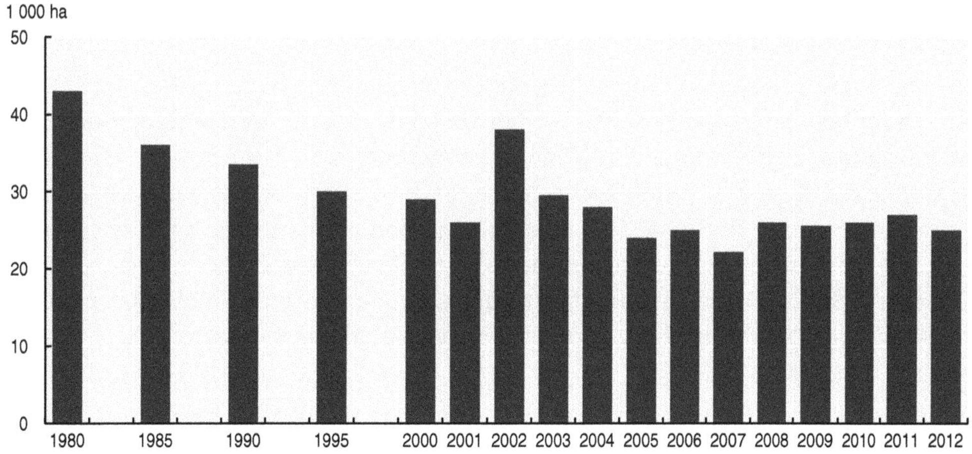

Source: LP (2013), *Forests in Poland 2013.*

StatLink http://dx.doi.org/10.1787/888933197788

Not all forests are suitable for selection-cutting. For example, it may be difficult in fast-growing, single-age monoculture stands. To eliminate clear-cutting, it is necessary to focus on forests where the trees are of multiple age classes and where preservation of endangered species is a key objective.

The received opinion is that selection-cutting instead of clear-cutting somewhat reduces forest productivity. But there is a lack of knowledge in this area. The debate between selection-cutting and clear-cutting illustrates the difficulty of a trade-off between forest biodiversity conservation and timber production objectives at the stand level. Since the mid-1990s, it has been common practice to leave trees for biodiversity purposes when clear-cutting in Finland, Norway and Sweden, and regulations for such "tree retention" are included in these countries' national laws and certification standards.

Sustainability of forestry practices

To a large extent, Poland has managed to increase timber harvesting and generate sustainable revenue while not compromising its natural capital. Despite limited productivity – 3-6 t/ha/year of dry matter – due to poor soil quality (podzolic soil is dominant), the growing stock (standing wood) has steadily increased since the first inventory of national forests in 1967. The total volume of standing wood is now 2.4 billion m^3, a 38% increase since 2000.[14] This amounts to 263 m^3/ha (up from 146 m^3/ha in 1967), higher than in most other OECD countries in terms of carbon stock in living forest biomass (FAO, 2011).[15] The 38% increase means Poland has far exceeded the timber security target set in the NFP (Table 4.2). In addition, the annual timber harvest potential increased to 36 million m^3 in 2013, again exceeding targets (Table 4.2).

The steady increase in the volume of standing timber over the last 45 years can be explained by improvement of the age structure and good timber harvest management. Though removal has continuously increased over the past decade, it has remained lower than incremental growth. The intensity of wood use in national forests (felling as a share of annual growth) was 68% in 1945-64, 71% in 1966-70, 60% in 1976-85 and 62% in 1986-95, continuing to fall to the current 55%, which is rather low compared to levels in other OECD countries (OECD, 2013). Afforestation and the fast growth of coniferous monoculture stands have also contributed to the increased volume of standing timber.

At the same time, many forest-dependent protected species have increased, and Polish forests host more game animals than those in most other EU countries. This is a result of Poland's long history of forest biodiversity protection. For example, efforts to save bison from extinction and protect wild horse, lynx, wildcat, beaver and predatory birds were initiated between the wars. The LP has always had programmes to protect threatened flora and fauna species. These programmes aim to preserve forest gene resources, restore fir (in Western Sudetes) and yew, and reintroduce grouse and lynx. Since 2000, populations of protected forest mammals have increased or remained stable (Figure 4.5).

The number of forest game animals in Poland is among the highest in the EU, indicating good game habitat management. The vast majority of populations of forest game mammals are found outside national parks (97-99% of wild boar, red deer, roe deer and fox, 90% of elk). Populations of game mammals have significantly increased. Since 2000, the elk population has increased by 559%, fallow deer by 212%, wild boar by 139%, red deer by 85%, mouflon by 59% and roe deer and fox by 47% each. These increases sometimes verged on posing a threat to forest stands, particularly young stands, as animals damage trees by browsing and bark stripping. Since 2000, protection of forest stands from damage by animals has been sustained at an annual average rate of 100 000 ha. Farmers whose crops are damaged by game species are eligible for financial compensation. Such payments increased from PLN 55 million in 2008 to PLN 69 million in 2013. The Polish Hunting Association paid more than 80% and the LP and voivodship governments paid the rest.

Figure 4.5. **Population of protected forest mammals and forest birds, 2000-13**

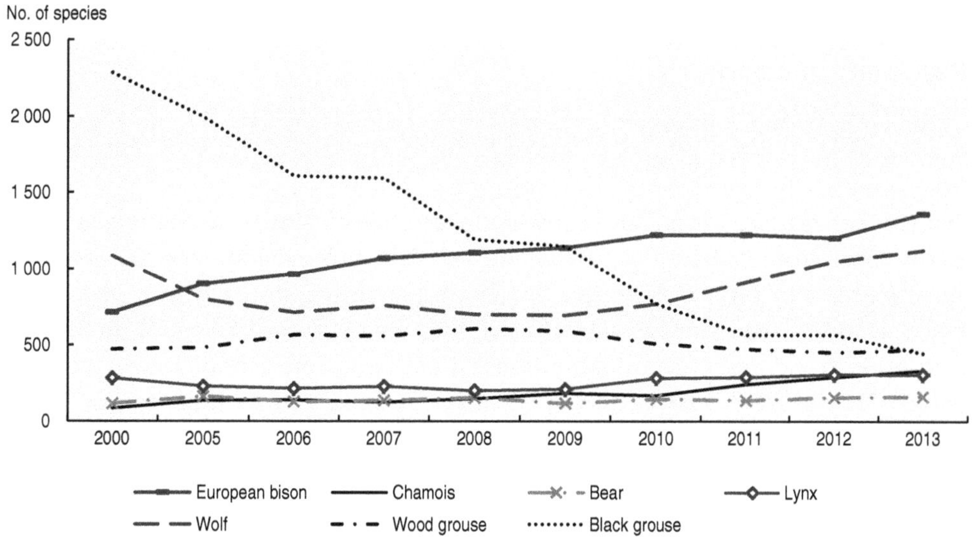

Source: CSO (2013), *Environment 2013.*

StatLink http://dx.doi.org/10.1787/888933197794

However, populations of some protected forest birds, such as black grouse, have significantly decreased (Figure 4.5). Reports from hunting districts indicate that the number of black grouse had already declined from 33 000 in 1977 to 5 000 in 1994. As a result, black grouse became a protected species in 1995. Its decline is attributed mainly to the increase in predators such as fox, badger and marten, and nest destruction by growing populations of the common raven, e.g. in coniferous lowland forests of the south-west (Merta et al., 2009). Another key factor is habitat destruction. The main habitat of the black grouse is wet forest. Such forest habitat used to be drained and developed for productive forestry or agriculture. As a result, the number of birds living in Polish wet forests decreased by 70% between 1982 and 1994 (Kamieniarz, 2003). Black grouse are also found on peat bogs, which have been drained as well. In mountain habitats, most bird refuges are on the borderland of lower subalpine forests and grasslands. Many grasslands have been developed for farming. Finally, the shrinking of black grouse populations in dry forests is related to the decline in area of young stands – an unexpected outcome of efforts to improve forests' age structure. A similar outcome can be expected from the shift from clear-cutting to selection-cutting.

Trends for game animals inhabiting open areas and forest borders have been varied. While the pheasant population has increased by 83% since 2000, the partridge population has continued to decrease (by 16%). The hare population has grown but has not recovered its pre-2000 level. Hare and partridge breeding programmes have been undertaken.

Forest certification has helped raise awareness and disseminate knowledge on sustainable forestry practices. Nearly all (98%) of the LP forests are certified under the internationally recognised Forest Stewardship Council (FSC) programme, making Poland the fifth largest FSC-certified area in the world (FSC, 2014). The world's largest forest certification system, the Programme for the Endorsement of Forest Certification (PEFC), was introduced in Poland in 2003. The Polish PEFC standards were accredited in 2008. Decisions to opt for FSC or PEFC certification are left up to the RDSFs. So far 9 of the 17 RDSFs have opted for PEFC. Because of their small size, private forests are not subject to certification (Kozioł and Matras, 2013).

4.2. Regulatory approaches

Direct regulation has played and will continue to play an important role in protecting forest cover and creating protected areas in forests, particularly in a context of still-unsettled claims for restitution of or compensation for property nationalised in the socialist era. Key regulations on land conversion and tree cutting have been used to protect the forest cover from destruction. However, regulatory provisions should better target nature protection in forests (through, for example, conversion permits or fees) while improving economic efficiency (e.g. by considering the opportunity cost of not converting forest to other uses). In 2012, an estimated 7% of Polish forest habitat was under legal protection for nature conservation. The share is expected to increase to 36% with implementation of the Natura 2000 network. A prerequisite, though, is to include Natura 2000 provisions in local land use plans. This requires revision of the 2003 Spatial Planning Act; in the meantime, the 2004 Nature Conservation Act should be applied in areas where no local land use plans are yet in place (see more discussion on land use planning in Chapter 2).

Forest protected areas

Taking all habitat categories together, not only forests, the share of land area in strict nature reserves, wilderness areas and national parks is lower in Poland than in many other OECD countries. Poland is among 14 OECD countries in which the share is 1% or less (OECD, 2013).

In 2012, the share of Polish forest habitat under protection was also low, with 644 000 ha or 7% of the forest area designated primarily for biodiversity conservation (Table 4.3), compared with the EU average of 10% in 2010, up from 4% in 1980 and 7% in 2000 (FAO, 2011).

Almost half the area of forest habitat under protection is protected by law, as part of national parks or nature reserves (Table 4.3). The rest, while not protected by nature

Table 4.3. **Areas of forest habitat protection, 2012**

	'000 ha	Forest area[b]	Land area[c]
		%	
National parks	195		
Nature reserves	104		
Total protected area by law	*299*	*3.3*	*1.0*
Forests of value to nature protection[a]	101		
Animal sanctuaries	150		
Seed stands	16		
Total protective forests	*267*	*2.9*	*0.9*
Areas of ecological utility	29		
Nature-and-landscape complexes	47		
Documentation sites	2		
Total other areas under LP inventory	*78*	*0.8*	*0.2*
Total	644	7.0	2.1

a) Excluding 104 000 ha of nature reserves with protected status.
b) Poland's forest area is 9.2 million ha.
c) Poland's land area is 31.2 million ha.
Source: CSO (2013); LP (2013).

conservation acts as such, is either classified as having a nature "protective" function, pursuant to the Forest Act, or is inventoried and registered by the LP for valuable nature protection attributes (see Section 4.4 for details on the inventory).

Poland has a long history of forest habitat protection. As early as 1921, attempts were made to manage the Białowieża Primeval Forest as a nature reserve and in 1932 it was made a national park. Other national parks were created in the 1930s, and administered then by the LP.

National parks are the highest level of nature protection. Poland has 23 of them, the most recent dating from 2001.[16] The forest area in national parks grew significantly in the 1980s and 1990s, slightly increased after 2000 and now totals 195 000 ha. Around 20% of the area of national parks is under strict protection. Most (80%) of the strictly protected area is forest. The area of strictly protected forest increased slightly between 2005 and 2012, from 52 000 ha to 57 000 ha.

Nature reserves constitute the second highest level of nature protection after national parks. Poland's 1 481 nature reserves include 174 established since 2000. The total land area in nature reserves increased from 150 000 ha in 2000 to 166 000 ha in 2012. By the end of 2012, the LP inventory included 267 nature reserves with total area of 122 000 ha, including 104 000 ha of forest.

Few "protective" forests meet explicit habitat and biodiversity protection objectives (Table 4.4). Since the interwar period, forests have been categorised as either protective or productive. In 1928, forest legislation recognised six categories of protective forests, one being "forests of value to nature protection", also called "forests representing valuable elements of indigenous nature".[17]

Table 4.4. **Categories of protective forests, 2012**

	Date of creation	'000 ha	% of forest administered by LP[a]
Water protecting	1928	1 517	21
Soil protecting	1928	331	5
Of military importance	1928	130	2
Of value to nature protection	1928	205	3
Located near health resorts	1928	56	1
Located near cities	1936	634	9
Damaged by industrial pollution	1992	473	7
Animal sanctuaries[b]	1992	73	1
Permanent research areas	1992	48	1
Seed stands[c]	1992	13	0.2
Total		**3 480**	**49**

a) The forest area administered by the LP is 7.1 million ha.
b) An additional 77 000 ha was registered in the LP nature protection inventory
c) An additional 3 000 ha was registered in the LP nature protection inventory.
Source: CSO (2013).

In 1992, rules granted protective forest status, set out management principles for such forest and defined new categories of protective forest (Table 4.4). There are three categories primarily aimed at nature protection: the one identified in 1928, forest habitats of protected species (so-called animal sanctuaries) and forest seed stands. Seed stands are important for nature protection as they allow native species and ecotypes to be included in forest renewal and afforestation.

In 2012, the area of protective forests under LP administration reached 3.5 million ha or 49% of the national forest area (Table 4.4). Most are in mountainous areas and have soil and water protective functions, though significant shares are designated near cities and in areas affected by industrial pollution. There are 65 000 ha of protective forests in private ownership, covering less than 4% of private forest area, and 25 000 ha in municipal forests, mostly peri-urban forests.

Forest habitat protection represents only around 4% of protective forests or 300 000 ha (Table 4.4). This includes 205 000 ha representing valuable elements of indigenous nature.[18] In addition, 3 146 zones have been created within LP forests to protect refuges of rare birds, mammals, reptiles, insects and lichens, covering 150 000 ha in all. And 16 000 ha of forest stands have been selected in protective forests to produce seeds and preserve the forest genetic pool.

Poland is not a member of the OECD Scheme for the Certification of Forest Reproductive Material, but has its own seed certification system primarily focusing on the use of forest seeds of Polish origin within the country. As an EU member Poland is reviewing the EU legislation on forest reproductive material covering trade in seeds from selected stands with third countries. The benefits of membership in the OECD programme would arise from expanding trade coverage to all registered seed provenances, as well as sharing information and best practices related to forest genetic resources and certification.

Natura 2000

A key challenge for enhancing forest biodiversity in Poland is to implement the Natura 2000 network. This implies an increase in forest habitat protection from the estimated 7% in 2012 to 36% of Polish forests (38% of LP forests). This does not necessarily mean that nature conservation should replace other forest functions; habitat and biodiversity protection objectives can coexist with other forest objectives. For example, productive forests often serve as wildlife corridors. However, there has been little progress in setting conservation objectives in the Natura 2000 network. By the end of September 2014, management plans had been approved for only 15% of the network area. Poland has started preparing management plans for a further 30% of the Natura 2000 area. More than 80% of the delineated Natura 2000 forest area is on LP-administered land.

The state of preservation of natural forest habitats in the Natura 2000 area is also of major concern. A survey conducted in 2006-11 by the Chief Inspectorate for Environmental Protection revealed that natural forest habitats in the network had predominantly poor or bad conservation status; only 30% of their area was in good condition (MoE, 2013). (It should be noted that the survey shows the non-forest Natura 2000 habitats to be in similar shape.) Natura 2000 also requires significant investments: financing needs for the network in 2014-20 are estimated at more than 12 times the level of spending in 2007-13 (Section 4.3). The next several years will be crucial if the network is to be successfully established and consolidated.

The Natura 2000 network is much larger than the area of Polish forest habitat previously under protection. As of January 2013, it amounted to 6.15 million ha, 20% of Poland's land area (MoE, 2013), compared with the estimated 7% of forest area under nature protection in 2012.[19] Forest accounts for more than half: 3.3 million ha or 36% of the total forest area (Table 4.5) Most forest mammals (except chamois) and birds are found outside national parks. This reinforces the need to speed up implementation of Natura 2000 in forests outside national parks.

Table 4.5. **Natura 2000 network, January 2013**

	'000 ha	Forest area	Poland
		%	
Forest	**3 320**	**36**	
of which:			
Deciduous	630		
Coniferous	1 923		
Mixed	767		
Semi-natural ecosystems (shrubs, grassland, open land)	147		
Areas with human development (urban, industrial)	51		
Agricultural areas	2 265		
Wetlands	79		
Freshwater and sea water	981		
Total	**6 843**		
of which:			
Land area	6 150		20
Coastal waters	693		

Source: MoE (2013).

Upon EU accession, Poland initiated its Natura 2000 programme and transposed the Habitats and Birds Directives (92/43/EEC and 2009/147/EC) into national legislation. The requirements of Natura 2000 are not unfamiliar to Polish foresters, who have been European pioneers in forest nature protection. Forest districts have included nature protection as an integral part of management since the interwar period, and under the 1991 Forest Act the districts must report on achievements. This is done through forest district nature protection programmes, which produce a companion report to the forest management plan (Section 4.4). The question that remains is the extent to which Natura 2000 requirements will affect timber production, the key to the financing of national forest (Section 4.3).

Pursuant to EU requirements, the Natura 2000 network is made up of Special Protected Areas (SPAs) for birds and Special Areas of Conservation (SACs) for habitats. Poland has designated 5.6 million ha in SPAs and 3.8 million ha in SACs; the two categories cover almost 20% of the territory.[20] Of this, LP forests account for 2.2 million ha in SPAs and 1.6 million ha in SACs, together representing 38% of the area administered by the LP.

Natura 2000 areas come in addition to existing landscape protection areas in Polish forests (Box 4.3). The 3.5 million ha of existing landscape parks and protected landscape areas coexist with the Natura 2000 network. Their level of forest biodiversity protection is

Box 4.3. **Landscape protection areas**

In addition to forest habitats protected by law and forest habitats with a protective function, local authorities have created landscape parks. Limited recreational activity is permitted in landscape parks. They contain wide silence zones, and industrial, residential and tourism development is prohibited (tourist facilities are situated in marginal zones). Each landscape park has its own administration and management plan. The 122 landscape parks in Poland cover 2.6 million ha, of which 1.3 million ha is forest. In addition, 2.2 million ha of forest is part of a category called "protected landscape areas".

Source: MoE.

generally much lower than in the 644 000 ha of forest habitats designated primarily for biodiversity conservation (Table 4.3).

Permits and fees for land conversion

Land conversion policy in Poland is quite restrictive. As a result, only around 500 ha of forest (mostly public) is converted to other uses (mostly industrial) each year, pursuant to the 1995 Act on Protection of Agricultural and Forest Land. Under the act, exclusion of more than 1 ha of private forest from forest production requires the consent of regional governor (voivod).[21] If the exclusion refers to forest land owned by the Treasury, the decision must be issued by the environment minister,[22] irrespective of the exclusion area.[23]

The possibility of excluding farmland or forest from production must be specified in the local master plan. If there is no master plan, such exclusion may be impossible. A recent report of the Polish Academy of Sciences revealed that only 28% of the territory is subject to plans that define uses for land, such as housing, industrial or green areas (Kowalewski, 2014).

Exclusion of land from production is subject to a one-off payment plus annual fees for 10 years. The payment and fees depend on the timber value of excluded stands. Higher rates apply to protective forests, providing an incentive to restrict their deforestation.

The payment obligation, however, does not apply if market prices for excluded land exceed the amount of the payment, which is usually the case. Moreover, exclusions for housing on less than 0.05 hectare (0.02 hectare for multiple dwelling buildings) are exempt from payment and fees. A one-off compensation payment may still be due if trees on the land have been prematurely cut. It equals the difference between the estimated commercial value of the forest stand at optimum rotation age, specified in the forest management plan, and the value when it was cut down. Instead of reflecting the actual or projected timber value of converted forest land, conversion fees should be based on the biodiversity value of stands, with higher rates for threatened ecosystems.

More generally, the direct regulatory approach to land conversion only considers the risk associated with deforestation. It fails to consider the opportunity cost of not converting the land, i.e. the development risk. Decisions on land conversion should reflect trade-offs between the two types of risk. How important is this land for meeting current and future development needs, including nature protection? Are there alternative land resources that mean conversion of this land is not required?

Penalties for tree cutting

The 2004 Nature Conservation Act imposes fees on private landowners who cut trees on their property (Table 4.6).[24] Without the required permit, penalties are three times the value of the fee.[25] The level of fees and penalties reflects the market value of the trees, with higher rates for older trees and for trees with higher timber quality. However, ideally the rate should reflect the trees' biodiversity value, with higher rates for threatened species, possibly based on the priority ranking of threatened forest tree species (see Kozioł and Matras, 2013).

Table 4.6. **Fees for tree removal on private land,[a] 2014**

Tree species[b]	Unit rate[c]	Coefficient							
	PLN/cm	Trunk size in cm (circumference at 130 cm height)							
		< 25	26-50	51-100	101-200	201-300	301-500	501-700	> 700
Poplar, alder	13.52	1	1.51	2.37	3.7	5.55	7.77	10	12.96
Spruce, Scots pine, Douglas fir, birch	36.75	1	1.51	2.37	3.7	5.55	7.77	10	12.96
Oak, beech, silver fir, other species of birch, spruce and pine	89.39	1	1.51	2.37	3.7	5.55	7.77	10	12.96
Other species of fir	337.21	1	1.51	2.37	3.7	5.55	7.77	10	12.96

a) Pursuant to the 2004 Nature Conservation Act (articles 88 and 89).
b) Only the main forest tree species have been included in this table.
c) 2014 rates represent a 25% increase over 2004 rates.
Source: Monitor Polski (Official Journal) No. 835 of 31 October 2013.

4.3. *Finance and other economic instruments*

Biodiversity financing

Since EU accession in 2004, national budgetary support to nature conservation has been increasingly supplemented with EU funding. Most expenditure on nature protection on private land over 2007-13 was financed by the European Agricultural Fund for Rural Development (EAFRD) as part of the Common Agricultural Policy (CAP). As regards public land, there is uncertainty as to the amount of LP budget devoted to nature protection, but budgetary expenditure on nature protection in LP forests has remained very limited. To meet Natura 2000 requirements, Poland must increase the management of forest protected areas from the current 7% of Polish forests (Table 4.3) to 36%. It is not clear how the gap in financing to accomplish this will be closed.

Over 2007-13 the EAFRD allocated EUR 235 million to Poland to afforest farmland and wasteland, and EUR 134 million to manage Natura 2000 sites[26] (Table 4.7) under the RDP. Natura 2000 payments were made available under the CAP for 2007-13, but there was little uptake by private forest owners, who were reluctant to prepare the required forest management plans. As for the CAP's on-farm afforestation programme, part of the eligible farmland has been returned to agricultural production in recent years.

Some afforestation and agri-environmental payments under the RDP can help improve on-farm forest biodiversity. This includes support for protection of endangered bird species and natural habitats, both inside and outside Natura 2000 areas.[27] In 2007-13 some 19 000 farmers participated in the agri-environmental programmes on around 250 000 ha. The number of farmers participating in afforestation projects rose from 8 000 in 2004-06 to 16 000 in 2007-13, representing afforestation of around 70 000 ha to date (FAPA, 2014).

However, most RDP payments are not targeted at environmental protection (FAPA, 2014). Moreover, from 2007 to 2013, eligibility criteria for afforestation finance took little account of habitat and biodiversity protection on abandoned farmland. As a result, afforestation took place on areas with low potential for agricultural production rather than in locations that would have enhanced nature protection (e.g. creation of ecological corridors). The eligibility criteria were changed for 2014-20, however, and now promote afforestation in support of erosion control, establishment of ecological corridors and enhancement of "ecological stability".

Other types of agricultural policy support – particularly market price support – create incentives to intensify agricultural production, which can lead to disincentives to protect

Table 4.7. **Budget allocated to nature protection, 2007-13**

Million EUR

European Agricultural Fund for Rural Development	**2 608**
Agri-environmental payments	2 303
of which support to Natura 2000 sites	134
Advisory services	70
Afforestation of farmland and wasteland	235
Structural funds and cohesion fund	**277**
Promotion of biodiversity and nature protection[a]	124[a]
Promotion of natural resources	69
Protection and valorisation of natural heritage	84
LIFE +	34
National Fund for Environmental Protection and Water Management[b]	**44**
Nature conservation and sustainable forest management	27
Environmental education	17
Provincial Funds for Environmental Protection and Water Management[b]	4
Norwegian Funds[c]	3
Swiss-Polish Co-operation Programme	1
State budget[d]	125
Total	**802[e]**

a) Includes EUR 90 million under the Infrastructure and Environment Operational Programme.
b) 2007-11.
c) 2007-12.
d) 2008-12. Covers administrative costs.
e) Excluding agri-environmental payments other than support to Nature 2000 sites, and the national budget.
Source: MoE (2013).

habitat and biodiversity, including on farm woodland. Market price support and direct payments have boosted farmland prices, creating incentives for farmers to reduce land set aside or abandoned, a trend in many regions of Poland that reduces LP ability to buy land for afforestation.

In addition to RDP payments, Polish farmers can apply for many other direct payments as part of the CAP. In particular, EUR 2.7 billion was allocated on single area payments in 2013, accounting for 80% of all direct payments that year.[28] The last reform of the CAP introduced the possibility of applying single area payments to forest areas from January 2015. Single area payments can help enhance nature protection in forests on farms since i) farmers are not required to produce commodities to be entitled to payments, ii) there are general obligations to keep land in "good environmental and agricultural condition" and iii) there are specific obligations to comply with the EU Birds and Habitats Directives.

Overall, there is a significant gap to cover the financing needs to properly establish and maintain the Natura 2000 network in years to come. The Priority Action Framework (PAF) for Natura 2000, published in 2013, sets priorities for action to develop the Natura 2000 network and estimates the financing required. It calculates that around EUR 1.6 billion is required to manage the Natura 2000 network over 2014-20 – a significant increase (12 times) from the EUR 134 million budget allocated by the EAFRD for the purpose over 2007-13.

Some 80% of PAF activities relate to extensification of production – essentially on farmland (700 000 ha) and grassland (200 000 ha) – and the creation of ecological corridors, essentially on afforested areas (50 000 ha) and in natural habitats of large carnivores such as lynx and wolf, whose migration is forest dependent. The PAF also refers to biodiversity preservation in decaying wood and to protection of old trees that provide refuges for forest biodiversity. The PAF provides support to ensure that nature protection is well covered in the forest management plans of forest districts.

In addition to the CAP, structural funds contribute to EU spending on nature protection (Table 4.7). In particular, the European Regional Development Fund allocated EUR 124 million to habitat and biodiversity protection in 2007-13. LIFE+ (renamed LIFE in 2014) is another key source of nature conservation funding by the EU, with EUR 34 million allocated over the period (Table 4.7). LIFE biodiversity protection projects are managed directly by the European Commission, as in all EU countries.

Bilateral assistance for biodiversity protection includes the Norwegian Funds (of which Poland became a beneficiary upon accession to the EU), which allocated EUR 3 million over 2007-12. The Swiss-Polish Co-operation Programme allocated EUR 0.8 million in the same period (Table 4.7).

The National Fund for Environmental Protection and Water Management, created in 1989, and similar funds established since 1993 at regional level allocated close to EUR 50 million to nature and biodiversity protection over 2007-13 (Table 4.7). These Polish funds are used to manage revenue from, and provide co-financing to, the EU structural funds. They complement budgetary support to nature conservation by collecting the proceeds from pollution charges to support financing of environmental investments, including biodiversity (Chapter 2). However, such earmarking limits flexibility in public spending and may mean that resources are not allocated efficiently. It may also lead to environmental issues being marginalised in the mainstream budget process. The lack of cost-benefit analysis in project selection is likely to lead to inefficiencies.

Forestry financing

Pursuant to the Forest Act, the operating costs of LP forests' management must be entirely covered by revenue from timber sales, as the LP is required to be financially self-sufficient. Until recently the LP could use any surplus money from timber sales to finance investment in the forests it administers. But available evidence suggests that little of this investment was targeted for nature. In a recent fiscal consolidation, the government decided that the LP should contribute to the central budget, first via a lump sum payment and then, from 2016, via a 2% fee on income from timber sales. This fee will come on top of a steady increase in the property tax on forest land (the so-called forestry tax) over the last decade (see discussion of property tax). At current timber sales and price levels and the current forestry tax rate, a 2% income fee plus the forestry tax would total some PLN 300 million (EUR 70 million) a year. This taxation should not affect LP core forest management activities, but will clearly affect LP investment unless demand for timber and timber prices both increase. Thus nature protection in LP forests will increasingly have to rely on funding other than profit on timber sales. The Forest Act allows central budget funding of nature protection in LP forests. DGSF annual economic and financial reports show that in recent years the central budget granted PLN 3 million (EUR 0.7 million) a year to the LP to carry out tasks beyond LP forest management. This included funding not only of nature protection but also of many other tasks (e.g. drawing up afforestation plans on private land, inventorying forest condition).

The LP internal financial allocation practice revolves around the Forest Fund, established by the 1991 Forest Act. The forest districts pay into this fund in amounts that vary by district, in accordance with prevailing local natural and economic conditions. A small part of the LP's income – most of its revenue other than from timber sales[29] – is also deposited in the fund. The fund balance has increased in recent years and stood at PLN 800 million at the end of 2012 (Table 4.8).

Table 4.8. **Forest Fund, 2005-12**

Million PLN

	2005	2006	2007	2008	2009	2010	2011	2012	2005-12
Opening balance	300	230	299	426	492	625	742	784	
Timber sales	550	577	690	671	543	525	657	916	5 129
Fees and fines for forestland conversion[a] and damage to forests[b]	83	69	70	88	91	84	109	114	708
Other income from the LP	8	35	26	76	39	41	40	56	321
Other income from national parks and private forests	1	2	2	4	5	6	8	11	39
Income from non-LP forests[c]	12	17	20	23	25	25	32	35	189
Total income	*653*	*699*	*809*	*863*	*703*	*682*	*846*	*1132*	*6 387*
Funds put at disposal of forest districts (equalisation)	455	467	455	636	449	409	525	744	4 140
Overhead:	268	164	226	160	121	156	281	380	1 756
Joint undertakings between LP and others in managing forests	18	29	36	32	36	56	68	90	365
Scientific research	23	25	29	30	26	18	29	42	222
Forest management infrastructure	170	61	102	39	4	26	130	172	704
Drawing up of forest management plans	45	47	43	48	46	49	47	51	376
Other management tasks	11	0	7	11	9	0	1	9	48
Afforestation and management of non-LP forests[c]	1	2	9	0	0	7	6	16	41
Stabilisation fund (to respond to unpredictable events[d])	0	0	0	0	0	22	36	0	58
Total expenditure	*723*	*631*	*681*	*796*	*570*	*587*	*842*	*1124*	*5 954*
Closing balance	230	299	426	492	625	720	748	*793*	

a) Pursuant to the Act on Protection of Agricultral and Forest Land.
b) Such as damage from industrial air pollution and arson.
c) Forests not owned by the Treasury and forests administered by the national parks.
d) Such as flooding in 2010.
Source: DGSF (2014).

The Forest Fund primarily acts as an equalisation mechanism, channelling money from the more prosperous districts to less prosperous ones. In other words, it finances deficits incurred by forest districts that are disadvantaged because of unfavourable natural or economic conditions – for example, a predominance of tree stands that are too young to be harvested.

Any surplus in the fund can only be allocated to LP basic forest management activities,[30] thus excluding the funding of nature protection in LP forests. Over 2005-12, the fund surpluses financed activities worth PLN 230 million a year on average, and as much as PLN 400 million in 2012 (Table 4.8). It is not clear whether the allocation of such resources was based on cost-benefit analysis of proposed projects. In 2010, the finance minister proposed using the Forest Fund to reduce the central budget deficit. A petition against this proposal gathered 200 000 signatures. Critics felt the move would threaten the LP's self-financing and the availability of funds supporting non-productive forest functions.

Taxes

The increasing demand for nature conservation in LP-administered forests, particularly in the context of consolidation of the Natura 2000 network, comes at a time of increasing fiscal pressure on the LP in terms of property and income taxation (see discussion of income fee in Section 3.1). Introduced in 1991 by the Forestry Tax Act, the property tax on forests was designed in a way similar to the property tax on farmland, introduced in 1984.

It is a progressive tax: the higher the soil quality and the more productive the type of forest, the higher the rate.[31] In other words, wealthy forest stands are taxed more than stands of poor quality. The same is true for farmland: high-yield crops on fertile arable land are taxed more than extensive meadows and pastures. The tax is payable to the local authority in which the forest is located.

Since 2003, calculation of the forestry tax has been simplified under the 2002 amendment to the Forestry Tax Act. The unit tax rate (per hectare) is now calculated according to the average sale price of wood by forest districts for the first three quarters of the year preceding the tax year. As a result, the maximum forestry tax rate has increased by more than 60% over the last decade (Pater, 2013). In 2013, the maximum rate was PLN 41/ha (10 EUR/ha), compared with a maximum rate of PLN 205/ha (50 EUR/ha) for the property tax on farmland. The forestry tax payment to municipalities increased from PLN 140 million in 2005 to PLN 230 million in 2012 (CSO, 2013).

A 50% rebate is granted to forests in nature reserves and national parks (i.e. protected forests). Forest stands "used for ecological purposes" are tax exempt.[32] These tax concessions provide incentives to protect nature in forests. Municipalities located in conservation areas have long claimed some form of compensation for the loss of tax revenue. In 2014 it was decided to abolish property tax relief on protective forests.[33] This will translate into an additional PLN 60 million transferred to municipal budgets from 2015 (The Voice of the Forest, 2014).

Overall, taxing property (wealth) instead of people (income) contributes to a fairer society. It is also less harmful for economic growth (Johansson et al., 2008). Taxes on land values (or a proxy) do not depress or distort wealth creation and are easy to assess, cheap to collect and hard to avoid. However, the decision to end tax relief on protective forests sends the wrong signal on nature protection in forests.[34] Fairness of forestry tax revenue distribution among municipalities should instead be addressed via a broader income equalisation policy. Proceeds of the forestry tax represent a very small share (0.3% in 2012) of total municipal income.[35] Moreover, due to tax exemptions and the varying age of forests, the tax proceeds vary significantly among forest districts and thus among municipalities.

Payments for ecosystem services

An interesting development in nature protection policy in the OECD is the rapid increase in PES programmes in the past decade. As a voluntary, flexible, incentive-based and site-specific instrument, PES can provide potentially large gains in cost-effectiveness compared to indirect payments or other regulatory approaches used to meet policy (e.g. forest biodiversity) objectives (OECD, 2010). PES is a mechanism by which the user or beneficiary of an ecosystem service makes a direct payment to the service providers – i.e. to those whose management decisions influence provision of such ecosystem services as reducing biodiversity risks. Individuals such as farmers and foresters are paid for the additional costs of achieving biodiversity conservation beyond what is required by law.[36] Instead of compensating forgone revenue from timber sales or farming, PES should reward the provision of well-targeted and otherwise unremunerated nature protection services.

Even though the term "ecosystem services" (and its variants) appears 13 times in the 1997 NFP, the application of this approach is still to be developed in Polish forestry (Mączka et al., 2014). One reason is that PES programmes are generally easier to apply to private forests and so are currently used on a larger scale in countries with predominantly private forest ownership (UNECE/FAO, 2014). Poland could consider introducing PES to reward biodiversity protection beyond what is required by law in both public and private forests.

4.4. *Information*

Promotional forest complexes

Impressive efforts have been made to improve information on forests through the creation of "promotional forest complexes". They constitute a major step forward in raising public awareness of forests' multiple roles, including nature protection. Such complexes are contributing to an increase in willingness to pay for nature-friendly forest management or to accept public spending to that end. The LP was awarded the 2013 UNESCO Sultan Qaboos Prize for Environmental Preservation in recognition of its outstanding contribution in the fields of research, education and awareness raising on the preservation of the environment and natural resources.

The LP established its first promotional forest complex in 1994 and has since created 24 others on 1.2 million ha, representing the various forest habitats of Poland and 15.5% of the area administered by the LP. More than 750 000 people visit the complexes every year. Forest research stations have been attached to them. Public expenditure on forest education has been increasing in recent years and reached PLN 25 million in 2012.

Nature protection inventories

In compliance with the 1991 Forest Act, the LP keeps an inventory of all forms of nature protection on the 7 million ha of forest it administers. This is done through forest district programmes for nature protection, which produce a companion report to the forest management plan that is unique in Europe (and probably in the world). Data provided by the forest district programmes are regularly used to update the inventory. Since 1998, the nature protection programmes have been an obligatory part of each district's forest management plan. The aim is to create a knowledge base to aid in increasing biological diversity in LP forests.

Beyond the 122 000 ha of nature reserves, including 104 000 ha of forest (Section 4.2), the LP inventory includes more than 9 000 "areas of ecological utility" (aka ecological sites) covering 29 000 ha. Areas of ecological utility host valuable habitats and species, but are too small for designation as nature reserves. They contain remnants of ecosystems, such as natural water bodies, mid-field and mid-forest ponds, clumps of trees and shrubs, swamps, bogs, dunes, and strands of rare or protected plants and animals. Taking all habitat categories together, areas of ecological utility increased from 45 000 ha in 2000 to 52 000 ha in 2012.

Another category in the LP inventory is "nature and landscape complexes", of which there are 126 covering 47 000 ha. Smaller than landscape parks, they include fragments of natural and cultural landscapes that are protected for their scenic and aesthetic values. In all habitat categories together, nature and landscape complexes increased from 78 000 ha in 2000 to 96 000 ha in 2012.

The LP inventory includes 147 documentation sites totalling 1 700 ha and some 11 000 natural monuments (e.g. single trees or groups of trees). There are 161 documentation sites in all, which are important for research and education. Natural monuments have particular scientific, cultural or landscape value; Poland has a total of 36 316, including glacial boulders, rocks, grottos, caves and springs.

Despite considerable monitoring and fieldwork, there is no comprehensive assessment of the economic value of ecosystem services provided by forests as a basis for PES.

Environmental and social functions of Polish forests have long been recognised in forest management, which began to distinguish categories of "protective" forests as early as in the 1920s (Section 4.2). However, this has not been accompanied by an economic valuation of environmental services (e.g. carbon sequestration, air and water purification, biodiversity) and social benefits (e.g. employment, recreational opportunities, cultural values) associated with the protective functions. Doing so would allow the gearing of forest policies towards maximising the social, economic and environmental services provided by forests.

Notes

1. Including forestry, manufacturing of wood, paper products and furniture.
2. Threatened species are endangered, critically endangered and vulnerable species.
3. More generally, Poland is host to 40% of all animal and plant species described in Europe.
4. The Pan-European (Helsinki) process focuses on the development of criteria and indicators for sustainable management of European forests. It is overseen by Ministerial Conferences on the Protection of Forests in Europe. In 2007, Poland hosted the fifth Ministerial Conference.
5. As agreed in 2010 at the tenth Conference of the Parties to the CBD.
6. As is the National Fund for Environmental Protection and Water Management.
7. As is the Chief Inspectorate of Environmental Protection, which enforces environmental policy.
8. Forest Europe implements the Helsinki Process.
9. With financial support from the European Union, tens of thousands of hectares of farmland were afforested between 2004 and 2006.
10. Balanced age classes, with roughly equal areas of forest in each age class, are essential to ensure a steady supply of wood while maintaining the diversity of forest ecosystems.
11. Relatively few stands are older than 120 years, reflecting the predominance of conifers, which usually have a shorter lifespan than broadleaved trees.
12. Poland has two main regions: the Polish Plain and the Southern Uplands and Mountains. The Polish Plain covers the northern two-thirds of the country. The Southern Uplands (hilly areas) and Mountains (the Sudeten and Carpathian ranges) cover the southern third.
13. In 2007, Polish forests were hit by several bad windstorms.
14. Fronczak (2013) estimates the volume of standing timber in national forests in 1946 at 700 million m^3.
15. Growing stock is an indicator of living forest biomass (above-ground living tree material), which is about 50% carbon.
16. Warta River Mouth National Park, essentially a freshwater area containing little forest.
17. A seventh category, forests in and around cities, was added in 1936.
18. Nearly half (49%) of this area has protected nature reserve status.
19. In addition the proposed network extends over some 700 000 ha of Baltic Sea coastal waters.
20. The SPA and SAC categories overlap, so they cannot be simply added.
21. The same provision applies to exclusion from agricultural production of poor quality arable land (classes IV and V-VI) comprising organic soil and peat bog.
22. The same provision applies to exclusion from agricultural production of good quality arable land (classes I-III), for which consent must be obtained from the minister of agriculture and rural development.
23. Until 2013 such consent was not required for areas of less than 0.5 ha.
24. If the owner has been granted a cutting permit, exemption from payment of the fee applies in some cases (e.g. for safety reasons).
25. The act also imposes a penalty for damaging trees through "inappropriate execution of maintenance procedures".

26. The latter as part of agri-environmental measures.
27. The creation of buffer zones is also eligible for agri-environmental payments.
28. Data from the Agency for Restructuring and Modernisation of Agriculture as of end August 2014.
29. The LP may receive payments for forest management services on land other than that under its administration (e.g. private forests, municipal forests, national parks). The small additional income derived from such payments, as well as from various fees and fines that the LP is authorised to collect from forest users or abusers, accrues to the Forest Fund.
30. Including activities in silviculture, forest protection, research and the development of infrastructure "necessary for managing the forest economy".
31. It is obtained by using a set of coefficients applied to the unit tax rate. Forest stands less than 40 years old are tax exempt.
32. Similarly, agricultural land under "ecological zones" and afforestation are exempt from the farmland property tax.
33. Until 2014, a 50% rebate was also granted to protective forests.
34. Protective forests include forests of value to nature protection and animal sanctuaries (Table 4.4).
35. Most municipal income comes from corporate and personal income taxes and the central budget.
36. CAP payments to compensate farmers for conserving biologically rich habitat in Natura 2000 sites do not fulfil this requirement.

References

APA (2014), Agricultural Property Agency, *www.anr.gov.pl/web/guest/welcome.*

Bartczak A. et al. (2008), "Valuing Forest Recreation on the National Level in a Transition Economy: The case of Poland", draft 21 January, *www.lindhjem.info/Polandpaper.pdf.*

CSO (2013), *Forestry 2013*, Central Statistical Office, Warsaw.

Convention on Biological Diversity (CBD) (2013), "Sectoral Integration of Biodiversity in Poland", in *Resource Mobilization Information Digest*, No. 90, February.

Council of Ministers (2007), "National Strategy for the Conservation and Sustainable Use of Biodiversity and the Action Programme for 2007-13", Annex to Resolution No. 270/2007, Council of Ministers, Warsaw (in Polish).

FAO (2011), *State of the World Forests 2011*, Food and Agriculture Organization of the United Nations, Rome.

Forest Europe (2013), *State of Europe's Forests 2011, Status and Trends in Sustainable Forest Management in Europe*, UNECE/Food and Agriculture Organization of the United Nations, Rome.

FSC (2014), "Global FSC Certificates: Type and Distribution", Forest Stewardship Council, Bonn, June.

Forestry Commission (2011), *Forests and Biodiversity, UK Forestry Standard Guidelines*, Forestry Commission, Edinburgh, *www.forestry.gov.uk/PDF/FCGL001.pdf/$FILE/FCGL001.pdf.*

FAPA (2014), "Changes in the Instruments of Agricultural and Fisheries Policy (Monitoring for OECD)", February, Foundation of Assistance Programmes for Agriculture, Warsaw.

Fronczak, K. (2013), *Signs of the Times, The State Forests: Past and Present*, LP Information Centre, Warsaw.

Gerasimov, Y. (2013), "Atlas of the Forest Sector in Poland", *Working Papers of the Finnish Forest Research Institute* (METLA) No. 268, Vantaa, Finland.

Humphrey, J. and S. Bailey (2012), *Managing Deadwood in Forests and Woodlands*, Practice Guide, Forestry Commission, Edinburgh.

IUCN (2013), *Poland's Biodiversity at Risk, A Call for Action*, IUCN, May 2013.

Johansson, Å. et al. (2008), "Tax and Economic Growth", *ECO/WKP(2008)28, OECD Economics Department Working Paper* No. 620, OECD Publishing, Paris.

Kamieniarz, R. (2003), "Black Grouse Habitats in Poland", *Sylvia*, No. 39 (suppl.).

Kowalewski, A. et al (2014), "Report on the Economic Loss and Social Costs of Uncontrolled Urbanization in Poland ", *Samorząd Terytorialny*, No. 4, pp. 5-21, Warsaw.

Kozak, J. (2010), "Forest Cover Changes and their Drivers in the Polish Carpathian Mountains since 1800", Chapter 11 in *Reforesting Landscapes, Linking Pattern and Process*, Springer.

Kozioł C. and J. Matras (2013), *The Country Report on Forest Genetic Resources*, Poland, LP Information Centre, Warsaw.

Król, M. (2013), "Legal Framework of Environmental Law for Agricultural Production", National Report for Poland, European Congress on Rural Law, Lucerne (Switzerland), 11-14 September.

LP (2013), *Forests in Poland 2013*, Lasy Państwowe (LP) Information Centre, Warsaw.

LP (2013), *The State Forests in Figures 2013*, LP Information Centre, Warsaw.

LP (2013), *For Forest, For People; Poland: the State Forests*, LP Information Centre, Warsaw.

LP (2013), "Nature Conservation Plan, Forest District of Choczewo", LP, Warsaw.

Lundel, M. (2013), "Clear-cutting or Selection cutting – which Method Allows most Life in the Forest?", *Sustainability*, Issue 4, December.

Mączka, K. et al. (2014), "Environment as a Stock: does the Ecosystem Services Approach exist in the Polish Environmental Policy?", presentation at the International Symposium on Society and Resource Management, Hannover, Germany, 8-13 June.

Merta, D. et al. (2009), "Distribution and Number of Black Grouse, Tetrao tetrix in Southwestern Poland and the Potential Impact of Predators upon Nesting Success of the Species", *Folia Zool.*, No. 58 (2).

MoE (2013), "Priority Action Framework for Natura 2000, Long-term EU Financing over 2014-20", Council Directive 92/43/EEC on the Conservation of Natural Habitats and of Wild Fauna and Flora and Directive 2009/147/EC of the European Parliament and of the Council on the Conservation of Wild Birds, Ministry of the Environment, Warsaw, April (in Polish).

OECD (2013), *Environment at a Glance 2013: OECD Indicators*, OECD Publishing, Paris, *http://dx.doi.org/10.1787/9789264185715-en.*

OECD (2010), *Paying for Biodiversity: Enhancing the Cost-Effectiveness of Payments for Ecosystem Services*, OECD Publishing, Paris, *http://dx.doi.org/10.1787/9789264090279-en.*

OECD (2005), *Taxation and Social Security in Agriculture*, OECD Publishing, Paris.

Parlińska, A. (2008), "Legal Aspects of Polish Tax and Social Security in Agriculture", *Aestimum*, No. 53, December.

Pater, B. (2013), "The Structure of Forest Tax in Poland", in *Business and Non-Profit Organisations Facing Increased Competition and Growing Customers' Demands*, Vol. 12, National-Louis University, Nowy Sącz.

Pater, B. (2011), "National Parks – their Operations and Financing", in *Business and Non-Profit Organisations Facing Increased Competition and Growing Customers' Demands*, National-Louis University, Nowy Sącz.

Simon, L., J. Mozgawa and C. Cieslak (1997), "La Pologne forestière entre permanences et mutations", *Revue Forestière Française*, XLIX, 3-1997.

The Voice of the Forest (2014), "State Forests Will Pay, but not Workers", Monthly of LP Information Centre, Warsaw, January.

UNECE/FAO (2014), "The Value of Forests, Payments for Ecosystem Services in a Green Economy", *Geneva Timber and Forest Study Paper* No. 34, ECE/TIM/SP/34, UNECE/FAO, Geneva.

Van Benthem M. (2013), "Timber Market Trends in the EU and Opportunities for Polish Wood products", Presentation, Probos (Dutch Institute for Forestry and Forest Products).

Wibe S. (1992), "Policy Failures in Managing Forests", in *Market and Government Failures in Environmental Management, Wetlands and Forests*, OECD Publishing, Paris.

PART II

Chapter 5

Waste and materials management

Poland has recently undertaken major reforms of its waste management policies. This chapter examines trends in materials use and waste generation, as well as related policy and institutional frameworks. It discusses the reform of municipal waste management and investment in treatment facilities. It also analyses the performance of extended producer responsibility programmes and reviews progress in managing industrial, hazardous and construction waste. Opportunities for strengthening policy instruments, including economic instruments, are identified and progress in remediating contaminated sites is examined.

The statistical data for Israel are supplied by and under the responsibility of the relevant Israeli authorities. The use of such data by the OECD is without prejudice to the status of the Golan Heights, East Jerusalem and Israeli settlements in the West Bank under the terms of international law.

Assessment and recommendations

Since the last OECD Environmental Performance Review in 2003, Poland has undertaken major changes in waste management. National Waste Management Plans (NWMPs), together with EU and national targets, have provided the basis for the reform agenda. The legal framework for waste management has been transformed with the adoption of EU legislation. Nevertheless, further steps are needed to establish a comprehensive and coherent framework. Waste prevention and minimisation have not received sufficient attention. The adoption of a National Waste Prevention Programme by the Council of Ministers in June 2014 provides a good basis for addressing this gap. While the NWMPs and the 2013 Strategy for Innovative and Efficient Economy address the need to improve materials productivity, as yet few concrete actions have been proposed to improve performance in this area. A major impediment to effective waste management policy is poor-quality and incomplete data.

Materials productivity improved in 2000-10, but these gains were largely offset in 2011 by a sharp rise in domestic materials consumption driven by a boom in construction and civil engineering projects. Due to its relatively large mining and industrial sectors, Poland is a relatively materials-intensive country, both in per capita and GDP terms.

In the context of rising GDP and private final consumption, waste generation appears to have been largely stable. If the data are accurate, this is an important achievement. The stable trend in municipal solid waste (MSW) is partly due to declining collection in the first half of the 2000s. Waste generation per capita is below the OECD average, mostly due to lower average income.

For most of the review period, Poland made slow progress in achieving its objectives of providing MSW collection for all inhabitants and separate collection of recyclable waste. The 2013 reform of MSW management replaced a poorly regulated system in which each household or building contracted separately for waste collection with one in which municipalities are responsible for MSW. Preliminary evidence suggests that this reform is helping achieve the main MSW policy objectives. Nevertheless, a range of challenges remains. In particular, municipalities need significantly more capacity and support to carry out their responsibilities and to ensure that waste management services are provided efficiently and effectively. This involves a complex series of tasks, including tendering for the provision of waste management services, establishing tariffs at an appropriate level and entering into public-private partnerships.

Since 2001, extended producer responsibility systems have been responsible for the collection, recovery and recycling of six important waste streams, including packaging, tyres and batteries. They have played an important role in establishing infrastructure and increasing separate collection, recovery and recycling for the waste streams concerned. Although published results suggest that they are by and large achieving their targets, there are concerns about the reliability of the information they generate and the "grey zones" of waste that fall outside these systems. Recent reforms, such as the revision of Poland's packaging waste legislation, have addressed some of the problems but further efforts are needed to improve the systems' reporting and performance.

Poland has made important progress in reclaiming former mining areas, cleaning up contaminated sites and closing landfills that do not meet EU standards. However, the area covered by unremediated mining and contaminated sites is still extensive. Further efforts are needed to address these legacy sites and to protect soil and groundwater. Establishing a comprehensive inventory of contaminated sites is a key step in this direction.

From 2000 to 2012, EUR 2.4 billion was invested in waste management. Enterprises, including municipal utilities, provided a large share of the financing. Poland's environmental funds and EU financial support also played important roles. This level of funding, however, was not sufficient to achieve national and EU targets. While there was a significant expansion of biological and mechanical treatment and composting, more than half of MSW is still landfilled. Further investment is needed to meet the 2020 targets, notably for the recycling and composting of MSW. Current plans also call for high levels of investment to build MSW incinerators. Given the large costs involved, it is vital to develop a coherent strategy for investment in this sector in which the cost and benefits of alternative approaches are carefully assessed and support is provided to municipalities. Implementation of the strategy should be carefully monitored and adjusted in the light of experience.

Recommendations

- Strengthen efforts to improve resource productivity and reinforce implementation of the material productivity components of the Strategy for Innovative and Efficient Economy.
- Update national and regional (vovoidship) waste management plans, integrating a coherent investment approach for MSW treatment facilities that aims to meet EU targets for municipal waste recycling and reduce the share of biodegradable waste sent to landfill, and avoiding the development of incineration capacity that outstrips demand or competes with other forms of waste treatment; focus implementation of the National Waste Prevention Programme on priority waste streams.
- Consider setting recycling targets for municipal waste at the level of waste regions or vovoidships rather than municipalities.
- Assess how greater use of economic instruments could support the more efficient achievement of waste management goals, enhance material productivity and support the financial sustainability of waste utilities, including by increasing landfill charges; strengthening the incentive effect of the tax on minerals extraction, including aggregates; and introducing a tax on single-use carrier bags.
- Expedite the completion of the National Database on Products, Packaging and Waste; adopt measures to improve the accuracy of waste data.
- Reinforce efforts to improve public awareness of waste management and resource productivity issues.
- Consider establishing a mechanism to support and oversee municipalities in providing efficient and effective waste management services (e.g. through tendering, project preparation and tariff setting); further support the strengthening of capacities in municipalities to promote compliance with waste management legislation and regulations.

Recommendations *(cont.)*

- Consider ways to strengthen the reliability and performance of environmental producer responsibility systems, including by requiring the certification of producer responsibility organisations and their adherence to an environmental management system (such as EMAS), and the adoption of common reporting formats.
- Further develop the national register of contaminated sites; provide funding for both remediation and the identification of degraded sites; prioritise sites for remediation on the basis of the risks they pose to human health and the environment.

1. Objectives, policies and institutions

1.1. *Policy framework*

Poland adopted a series of waste management plans over the review period. The National Waste Management Plan 2006 (NWMP 2006, published in 2002) was updated by the NWMP 2010, (published in 2006), and that was in turn revised by the NWMP 2014 (published in 2010). Each plan identifies key problems and issues for waste management and sets policy objectives, targets and actions. Overall policy objectives have remained fairly constant, partly because many are linked to EU waste objectives. Major common objectives found in both the 2010 and 2014 NWMPs include:

- continuing the decoupling between waste generation and GDP growth
- increasing the levels of recovery, including energy recovery, and recycling of waste
- reducing the quantities of waste sent to landfill
- closing landfills that do not meet EU standards
- eliminating illegal waste storage practices
- creating a database for products and waste management.

The plans include quantitative targets: Figure 5.1 presents an overview of key targets in the NWMP 2014, which sets out actions and identifies targets and directions for waste management to 2022 (described further in Sections 3-5). As not all actions and targets in earlier plans were met, some are repeated in the current plan. For example, the target to provide separate waste collection for all was first set for 2007 in the NWMP 2010; it is set for 2015 in the NWMP 2014.

The plans also estimate needed investment: in 2010, the NWMP 2014 indicated PLN 6.8 billion was required (EUR 1.7 billion at 2010 exchange rates). However, this estimate included investment where financing was expected, rather than all investment to meet objectives and targets. Thus in 2014, the Ministry of the Environment (MoE) identified major investment needs to 2020 (Section 6).

The NWMP 2014 sets out key principles highlighted in EU waste policy, including the proximity principle of waste treatment and the waste hierarchy, which calls for priority first on prevention, then reuse, recycling, other recovery and disposal. The plan calls for waste prevention and eco-innovation but lacks concrete initiatives in these areas. In June 2014, the Council of Ministers adopted the National Waste Prevention Programme.

Voivodship (regional) waste management plans were prepared following each national plan. The most recent voivodship plans identify investment and other action to implement the NWMP 2014, focusing in particular on municipal waste management. These plans were

Figure 5.1. **Key targets from the National Waste Management Plan 2014**

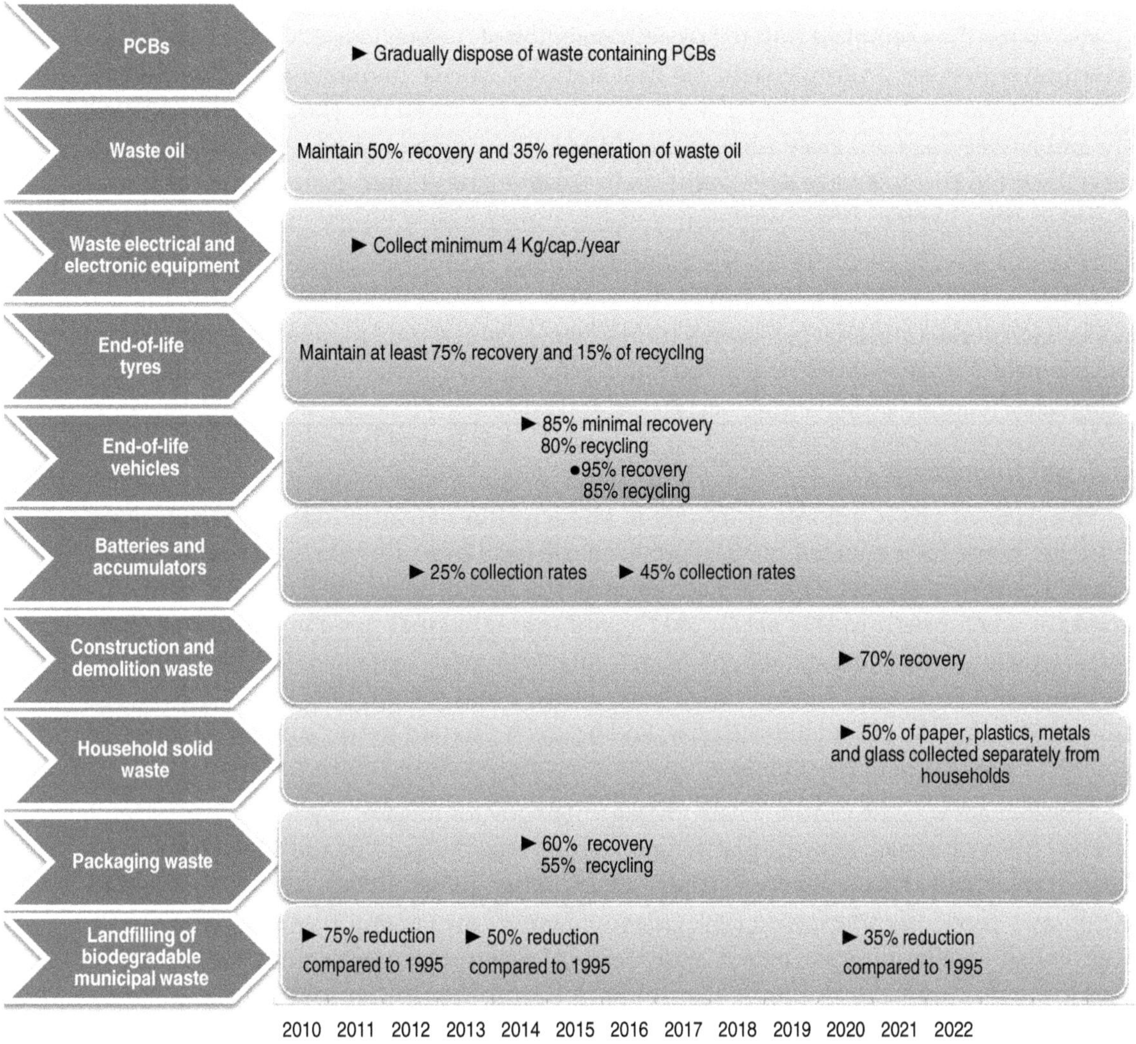

Source: Ministry of Environment (2010), *National Waste Management Plan 2014.*

adopted in 2012; most have time frames to 2017 with outlooks to 2022 or 2023. Previous planning cycles had a more complex, cascading system of waste planning at four levels, including powiats (counties) and gminas (municipalities): each plan had to be consistent with the one above, with reporting in the opposite direction, flowing from lower to higher levels. This four-level approach proved too complicated to co-ordinate and was changed to a two-level approach for the most recent planning cycle.

The national plans include provisions for monitoring results. Regular implementation reports have detailed progress towards targets and have identified shortfalls. Their conclusions help strengthen continuity across the plans. The most recent implementation report, published in late 2011, described the results of the NWMP 2010. The next NWMP is expected for 2016, extending the original time frame for revision by two years. A report on implementation of the NWMP 2014 and related voivodship plans will present results for 2011-13: it is expected to be completed in December 2014 (voivodship reports) and June 2015 (national report), a gap compared to previous implementation reports, which appeared every two to three years.

Poland has thus complied with the recommendation of the previous OECD Environmental Performance Review: to implement its first national waste management plan and to establish regular progress reviews. The review system informed the NWMP (2006), NWMP 2010 and NWMP 2014. An evaluation of the NWMP 2014 implementation would be useful, especially given the extensive developments in waste management policy in recent years, detailed in this chapter.

Poland's Energy Security and the Environment Strategy, adopted in April 2014, summarises and updates some broad objectives for waste management. It calls for increasing materials and energy recovery from waste; ensuring the functioning of the system of municipal solid waste (MSW) collection put in place in 2013, including selective collection; closing small landfills for MSW and inert waste; and putting in place low-waste technologies.

1.2. *Legal framework*

The 1996 Act on Cleanliness and Order in Municipalities and the 2001 Waste Act, along with other waste laws enacted in 2001, provided the legal basis for waste management for most of the review period. The 1996 act governs the institutional structure for MSW. An important amendment to this act in 2011 made the municipalities the owners of MSW generated within their jurisdiction, as from 1 July 2013, with responsibility for collection and treatment. Previously, individual property owners and building managers contracted with waste collection companies directly, an approach that led to incomplete coverage of collection and treatment (Section 3).

The 2001 act was the central waste management law for most of the review period, and it set out the waste management planning system. It was replaced by the 2012 Waste Act,[1] which transposed the EU Waste Framework Directive (2008/98/EC). The 2012 act also incorporates previously transposed EU legislation, notably the Landfill Directive (1999/31/EC). Other Polish legislation transposed additional EU waste legislation in areas including mining waste, recycling of end-of-life vehicles (ELVs), waste electrical and electronic equipment (WEEE), batteries and accumulators. The 2013 Act on Packaging and Packaging Waste Management updated previous legislation following a formal opinion from the European Commission concerning the original transposition; among the issues strengthened were provisions for data and reporting (European Commission, 2011).

Overall, EU legislation sets the framework for waste management policy and legislation in Poland and has been the main driver for action. Many of the quantitative targets in the 2010 and 2014 NWMPs are established in EU law. The preparation of national waste management plans is itself a requirement of the EU Waste Framework Directive and earlier EU legislation, as is the preparation of a national waste prevention programme.

In addition to setting the legal framework and key policy targets, the EU provides financing for waste management investment through its cohesion policy (Section 6).

1.3. *Materials and resource efficiency policy*

Poland's National Development Strategy to 2020 (NDS), published in 2012, calls for improving the energy and resource efficiency of the economy. It lays out nine strategies on specific issues; the most relevant for materials consumption and resource efficiency is the Strategy for Innovative and Efficient Economy, published in January 2013. This strategy aims to strengthen innovation, improve knowledge and human resources for economic growth, increase the international dimension of the economy and improve sustainability of resource use. It has four objectives, including "increased resource and raw materials efficiency" with actions involving:

- promoting sustainable public procurement
- supporting innovation for sustainable development
- addressing energy and material consumption in supply chains
- raising awareness of environmental challenges and increasing related education and training
- supporting sustainable construction, including the use of renewable materials, recycling and reduced use of resources, materials and water.

Three ministries – for the environment, economy, and science and higher education – oversee work on this objective. EU funding is seen as the main financing source for the strategy overall. The strategy provided for allocating about PLN 5 billion for resource and raw materials efficiency until 2020. However, only PLN 1 billion funding (4% of total funding) was allocated to the related objective in the 2014 Enterprise Development Programme implementing the strategy. A mid-term evaluation of the overall strategy is expected in 2015 or 2016. The strategy identifies indicators to monitor results, though for resource and raw materials efficiency it lists only an indicator on energy consumption; work on materials indicators is under way.

Previous policy documents addressed materials consumption. A 2003 strategy of changing production and consumption patterns to favour implementation of sustainable development principles called for decoupling resource consumption and environmental impacts from economic growth. Areas of action included stronger environmental management systems and research to support new production and consumption patterns. The 2005 Integrated Product Policy Implementation Strategy sought to improve market conditions for environment-friendly products as a mechanism for more sustainable use of natural resources. It called for eco-labelling of products, use of the Environmental Management and Audit Scheme (EMAS) in organisations, green public procurement and imposition of environmental taxes, including on fuels (Andrykiewicz, 2012). The NWMP 2014 called for developing a circular economy based on waste recycling and recovery, along with reduced raw materials consumption, though it set no targets in this area.

1.4. *Institutional framework*

The MoE is the central institution dealing with the policy and regulatory framework for waste management. It elaborates national strategies and plans, and prepares legislation in this field. The Ministry of Economy supports the MoE in preparations to implement regulations on waste, particularly as regards industrial waste management. Other ministries, such as the Ministry of Health, are involved in regulating specific waste types.

The self-government administrations (marshals' offices) of the 16 voivods prepare waste management plans for their territories and issue most permits for waste treatment (some permits are issued at the level of powiats). Responsibility for municipal waste management is delegated to municipalities. Small municipalities are encouraged to jointly oversee MSW collection.

In addition, the NWMPs have called on marshal's offices to designate waste regions for joint management of MSW facilities. This approach was set out in the NWMP 2010, and by its completion 123 regions had been designated, though some adjustments were made afterwards. Each region should have designated facilities with mechanical-biological treatment (MBT) or incineration, composting facilities, and large landfills with sufficient capacity to treat waste generated in the region, the objective being to achieve economies of scale and close small landfills.

Overall monitoring and enforcement of waste management is carried out by the Chief Inspectorate for Environmental Protection (GIOS) and voivod inspectorates (Section 6.2). Municipalities are responsible for monitoring and enforcing MSW legislation for the collection and treatment companies they contract with.

The National Fund for Environmental Protection and Water Management plays a leading role in financing waste investment, working closely with the 16 voivodship funds. At both levels, funds bring their own resources and manage the Operational Programme for Infrastructure and Environment (OPIE), which provides EU financing. The national fund supports projects above EUR 25 million while regional funds lead on smaller projects (World Bank, 2011). Voivodship operational programmes can also support waste projects. A working group on waste management, supported by EU funds, brings together national and regional waste officials and fund managers.

Enterprises, both private and public, have played an important role in MSW collection and treatment and in other waste sectors. In 2011, private firms had about 58% of the market for MSW collection, with municipally owned firms holding about 40% and the remaining 2% going to mixed-ownership firms (Przygoński, 2014). Private firms have also provided recycling and other treatment services, along with public enterprises. Through producer responsibility organisations (PROs), producers have organised treatment for waste streams including packaging waste and WEEE (Section 4).

2. Trends in materials consumption and waste generation

2.1. Materials consumption

Between 2000 and 2010, materials consumption increased more slowly than economic activity, leading to a 22% improvement in materials productivity. However, productivity gains were offset by a sharp rise in domestic materials consumption (DMC) in 2011. For the period from 2000 to 2011 as a whole, DMC increased about 50% (Figure 5.2).

On a per capita basis, DMC in 2011 reached 20.8 tonnes, about 25% higher than the OECD as a whole, though some other European economies, such as Austria's, had higher DMC per capita (see statistical annex). In terms of GDP, Poland is one of the most material-intensive OECD countries.

One factor behind the high material intensity is the large mining sector, particularly coal and non-ferrous metals. Poland also has a larger share of industry than most EU countries, about one-third of GDP (including construction) compared with one-fourth for the OECD overall.

Since 2000, however, consumption of metal ore has decreased and that of fossil energy carriers has remained stable. While biomass consumption has increased slightly, the main area of growth has been in construction minerals, which rose 150% from 2000 to 2011 to reach 10.4 tonnes/capita in 2011, accounting for half of DMC. Growth in construction and other civil engineering has been a key driver of construction minerals use and thus of DMC. Private investment in building construction has grown rapidly in recent years. So has public investment in highways and other infrastructure, in part due to support from EU funds.

Figure 5.2. **Resource productivity**

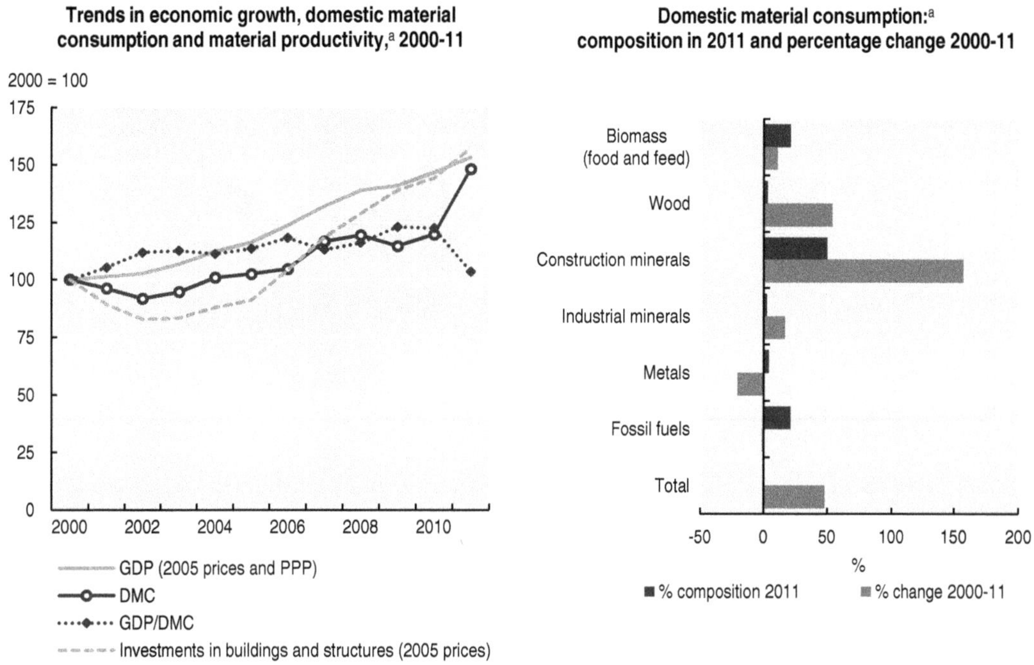

a) Domestic material consumption (DMC) is the sum of domestic raw material extraction used by an economy and its physical trade balance (imports minus exports of raw materials and manufactured products). Material productivity designates the amount of GDP generated per unit of materials used. It refers to the ratio of GDP to domestic material consumption. A rise in material productivity is equivalent to a decline in material intensity (i.e. DMC/GDP).

Source: OECD (2014), *OECD Environment Statistics* (database); OECD (2014), *OECD National Accounts Statistics* (database).

StatLink http://dx.doi.org/10.1787/888933197801

Consumption of construction minerals accounts for much of the 24% jump in DMC from 2010 to 2011. One driver was additional infrastructure construction in preparation for the Euro 2012 football competition, which Poland hosted jointly with Ukraine.

2.2. *Waste generation*

From 2000 to 2012, total waste generation remained largely stable while GDP grew by over 50% (Figure 5.3). According to the Central Statistical Office (CSO), the total amount of waste generated in 2012 was over 135 million tonnes; of this, 40% was generated in mining and quarrying and 19% in manufacturing (Figure 5.3). MSW made up about 8% of total waste generated (included under "other" in the figure).

The decoupling between GDP and total waste generation is an important achievement. There are uncertainties, however, about the accuracy of data collected and estimated, including for significant components such as construction waste and mining and quarrying waste.

Municipal solid waste

While GDP increased over 2000-12 (Figure 5.3), MSW collected per capita was reported as declining from 2000 to 2005 – partly because collection fell – and as remaining level from 2005 to 2012. In 2012, Poland generated an estimated 310 kg/capita of MSW, one of the lowest levels in the OECD – well below the OECD average of 530 kg/capita.

Figure 5.3. **Waste generation**

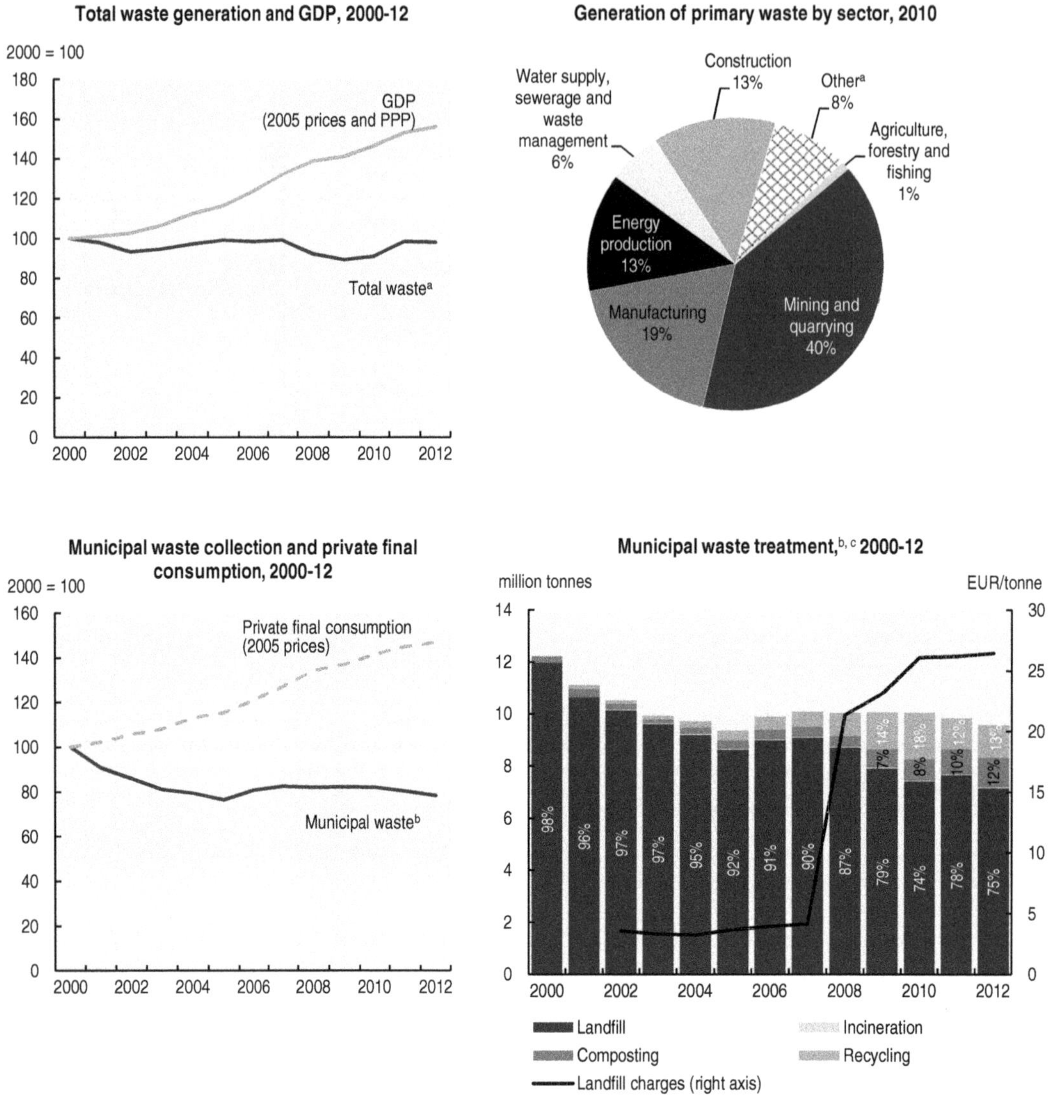

a) Including municipal waste.
b) Waste collected by or for municipalities including household, bulky and commercial waste, and similar waste handled at the same facilities.
c) Break in time series in 2011.
Source: CSO (2013), *Environment 2013;* OECD (2014), *OECD Economic Outlook No. 95* (database)*;* OECD (2014), *OECD Environment Statistics* (database).

StatLink http://dx.doi.org/10.1787/888933197816

In terms of treatment, about 75% of managed MSW was disposed of in landfills in 2012 (corresponding to about 60% of MSW generated, according to national estimates), with recycling accounting for 13% and composting for 12%.

The data on MSW, however, are affected by a number of uncertainties. In 2012, some 20% of MSW generated was not collected. Although households were obliged to contract for waste collection services, many did not (Section 3). In addition, underreporting appears to have been a problem in the previous MSW system, with waste collection companies allegedly underestimating data to reduce landfill fees. There was a lack of strong enforcement for MSW (World Bank, 2011). Calculating waste per capita can entail uncertainty about population due to internal and external migration, including Polish citizens working abroad.

The MoE (2013b) has projected that the quantity of MSW will increase by about 14% from 2011 to 2014. In addition to the uncertainties affecting past data, future levels will depend on the effect of GDP growth on waste levels. Data are expected to improve with the new MSW system introduced in 2013.

Mining and manufacturing waste

The mining sector is the largest single source of solid waste. The southern mining region of Silesia (two voivodships, Slaskie and Dolnoslaskie) accounts for the majority of mining waste and over 50% of waste from industry, mining and construction. Large amounts of industrial waste have accumulated at industrial sites. In 2012, accumulated industrial waste amounted to over 1.6 billion tonnes, the largest share of which came from mining; about 70% of the accumulated industrial waste is found in Slaskie and Dolnoslaskie voivodships.

Hazardous waste

According to Eurostat, the share of hazardous waste in total waste generated is relatively low: about 1% in 2010, compared with an EU27 average of 4.3% (Table 5.1). One reason has to do with the structure of industrial waste and the high share of non-hazardous mining waste. About 46% of hazardous waste is generated in manufacturing. Water supply, waste management and remediation activities generate a further 26%.

Table 5.1. **Hazardous waste generation, 2010**

Sector	Total amount of hazardous generated (tonnes)	Hazardous waste as a share of total waste generated by sector (%)	Hazardous waste produced in the sector as a share of total hazardous waste (%)
Agriculture, forestry and fishing	5 400	0.35	0.36
Mining and quarrying	8 596	0.01	0.58
Manufacturing	691 672	2.42	46.36
Electricity, gas, steam and air conditioning supply	14 117	0.07	0.95
Water supply, sewerage, waste management and remediation	401 401	2.98	26.91
Construction	66 466	0.32	4.46
Households	11 442	0.13	0.77
Other	292 751	6.84	19.62
All sectors	1 491 845	0.94	100.00

Source: Eurostat database.

Construction and demolition waste

In 2010, construction and demolition waste represented about 13% of all waste generated. Trends are difficult to assess, as it appears that official statistics previously captured only a small share of waste in the sector. CSO data show a fourfold increase in construction and demolition waste between 2010 and 2012. This jump may in part be due to the boom in construction, some of it linked to the Euro 2012 cup, but it also raises concern about the reliability of the time series.

3. Performance in managing municipal solid waste

Poland is undergoing two major transformations in MSW management. The first involves the recently introduced reforms in governance, giving a central role to municipalities. The second is extensive investment in new facilities to improve treatment and meet EU requirements, with their targets for recycling and composting.

3.1. Key policy goals and targets for municipal solid waste

All three NWMPs to date have had objectives to improve MSW collection coverage and increase investment in facilities for waste recovery and recycling.

Not all the targets have been met. The NWMP 2010 aimed to extend municipal waste collection and separate collection to everyone and close all MSW landfills not meeting standards. When these targets were not met by 2010, the NWMP 2014 adopted new deadlines (Table 5.2). It also set other objectives and targets, including several – such as those for biodegradable waste and the reuse and recycling of paper, metals, plastics and glass from households – that are part of EU legislation.

Table 5.2. **National Waste Management Plan 2014: Key targets for municipal solid waste**

Waste fraction or infrastructure	Target	Related EU legislation	Achievement
Landfills	Close all municipal landfills not meeting EU requirements by 1 January 2012*	Landfill Directive (1999/31/EC)	Yes
MSW collection	Ensure collection of MSW for all inhabitants by 2015*		Strong progress with 2013 reforms
Landfills	Decrease landfilled MSW to max. 60% of MSW generated by end of 2014 and max. 50% of MSW generated by 2016	Not an EU target, but reflects EU waste hierarchy	2014 target met in 2012 according to national estimates
Collection of separated waste	Separate waste collection system for all inhabitants by 2015*	Waste Framework Directive (2008/98/EC)**	Strong progress with 2013 reforms
Paper, metals, plastic and glass	Prepare for reuse and recycling of at least 50% of paper, metals, plastic and glass from households by 2020	Waste Framework Directive (2008/98/EC)	2012 levels: 18% across all four
Municipal biodegradable waste disposed of at landfills	Maximum levels, compared to 1995: 75% in 2010*** 50% in 2013 35% in 2020	Landfill Directive (1999/31/EC); dates for Poland set in accession agreement	2010 and 2013 targets not met

* The NWMP 2010 had set a deadline of end 2007.

** The directive calls for "separate collection of waste where technically, environmentally and economically practicable and appropriate to meet the necessary quality standards for the relevant recycling sectors" (Art. 11[1]).

*** The NWMP 2010.

Source: NWMP (2014), EU legislation, MoE, CSO.

3.2. Reforming municipal waste management

At the start of the economic transition, Poland gave the main responsibility for municipal waste to individuals: property owners, building administrators and service-sector organisations were required to contract with waste collection companies individually. In many municipalities, trucks from various companies collected waste from the same streets, increasing traffic, air and noise pollution, and greenhouse gas emissions. While municipal governments oversaw collection, most did not take a strong role. The capacity of some small companies was weak and disposal practices varied. Illegal dumping by individuals and some collection firms was a concern (EEA, 2013): some MSW reportedly ended up in closed mine pits and quarries or tipped illegally in forests. To avoid paying for waste collection, some households that used coal or wood for heating burned part of their waste, contributing to local air pollution. Some households simply never contracted with collection companies: some 20% of households were not part of an MSW collection system in 2012 (although this was an improvement from 2005, when about 30% of households were not covered). As a result, Poland failed to achieve the goal of universal coverage by 2007, set in the NMWP 2010.

The reform

To address these problems, the NWMP 2014 called for a reform of MSW management. This was set out in 2011 via amendments to the Act on Cleanliness and Order in Municipalities, which made municipalities responsible for MSW management as from 1 July 2013, requiring them to choose waste companies via open tender, following public procurement rules. The amendments also require municipalities to organise separate collection of recyclable waste. Municipalities had to set and collect fees from residents and service sector businesses to cover the full costs of MSW collection and treatment. Multiple municipalities could undertake joint collection and treatment, a mechanism especially useful for small, rural communities.

The change was controversial. Some individuals feared higher rates, probably including those who had not participated in the previous system and hence paid nothing. The waste management industry was concerned about upheaval, and indeed, the number of companies in an industry with many small players was reduced: in Warsaw, over 140 waste companies had been registered and had to compete for contracts to cover 14 districts.

Municipal governments had to take on new roles. The national government supported them through a range of activities. Surveys of municipalities pinpointed capacity needs. The MoE published a manual on the new system and ministry officials held conferences and meetings. For eight months, the ministry operated an internet hotline staffed by experts on waste technology, fee systems and tendering methods. The ministry also prepared materials for municipalities to distribute to residents informing them about the changes. The National Fund for Environmental Protection and Water Management (NFEPWM) supported training for local government officials in most regions.

One key task for municipalities was setting fees. The legislation identified three options: per head for each household; on the basis of the area of home; or on the basis of water consumption. The NFEPWM set up a short-term loan facility for municipalities where rates were too low and a temporary shortfall in revenue resulted (the loans required due diligence to show that the municipality had used reasonable estimates for its rates).

Initial results

As the reforms are still new, data on results are limited. What information is available points to a positive trend overall, with full coverage of waste collection services and improved separate waste collection.

As of early 2014, all but 14 of 2 479 municipalities had adopted the new system, which was upheld in legal challenges. A GIOS report in late 2013 surveyed about 10% of municipalities (GIOS, 2013). One finding was that household fees varied significantly. The average in the sample was just over PLN 15.00 (about EUR 3.50) per capita per month for mixed waste, but some charged only PLN 3.00. (To provide an incentive for recycling, national legislation requires municipalities to set lower waste collection fee rates for residents who separate waste.)

Official data on separate collection of waste were not available in mid-2014. One indication that the reforms had led to improved separate collection came from Rekopol, Poland's largest PRO for packaging waste. It reported that the municipal waste collection companies it worked with had seen large increases in separate collection of glass, paper and, especially, plastic packaging in the nine months immediately following the reform (Tyczkowski, 2014). These informal results, of course, represent only part of national MSW collection.

Still, the change can be seen in Izabelin, a municipality of about 10 000 outside Warsaw and a pioneer of the new system (Box 5.1).

Box 5.1. **The reform in MSW management in Izabelin municipality**

Izabelin, a town of about 10 000 on the outskirts of Warsaw, was a pioneer because its residents voted in a referendum to start the new waste management approach before the national law took effect. Previously, over a dozen waste operators offered their services in Izabelin. With the reform, the town administration organised a tender procedure that received eight bids, and it put in place fees for all residents, based on the number of people per household. Warsaw's municipal waste service company won the tender. Officials said that for most households, fees did not change significantly; in some cases they were lower than before due to the economies of scale that could be achieved through more complete coverage. The municipality set the fees after the tender procedure, so it knew the level of costs to be recovered.

Town officials report that the new system has led to an increase in separate collection, now available kerbside throughout the town, and a reduction in illegal dumping. The collection trucks have GPS systems that allow town officials to monitor compliance with collection and delivery requirements. Izabelin also has a central collection point for bulk waste, WEEE and batteries, as required under the 2001 amendments to the national law. The town's early experience led to two of its officials providing training to other towns in seminars financed by the NFEPWM.

A few issues remain. For example, more yard waste is collected than a survey before the change had indicated. Construction and demolition waste is a larger concern, and an important one in Izabelin as the town's population is growing. Although construction sites formally comply with permit requirements for a waste dumpster, town officials believe illegal dumping continues, and the residential areas of Izabelin are next to Kampinoski National Park.

Source: Izabelin municipality.

Despite initial indications of progress, the transition has generated challenges. One issue is that the fees set by many municipalities do not cover full collection and treatment costs. In some cases, the city councils approving the final rates reduced the proposed levels, perhaps with an eye to the 2014 municipal elections. Some municipalities will likely need to increase fees to recover the full cost of waste management. Collection frequency varied as well, with some municipalities providing infrequent collection of mixed waste – and some providing collection of separated waste only once a quarter.

Public procurement practices have also raised concerns. The 2014 OECD Economic Survey of Poland notes that in many sectors, public tenders have typically focused on lowest price, with inadequate attention to company capacity to carry out complex projects, or to environmental outcomes (OECD, 2014). Another concern is that local governments have tended to support local public enterprises in the waste sector and might continue to do so (OECD, 2009). These issues were seen in the controversy over the award of waste contracts in Warsaw (Box 5.2).

Box 5.2. **Contested municipal waste contract awards in Warsaw**

In September 2012, the city of Warsaw awarded three companies contracts for combined waste collection and treatment services. The city-owned waste management company won in 9 districts out of 16. Two unsuccessful companies submitted a complaint to the National Chamber of Appeal, arguing that the city-owned company and another winner offered abnormally low prices – half the indicative level in the city's terms of references. The companies appealing also asserted that their technology was more advanced and environment-friendly than those used by the winners. The complaint procedure ended in April 2014, one of the longest in the chamber's history (eight months), with the complaints dismissed.

Source: Zubik (2014).

While the reform is leading to a consolidation of waste collectors and improvements in economies of scale, the association of private waste management companies has suggested that tenders favour municipally owned waste treatment sites. Another problem was that waste collectors, which typically provide customers with waste containers, did not have always enough containers for all their territories when they won several contracts, leading to disruptions early on (Przygoński, 2014).

The concern about standards is also linked to the approach municipalities take in tendering. They could choose to tender waste collection and treatment separately or as a joint service, and most chose the latter. When selection criteria focus on price, however, joint tendering may not promote high standards for waste treatment. One operator of an advanced sorting facility near Warsaw went bankrupt (Przygoński, 2014).

The capacity of municipalities to monitor waste contractors and ensure a high standard of treatment also remains a concern. Some municipalities, including Izabelin, have strengthened enforcement through systems that track contractors' waste collection trucks via GPS to help ensure that all waste is taken to legitimate treatment facilities.

A government commission led by former Environment Minister Andrzej Kraszewski reviewed the lessons from the transition and proposed legal modifications, including clarification of the roles and requirements for municipalities. The commission also proposed that contracts for waste collection and treatment be separated, with collected waste sent to regionally designated treatment facilities.

3.3. Investment in waste treatment facilities

All three NWMPs have called for investment in MSW treatment capacity, including for recycling. Since 2002, the NFEPWM, voivodship funds and EU funds have supported such investment. The plans also called for investment in incineration capacity: for the NWMP 2014, thermal treatment is the preferred way to handle mixed municipal waste in urban areas or regions with more than 300 000 inhabitants, as a component of the long-term goal of sharply reducing waste sent to landfill.

Mechanical and biological treatment facilities sorting and composting plants

Between 2010 and 2013, Poland built many new facilities to expand capacity for MSW treatment (Table 5.3). In this relatively short period, well over 100 mechanical-biological treatment facilities – which sort mixed waste, often shredding the output and composting biodegradable waste – were constructed. These plants play an important role in meeting a requirement under the Landfill Directive that waste to landfill must first be treated, and they reduce the volume of residual waste going to landfill. While many MBT facilities have started operation, some reportedly need further investment to ensure the quality of their output. Poland also more than doubled the number of separate composting plants, from 85 to 172, between 2010 and 2013. Both private waste management companies and municipally owned companies have built new MBT, composting and sorting facilities.

Table 5.3. **Municipal solid waste treatment facilities, 2010 and 2013**

Type of plant	2010		2013	
	Total no.	Total capacity (million t)	Total no.	Total capacity (million t)
Sorting plants	139	2.2	148	3.3
MBT plants	9	0.4	124	8.8[a]
Landfills	610	n.a.	538[b]	n.a.
Composting plants	85	0.6	172	1.3
Organic waste fermentation plants	4	0.05	6	0.2
Municipal waste incinerators	1	0.4	1	0.4

a) Mechanical treatment.
b) As of December 2012.
Source: MoE (2010) *The National Waste Management Plan 2014*, Ministry of the Environment, Warsaw; BiPro (2013a, 2013b); MoE (2014), *"Keep Your Soul Unpolluted": Summing-up the Campaign*, Ministry of the Environment, Warsaw.

As a result of this and earlier investment, the amount of municipal waste recycled and composted has risen steadily and the share sent to landfill has fallen. In 2012, 75% of waste collected was sent to landfill. This result, together with the continued increase in capacity for composting and other non-landfill forms of treatment, suggests that Poland will meet the national target of sending no more than 60% of MSW to landfill in 2014 and should be on track to reduce the level to 50% by 2015.

The EU's MSW targets for 2020 will pose further challenges. In 2012, Poland recycled 18% of the combined volume of glass, metal, paper and plastic in MSW, compared to a 2020 target of 50%.[2] The European Environment Agency has suggested that Poland will need to make an "extraordinary effort" to meet the much higher EU 2020 recycling target of 50% (EEA, 2013). Still, initial results of the 2013 reform, described above, suggest recycling levels could rise significantly.

In addition to the EU target, Poland has set minimum recycling targets for municipalities, rising from 10% in 2012 to 50% in 2020. While these targets build towards the EU target and ensure common efforts, a requirement on each municipality may be overly rigid; it might be more cost-effective to set targets for wider areas, such as waste regions or voivodships.

Both EU legislation and national policy call for reductions in biodegradable municipal waste to landfill. Poland cut the share to 79% in 2010, just above its national target of 75%. A considerable distance remains to the EU target of 35% in 2020. However, many composting plants have been built since 2010 (Table 5.3), and almost EUR 1 billion in further investment has been proposed for coming years (Section 6).

Thermal treatment

Although the 2010 and 2014 NWMPs called for construction of MSW incinerators, in early 2014 Poland had only one in operation, in Warsaw. Its capacity is 40 000 tonnes/year, though maintenance problems in recent years have reportedly led to it operating below capacity. As of mid-2014, construction had started on six incinerators: in Bydgoszcz, Kraków, Konin, Szczecin, Białystok and Poznań (with total capacity of 1 million tonnes), and at least three others were at the planning stage (Section 6).

Poland's capacity to prepare refuse-derived fuel (RDF) increased from about 350 000 tonnes in 2010 to about 750 000 tonnes in 2014. Most facilities are run by private companies. Cement kilns consumed about 1 million tonnes of RDF in 2010 and at least 1.3 million tonnes in 2013, the rise being due to growth in construction, with imports from Germany on top of national RDF. A short-term consequence of the reform in MSW management is that a growing share of waste is sent to designated regional plants, and some Polish RDF facilities have had difficulty obtaining sufficient amounts (Adamczyk and Schoenfelder, 2014).

Closing old landfills

As has been noted, the NWMP 2010 set a 2007 deadline for completing the closure of landfills that did not meet EU standards. This target was not met, and in 2010, the NWMP 2014 revised it to 2012, the date set in EU legislation (World Bank, 2011). Poland now appears to have met this important target, which was a recommendation in the previous OECD Environmental Performance Review. By early 2014, the MoE reported, substandard landfills had stopped operations, though preparation of closure plans and investment for closure were still under way for many. The NFEPWM, voivodship funds and EU programmes played an important role in financing closures, in many cases as part of projects to refurbish existing facilities or construct new MBT and sorting plants.

The formation of methane is an issue for landfills, though it also provides an opportunity for energy recovery. In 2012, about 60 landfills in Poland (both operating and closed) had installations for heat or electricity recovery.

Landfill closure is expected to continue, with the goal of consolidating operations and ending those of small facilities. In Mazowiecka voivodship, for example, about 30 landfills are to be closed. However, not all closures are following the original plans. For example, the large Radiowo landfill in Warsaw was originally to be closed in 2014, but on request of the city government and its waste company, the marshal's office of Mazowieckie voivodship extended its permit to the end of 2016. The regional inspectorate has limited the types of waste that can be deposited there, and authorities have stated that the landfill meets environmental requirements, despite protests by nearby residents, who established an association called "Clean Radiowo" (Kraj, 2014; Zubik, 2013).

3.4. Strengthening municipal waste management

Over the review period, Poland moved slowly to address the recommendation of the previous Environmental Performance Review on strengthening measures to increase municipal waste recovery rates, including via separate collection and promotion of recycling markets. These objectives were also part of the NWMPs. In 2013, the reform of MSW management, together with continuing investment in waste treatment (Section 3.3), played a key role in addressing the objectives.

The reforms have given municipalities a much stronger role, and recent efforts to strengthen capacity continue, yet further initiatives could be considered to provide support for the preparation of tenders and management waste contracts. In France, for example, the National Association of Mayors and the National Federation of Concessionary and Publicly Controlled Authorities created a consulting firm, Servicepublic2000, which supports local governments on tendering for waste management and other public services.[3]

More broadly, the system that has emerged from the 2013 reform, as well as the recent Kraszewski proposals, involves competition for waste collection but a more managed approach to waste treatment. An independent regulatory agency could be valuable in overseeing operation and results in this approach, to ensure that residents receive a high quality of service as well as a level playing field between private and public waste management companies, for example by establishing guidelines for tendering. The designation of regional waste treatment facilities can ensure high standards of waste treatment; other plants that operate to high standards, including those for RDF, should also have a role. Several OECD countries have established independent authorities to oversee municipal services such as waste collection and treatment. Portugal provides one example (Box 5.3).

Box 5.3. **A national regulatory authority: ERSAR in Portugal**

In Portugal, the Water and Waste Services Regulation Authority (ERSAR) oversees municipal water and waste operators to ensure that they provide a high level of service (OECD, 2011). ERSAR is independently financed by a tax on sector concessions. Its work includes:

- overseeing legal and contractual operations, including tender processes and concession requirements
- overseeing tariffs for services
- monitoring and providing public information on service companies and their activities
- assessing the execution of contracts
- monitoring and assessing the quality of service to end-users through quantitative indicators and benchmarks
- investigating consumer complaints.

The authority was set up to address issues related to the structure of Portugal's municipal services. An authority in Poland would address slightly different needs. For example, in addition to oversight of MSW management, a central authority could monitor the work of extended producer responsibility programmes (Section 4).

Source: OECD (2011).

4. Performance of extended producer responsibility programmes

In extended producer responsibility (EPR) systems, "a producer's responsibility for a product is extended to the post-consumer stage of a product's life cycle" (OECD, 2001), and thus to its end-of-life environmental impact. Several pieces of EU and Polish legislation set out EPR requirements. To meet these, producers often join PROs, which collect, recover and recycle their waste. Poland has EPR systems for six waste streams: packaging waste, ELVs, WEEE, used oil, tyres and batteries. Table 5.4 lists the main quantitative targets in the NWMP 2014 for these waste streams; most targets were established in EU legislation.

Table 5.4. **Targets for extended producer responsibility programmes**

Waste fraction	NWMP 2014 target	Related EU legislation	Achievement
Packaging waste	Reach 60% recovery and 55% recycling levels by 2014	Packaging Waste Directive 1994/62/EC	2012: recovery reached 57% and recycling 41%; data accuracy questions
Portable batteries and accumulators	Minimum collection rate: 25% collection by 2012 and 45% in 2016 Minimum recycling rate (from 2011): 75% for nickel-cadmium batteries and accumulators 65% for lead-acid batteries and accumulators 50% for other batteries and accumulators End landfilling and incineration of batteries and accumulators	Batteries Directive 2006/66/EC	2013: 30% collection rate; data accuracy questions
Waste oil	Maintaining recovery at least 50% and recycling with regeneration at least 35%		Ongoing
Waste electrical and electronic equipment	4 kg/end-user/year collection rate for WEEE from households from 2011*	WEEE Directive, 2002/96	For 2012 (latest data available), level of 3.8 kg/cap
	The 2012 WEEE Directive calls for:** By 2016, collect at least 40% of average weight of EEE placed on the market in the 3 previous years By 2021, at least 65% (or 85% of all WEEE generated)	Revised WEEE Directive, 2012/19/EU	
End-of-life vehicles	2014: 85% minimal recovery and 80% recycling of the mass of end-of-life vehicles admitted to dismantling stations 2015: 95% recovery and 85% recycling	Directive 2000/53/EC on end-of-life vehicles	See Section 4.2
End-of-life tyres	For 2022: maintain at least a 75% current recovery level and 15% recycling level		For 2012: 84% recovered and 24% recycled

* The NWMP 2010 had set 2008 as the target date.
** Targets are in new directive; not included in the NWMP 2014.
Source: NWMP (2014), EU legislation, MoE, CSO.

4.1. *Packaging waste*

Producer responsibility for packaging waste was introduced in 2002, together with product fees.[4] The government set required recovery and recycling rates that have steadily increased; enterprises that do not meet their targets, based on the amount of packaging, must pay non-compliance fees. Enterprises can meet their obligations via membership in a PRO that supports collection and recycling of packaging waste. By 2009, about 40 PROs were in operation. The largest, Rekopol, has covered at least one-quarter of packaging waste.

The system has faced a range of problems. The 2010 and 2014 NWMPs both note that most packaging waste is collected from businesses rather than households: it is secondary and tertiary packaging – used, for example, for wholesale storage and for transport and collected from distributors and retailers – and not primary packaging from products purchased by end-users. Both plans mention compliance issues. Several sources say some programmes have reported waste that is not recycled.

The NWMP 2014 sets out several actions for packaging waste, including:

- putting in place legislation and inspections "to eliminate [the] grey zone"
- expanding infrastructure for the collection of primary packaging waste
- expanding technical infrastructure for sorting and recycling packaging waste
- improving monitoring and establishing a national recycling register.

In 2013, Poland reformed its law on packaging waste. In addition, several court cases have been brought against recyclers and compliance programmes. The 2013 reform described in Section 3 has also had a major influence, increasing separate collection and thus the amount of primary packaging waste for recycling (Tyczkowski, 2014).

The CSO, citing reporting from PROs and enterprises, said that in 2012 recovery of packaging waste reached 57% and recycling reached 41% (CSO, 2013). These levels are below the EU averages: Eurostat reports that the average EU recovery rate is about 77%. While the levels reported in Poland have grown steadily and are close to the 2014 targets, the accuracy of reported data remains a concern due to the "grey zone".

The 2013 reforms are expected to strengthen the overall system and the accuracy of data on packaging waste. Several issues remain, however. One is whether the voivodship administrations have sufficient capacity and resources for enforcement. A further issue is ensuring high standards across PROs. While the total number of functioning PROs is reported to have fallen to about 20 by early 2014, there is no certification system for PROs, nor external auditing requirements.

4.2. Other producer responsibility systems

End-of-life vehicles

Carmakers selling new vehicles in Poland are required to organise a system to take back and recycle ELVs in accordance with the relevant EU directive. They do so via contracts with authorised recyclers. The network should be organised so that users do not have to travel more than 50 km to a recycler.

This system has existed since 2005, yet the 2010 and 2014 NWMPs both refer to problems with complete data, and as well as a "grey zone" of vehicles dismantled outside the system. The plans set targets for minimum recovery and recycling of ELVs, linked to the relevant EU targets. The NMWP 2014 also includes an action to "carry out legislative and inspection activities to reduce the grey zone".

In 2012 about 340 000 tonnes of ELVs went to dismantling stations; of this amount, 93% was recovered and 90% was recycled, so the targets were achieved.

From 2010 to 2013, Poland carried out about 200 inspections a year of facilities suspected of illegal treatment of ELVs, and about one-third of the inspections found violations. The "grey zone", however, still appears to be significant. Official data indicates that the volume of ELVs is far less than the level of over 1 million tonnes per year forecast by the NWMP 2014. Some of the difference may be due to slower turnover. Nevertheless, dismantling of automobiles outside the authorised system is suspected to remain a major activity. By one estimate, in 2011, out of some 23 million vehicles registered, 5 million no longer exist, having been dismantled and sold in parts without removing them from the register (Jarzab, 2011). Some old vehicles and parts with low value are reportedly discarded in forests, but this is believed to be a minor part of the problem given the value of residual metal. Factors contributing to the situation include the stringent requirements for legal dismantling stations (high targets for recovery and recycling). A more fundamental problem is that unauthorised dismantling is economically advantageous, including for the last users, who may receive a payment – which they would not from authorised recyclers.

One concern for the long-term sustainability of the system is that Poland imports a lot of used cars from other EU countries: over 1 million in 2008, most of them over 10 years old (Mehlhart et al., 2011). Polish legislation has required all importers of used vehicles, including individuals, to contribute PLN 500 (about EUR 120) to the NFEPWM; the revenue is used to support authorised recycling. However, the European Commission has raised questions concerning the compatibility of this fee with the requirements of the directive, by which individuals and small-scale operators should not be required to contribute (European Commission, 2012). In mid-2014, Poland was preparing to reform this provision.

Other EU countries have encountered problems with a high level of ELVs escaping the authorised system. Lessons from reforms in countries such as France could be useful (Box 5.4). These can include developing a national information campaign and label, and setting fines (including for the last owners) in the event of unauthorised disposal. It might also be useful to consider how the system could provide better payments for individuals who choose authorised treatment facilities.

Box 5.4. **Lessons from end-of-life vehicle treatment in other EU countries**

According to a 2010 study for the European Parliament, in several EU countries, including Austria and Denmark, less than half the cars and trucks removed from registration went to authorised recycling facilities. The reasons for such gaps vary: they can include private exports of used automobiles, illegal shipments and unauthorised disposal. This last had been identified earlier in the decade as a problem in countries including Belgium and France (Schneider et al., 2010). In France, reforms in 2005 set higher penalties and a public campaign raised awareness about proper treatment of ELVs, with the slogan, "If you leave your car in an unauthorised junkyard, Nature foots the bill. And so do you." A distinctive national label for authorised treatment facilities was created. Authorised treatment also was boosted by incentives for owners to replace old vehicles with newer, less polluting ones, contingent on proper treatment of the old vehicles (ADEME, 2010).

Source: Schneider et al., (2010); ADEME, (2010).

End-of-life tyres

Tyre manufacturers and importers are required to recover and recycle the target level of used tyres, and to pay non-compliance product fees if targets are not met. The system for waste tyres is reported to be working relatively well, with one main EPR programme that brings together the major manufacturers. End-of-life tyres that are collected are retreaded and reused, or their metal is recovered and they are made into rubber granulate that is recycled or used as fuel in cement plants. One reason for the relative success is that there is little competing demand for end-of-life tyres. The NWMP 2014 noted that some end-of-life tyres were sent to landfill or incinerated in improper facilities. National statistics indicate that, in 2012, 84% of end-of-life tyres were recovered and 24% were recycled,[5] levels already exceeding the policy targets for 2022.

Used oil

One major and two smaller EPR programmes operate for used oil. Out of some 150 000 tonnes of oil sold annually, official statistics show, the recovery rate is about 52% and the recycling rate 44% (CSO, 2013), exceeding the respective targets of 50% and 35%. The NWMP 2014 notes, however, that the collection rate from small enterprises and households is low.

Waste batteries and accumulators

About 30 waste brokers support the almost 2 000 companies selling batteries and accumulators in fulfilling their responsibilities for collection and treatment at the end of battery life. One large concern, REBA, covers about 30% of the market (Korkozowicz, 2014). Collection points are required at retail and wholesale points as well as educational and administrative establishments (NWMP, 2010).

Poland had a 29% collection rate in 2012, exceeding the 25% target for 2012. The achieved collection rate was 30% in 2013.

Regarding treatment facilities, the NWMP 2014 indicated that facilities for acid lead batteries and accumulators were sufficient for coming years (MoE, 2010). Poland has increased its capacity for recycling of alkaline batteries, and new facilities are in development. Facilities for nickel-cadmium batteries may need to be upgraded to meet new EU rules on recycling efficiency (Korkozowicz, 2014).

Waste electrical and electronic equipment

Poland has separate collection points for WEEE, and eight main PROs work to collect and treat such waste. The NWMP 2014 called for expanding facilities to collect and treat WEEE. It also noted that there was a "grey zone" of poor reporting. In addition, some large household appliances are not fully recovered but simply sold for scrap metal, and small devices are still likely to end in landfills. The NWMP 2014 set a range of targets for specific types of WEEE, as well as an overall target of collecting 4 kg per person per year from households as EU legislation specifies. The plan sets 2011 as the date to begin meeting the targets, many of which were also in the NMWP 2010 for 2008 but were not met.

Between 2007 and 2012, the amount of WEEE collected and recycled increased steadily. In 2012, total collection reached nearly 3.9 kg/person, close to the EU target level, which is likely to have been met in 2013 or 2014. It should be noted that the target is harder to achieve in Poland than in higher-income EU countries, as the amount and turnover of such equipment are lower.

PROs are required to spend 5% of their profit each year on improving public awareness. Each organisation does so separately. The MoE could consider other ways to strengthen public awareness as well, including by co-ordinating common campaigns.

The revised WEEE Directive (2012/19/EU) sets further targets, such as a minimum collection rate of 40% by 2016. From 2010 to 2012, Poland's collection rate (compared to WEEE placed on the market in the previous three years) rose from 21% to 32%, though further efforts will be needed to meet the 2016 target. The new directive introduces a requirement that retailers collect WEEE from customers, which is expected to increase recovery rates.

4.3. Improving producer responsibility performance

EPR systems have played an important role in establishing infrastructure and increasing separate collection, recovery and recycling for the waste streams concerned. Although published results suggest that these systems are by and large achieving the targets set, there are questions about the reliability of the information they generate. One issue is related to data aggregation, as most EPR systems have several competing programmes that do not always use common reporting formats. There have been reports of illegal practices as a result of competitive pressure, including improper reporting.

Poland has established new requirements for reporting, e.g. on recycling packaging waste, and has strengthened enforcement on ELVs. Further action is needed to strengthen EPR systems' reliability and performance. One option is to require certification of PROs and set operating standards for them, an approach taken in Norway (OECD, 2011). A parallel action would be to require them to adopt EMAS or ISO 14 000 procedures. Common reporting formats would help strengthen data comparability and activity.

5. Performance in managing industrial, hazardous and construction waste

The 2010 and 2014 NWMPs both set objectives for management of industrial waste:

- increasing the share of waste to recovery
- decreasing the share of waste to landfill
- increasing recovery of mine extraction waste.

The plans identified actions focusing on promoting recycling (e.g. using combustion ash and slag as aggregate) and developing new processes and products to reduce waste.

Table 5.5. **Selected targets for industrial, hazardous and construction waste**

Waste fraction	NWMP 2014 Target	Related EU legislation	Achievement
PCBs	From 2011, gradually dispose of waste containing PCBs at concentrations of less than 50 ppm	Directive 96/59/EC on disposal of PCBs and PCTs	In progress
Waste from construction, repair and demolition works	By 2020, preparation for reuse, recycling and recovery should reach at least 70% by weight	Waste Framework Directive	For 2011, 90% recovery reported; accuracy uncertain
Non-municipal biodegradable waste	Maximum of 40% to landfill by 2022		Information not available

5.1. *Industrial waste*

The 2001 Waste Act introduced a requirement for industrial enterprises to obtain permits for waste generation. The permitting process has reportedly focused attention on waste levels and treatment, and on waste prevention and recovery methods.

A growing share of mining waste is reported as recovered. The majority of coal mining waste, about 70%, is used to refill mining areas – mainly to reclaim open cast mines and refill underground mines. The rest is used in industrial processes, such as production of aggregates for construction and ceramics, and some is processed to extract fuel. Waste from mining of non-ferrous metals such as copper, zinc and lead is increasingly used to build barriers and tailing ponds for liquid waste. Waste from construction mineral extraction is used for some civil engineering work, such as road construction, as well as aggregate (Cała et al., 2013).

Two centuries of industrial coal mining, however, have left many mining waste heaps: over 100 in the Upper Silesia coal basin. Mining is no longer creating new ones, but some older heaps have come to be seen as part of the landscape and there have been local protests against proposals to process and extract their fuel content. In some cases, plans have been made to transform these mining areas into parks. However, some former heaps are subject to internal fires that consume the remaining fuel content (Cała et al., 2013).

Overall, reclamation of former mining areas remains an important challenge. In 2012, mining activities covered 380 km^2 and former mining areas a roughly similar area. The total reclaimed area that year was under 10 km^2. Moreover, the extent of reclamation of former mining areas has slowed since 2000 (Figure 5.4).

Figure 5.4. **Land under mining activities**

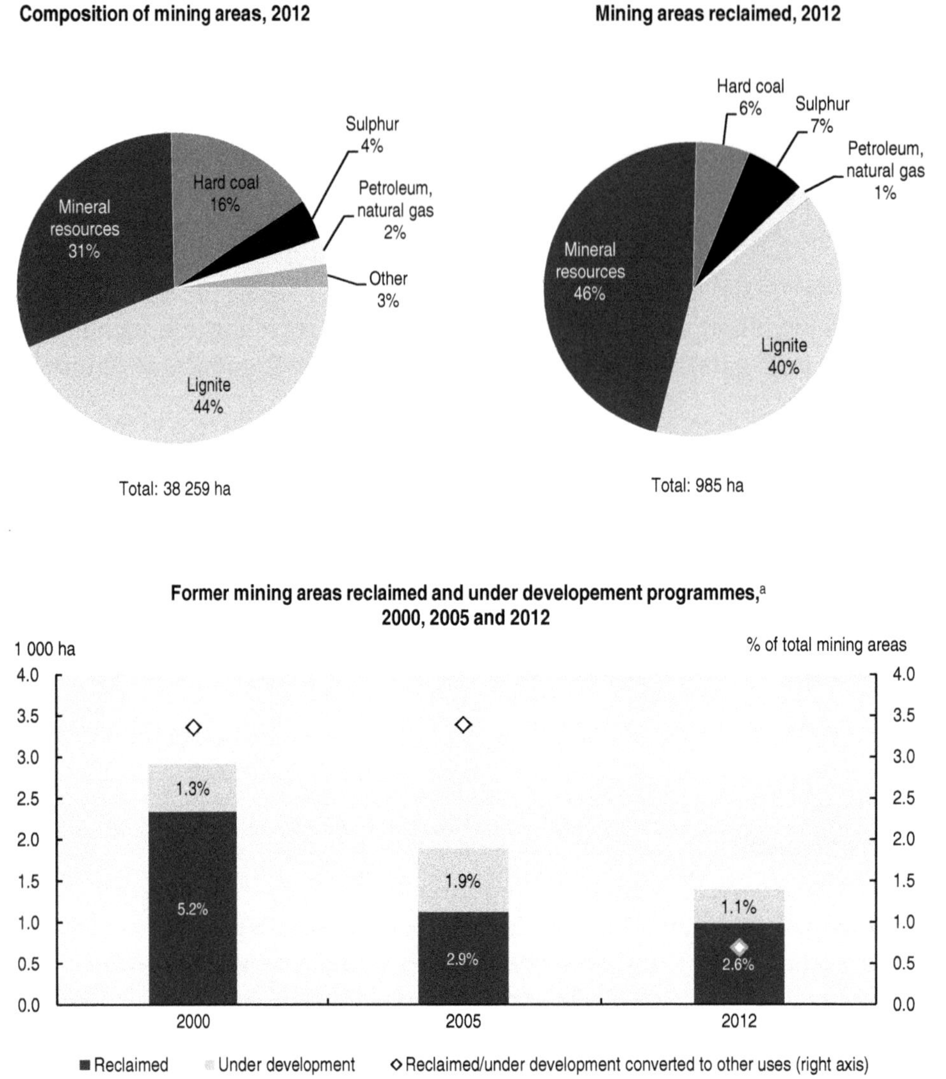

a) Land under development programmes for conversion to other uses (eg. agriculture and forest uses).
Source: CSO (2013), *Environment 2013.*

StatLink http://dx.doi.org/10.1787/888933197827

The second-largest type of industrial waste is from thermal power plants, mostly dust, slag and ash. Some is used for construction materials. It is reported, however, that power plants have difficulty finding uses for gypsum produced from flue gas desulphurisation.

Sewage sludge

Wastewater treatment plants generated about 6% of all waste in 2012. Production of sludge from urban wastewater treatment plants has grown steadily since 2000 as Poland builds new and improved plants to cover an increasing share of the population (Figure 5.5).

The latest two NWMPs called for reducing the landfilling of sewage sludge and increasing sludge treatment, including via incineration and energy recovery. Although data are incomplete, by 2012 Poland had reduced the amount of sewage sludge going to landfill

Figure 5.5. **Sludge generated by urban and industrial wastewater treatment plants, 2000-12**

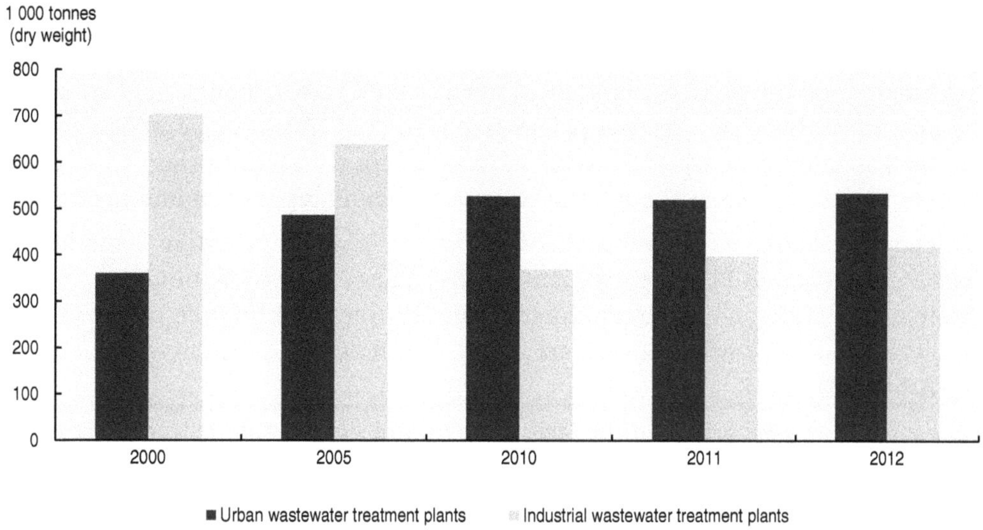

Source: CSO (2013), *Environment 2013.*

StatLink http://dx.doi.org/10.1787/888933197839

by two-thirds since 2005, while waste recovery and the application of sludge on farmland rose. Sewage sludge from some smaller cities in particular is used as fertiliser. In many of Poland's large cities, however, the sludge is not suitable for use as industries discharge to the sewer network, bringing a high level of heavy metals and other contaminants.

In contrast, levels of sewage sludge from industrial wastewater treatment plants have decreased. A problem for industrial sludge, however, is that high amounts of past sludge are accumulated and stored at treatment plants: some 6.3 million tonnes in 2012 (CSO, 2013).

5.2. *Hazardous waste*

Reducing hazardous waste generation is an objective of the current NWMP. Poland reportedly has enough capacity to incinerate most types of combustible hazardous waste. One concern relates to medical waste, including infectious waste. In the 1990s, 23 incinerators were built but 7 proved to have defects (OECD, 2003). The NWMP 2014 called for developing new incinerator capacity for medical waste. As several older facilities have been closed, in early 2014 waste was being transported long distances for incineration, while options for new facilities remained under study.

The 2003 OECD Environmental Performance Review highlighted problems with obsolete pesticides and PCBs. The obsolete pesticides were a legacy of the socialist period, stored in over 200 repositories around the country (OECD, 2003). By 2011, Poland had eliminated obsolete pesticides at 95% of these sites, according to the implementation report for the NWMP 2010 (MoE, 2011). In mid-2014, pesticides (and, in some cases, contaminated soil) remained at three sites where legal issues over ownership held up final removal and treatment.

Poland has also made important progress in removing and treating oil, liquids, capacitors and other products containing PCBs. The 2002 and 2006 NWMPs called for removing PCB-containing equipment in use by July 2010 and treating PCB-containing waste.

These targets were not fully met. By early 2014, in 11 of 16 voivodships, treatment of former PCB equipment had been completed, while it continued in the remaining five.

Poland's long history of industrial production left many contaminated sites, with total land area estimated at 8 600 km^2 at the turn of the century (OECD, 2003). There are no official statistics on the number or extent of contaminated sites, though data are collected on the broader category of "devastated and degraded land" (including eroded agricultural land as well as mining areas). The NWMP 2010 called for the identification of non-landfill sites contaminated by waste, though this does not cover all types of contaminated land.

Poland has cleaned up several sites, however, with support by national and EU funds. OPIE 2007-13 allocated EUR 200 million for the rehabilitation of industrial sites and contaminated land, including contaminated military sites. The original objective for this spending line was 170 km^2 of rehabilitated land; information on results was not available in mid-2014 (MRD, 2014).

The 2014 Energy Security and the Environment Strategy calls for better information on soil problems and land degradation. In mid-2014, the Environmental Protection Law was amended to establish a national register of contaminated sites and provide funding not only for remediation but also for the identification of degraded sites.

In addition to the historical contaminated sites, the GIOS environmental damage register recorded 452 new cases of "damage to land" from 2007 to 2013 (GIOS, 2014). Of these, 199 related to oil extraction, transport and storage (e.g. leaking pipelines) while 87 concerned power production.

Poland has addressed the recommendation of the previous OECD review to improve the treatment of hazardous waste, expanding capacity to destroy PCBs and pesticides, and improving controls on hazardous waste movements (Section 6.2).

5.3. *Construction and demolition waste*

While some construction and demolition waste is produced directly by households, for example in building or renovating homes, the vast majority is produced by construction and civil engineering companies. Municipalities set requirements for construction and demolition waste from households: some indicate days when it can be collected, and others specify a specific location or facility where it should be taken. Companies must contract with an authorised transporter and a treatment site for their waste.

A large share of construction and demolition waste is recovered: the MoE reported that 90% was recovered in 2011 and 73% in 2012, up from 67% in 2004 (MoE, 2013a), even though the total amount of waste from the sector quadrupled between 2004 and 2012 as construction activity boomed (CSO, 2013; MoE, 2011). The recent levels reported exceed the EU target of 70% for 2020. Nevertheless, large amounts have accumulated at construction and demolition sites: about 28 700 tonnes in 2008 (more recent data were not available).

The metal in construction and demolition waste is largely recycled. Other components, including earth and inert waste, are recovered for a range of uses, including road construction and refilling gravel and sand quarry sites. Thus the availability of sites for recovery of such waste is partly linked to activity in the construction industry, which has grown in recent years.

In general, companies transporting, treating and recovering construction waste need permits from the voivod marshal's office and report to it yearly. The main enforcement bodies are GIOS and the voivod inspectorates.

6. Strengthening policy instruments for waste management

6.1. *Waste data and reporting*

The three national plans all highlighted the need to improve the quality of data on waste and waste management. The 2010 and 2014 NWMPs refer to problems with data for several waste streams, including mining waste, health and veterinary waste and ELVs.

Data for some waste streams have improved, for example with stronger reporting requirements for veterinary and medical waste. Here and in several other sectors, penalties for inaccurate reporting have been increased for waste operators, industrial enterprises and EPR services, which should increase the accuracy of waste reporting. The reform of MSW management is expected to strengthen data accuracy, too, as households no longer evade the collection system. Yet many problems cited in the plans persist, such as poor data on ELVs (Section 4).

The NWMP 2006 called for the preparation of a database on waste management, and this has provided a central data repository. The NWMP 2010 called for the further development of this tool into a National Database on Products, Packaging and Waste Management, an objective that was to be completed for 2012. This timetable has slipped, due in part to funding issues: in early 2014, the MoE indicated that the database was expected to begin operation in January 2016. While an improved database will not solve problems with the accuracy of underlying data, it is hoped that it will make it easier for the ministry and other bodies to identify the issues.

6.2. *Enforcement*

GIOS leads on inspections of waste shipments, and the voivodship inspectorates carry out most inspections of waste management facilities. Other bodies involved in enforcement for specific waste streams include municipalities for MSW and the marshals' offices for packaging waste facilities. Table 5.6 presents an overview of the physical inspections that GIOS and the voivodship inspectorates carried out in 2004 and 2011, classified by relevant EU directive (the inspectorates also make desk reviews of reporting and other required documents).

The total number of enforcement activities remained relatively constant from 2004 to 2011. When a violation is discovered, written notification is sent to the company. Further enforcement action can include fines, temporary closure and referral to the courts for other sanctions. In 2011, the number of fines imposed for waste violations was more than 15 times higher than that in 2004, though the number of closures remained the same.

One concern stems from the fact that the topics and issues for enforcement broadened over the review period as Poland put in place the full range of EU waste legislation. GIOS sets yearly priorities among waste issues: for example, sewage sludge and mining waste were among the topics for 2014. The NWMPs have also identified priorities. The NWMP 2014, for example, called for GIOS and the voivodship inspectorates to verify that MSW landfills complied with the EU directive ahead of the 2012 deadline for closure of landfills that did not meet standards. While Poland has a relatively strong enforcement system compared to many EU and OECD countries, the inspectorates have difficulty ensuring sufficient capacity across all waste issues. For example, inspections of ELV facilities declined in 2013 from previous years as enforcement focused on other priorities, such as MSW management. Moreover, verifying and aggregating data directly reported by companies is a major challenge. For example, there has been no report

Table 5.6. **Waste inspections, fines and closures by national and voivodship inspectorates**

Topic	Number in 2004			Number in 2011		
	Inspections	Fines	Closures	Inspections	Fines	Closures
Framework waste laws (Directives 75/442, 2006/12, 2008/98)	7 539	3	7	8 662	285	8
Hazardous waste (Directive 91/689)	3 747	2	4	*	*	*
Landfills (Directive 1999/31)	1 040	14	5	412	4	6
Incineration (Directive 2000/76)	341	0	1	60	2	1
Hazardous waste incineration (Directive 94/67)	291	6	3	699	1	0
Waste shipments (Regulation 1013/2006)				172**	8	0
WEEE (Directive 2002/96)				525	50	1
ELVs (Directive 2000/53)				931	36	2
Batteries, accumulators (Directive 2006/66)				225	0	0
PCBs (Directive 96/59)				402	4	0
Mining waste (Directive 2006/21)				21	0	0
Total	12 958	25	20	12 109	390	18

* For 2011, included in inspections for the Waste Framework Directive (2008/98).
** Only inspections for the environmental inspectorates.
In addition to enforcement actions focused specifically on waste, industrial facilities may face checks on their waste generation as part of enforcement for integrated permits.

consolidating the data from over 2 000 companies selling batteries and accumulators for the last few years.

Before the 2013 reforms, municipalities did not always fulfil their role in overseeing the proper collection and treatment of MSW, a problem noted in the NWMP 2010. The 2013 reforms give municipalities a clearer role in terms of overall MSW management, but many lack sufficient capacity to ensure adequate controls. There is a similar concern about the marshals' offices, which have gained additional enforcement roles, including for packaging waste (Section 4).

Waste shipments

Between 2005 and 2010, imports of hazardous waste grew, and in tonnes they exceeded exports for the most recent years with available data, 2008 through 2010 (see Figure 5.6). Over the latter period, nearly all of Poland's imports and all of its exports (except one shipment to the US) involved other EU countries. The main non-EU imports – about 7% of the total in 2009 and 12% in 2010 – came from neighbouring Belarus and Ukraine. In 2006 and 2007, Poland made large shipments of waste oil for treatment in Germany.

Over the review period, Poland strengthened enforcement of hazardous waste shipments, addressing a recommendation raised by the previous OECD review. With EU accession, Poland applied the EU Waste Shipments Regulation and put in place further provisions, including penalties, through its national Act on International Shipments of Waste. A co-ordinated enforcement system was developed through agreements between the environmental inspectorates – which have power to carry out inspections at facilities but not at ports or on roads – and Poland's border guards, customs office, Road Transport Inspectorate and Rail Transport Office. These agreements established regular co-operation and joint actions. The environmental inspectorates also co-operate with police. Enforcement and inspection methods were strengthened, including through co-operation with other EU countries via the EU Network for the Implementation and Enforcement of

Figure 5.6. **Imports and exports of hazardous waste, 2005-10**

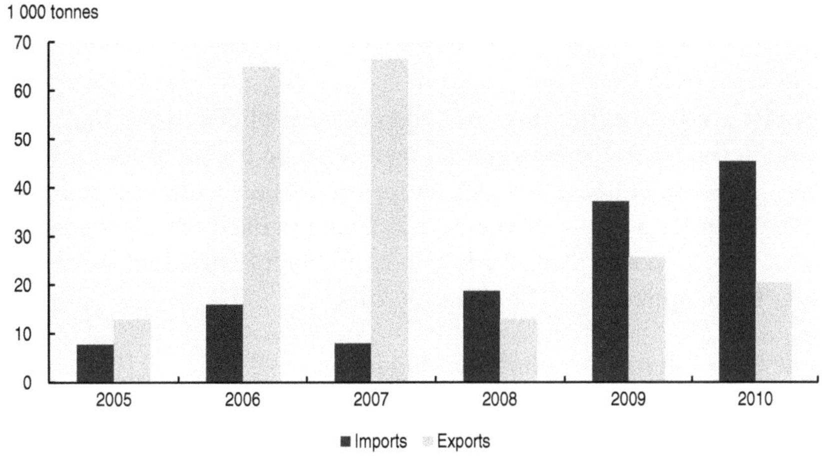

Source: Eurostat (2014), *Environmental Data Centre on Waste* (database).

StatLink http://dx.doi.org/10.1787/888933197849

Environmental Law (IMPEL) and its Transfrontier Shipment of Waste (TFS) cluster. Poland has also participated in EU-wide actions co-ordinated via IMPEL-TFS.

Until December 2012, Poland required permits for all shipments of waste, including waste on the "green list" of the Basel Convention. Since 2013, with the end of Poland's transitional period for implementation of EU Regulation 1013/2006 on waste shipments, only hazardous waste has required permits for imports and exports to other EU countries. Shipments of "green list" non-hazardous waste far exceed those of hazardous waste. Key imports include scrap metal, scrap paper, plastics, glass and textile waste used as raw materials for production in Poland. Another major waste import is refuse-derived fuel used in cement plants.

Over 2006-08, the major illegal shipments inspectors discovered were municipal waste, mainly from Germany: over 10,000 tonnes of illegal imports were found. In 2009-12, the main violations were imports of green list waste without authorisation, as some operators were not aware that Poland did not end authorisations until 2012 (MoE, 2012). Major cases of illegal waste shipments have not been found in recent years.

6.3. Public information and awareness raising

National and municipal awareness-raising campaigns have been an important element of the change in MSW management. One notable national campaign organised by the MoE, "Don't Litter Your Conscience", used TV and radio ads presenting a Catholic priest who instructed parishioners not to burn waste in their gardens, to stop illegal dumping and to separate recyclable waste. The spots reportedly reached a large share of the population and generated newspaper articles. The campaign also organised educational events and competitions in schools, with the theme of "eco-angels" teaching about waste. Information in supermarkets and articles in the press were other elements of the campaign, which was supported in part by EU funds (BiPro, 2013a; MoE, 2014).

The MoE has also carried out information campaigns to promote resource efficiency via websites as well as TV and radio advertising. In 2013, for example, a campaign sought to raise awareness among children and promoted the reuse of toys.

Further actions to raise public awareness on waste and resource issues are foreseen. Actions in other OECD countries may provide examples for consideration: Ireland, for instance, has conducted extensive information campaigns on fly tipping, which remains an issue in Poland (OECD, 2010).

Proposals for waste facilities have occasionally met public opposition. This has been the case for proposed MSW incinerators, as well as some incinerators for hazardous and medical waste. Other facilities, such as a proposed WEEE sorting plant, have also faced opposition. The plan for a waste incinerator in Poznań raised local questions. Polish and European NGOs have opposed plans for the construction of MSW incinerators and the use of EU funds for these projects (CEE Bankwatch, 2014).

6.4. *Economic instruments for waste management*

National landfill charges for industrial waste were introduced in 1980. Major changes in 1998 simplified the system into four rate levels based on risk level (Fischer et al., 2012).

A landfill charge for municipal waste was introduced in 2001 (Fischer et al., 2012). From 2007 to 2008, the charges for MSW were raised sharply to reduce the amount sent to landfill. In 2012, the charge for residual municipal waste reached PLN 110.65 (about EUR 25.00) per tonne (Fischer et al., 2012). The increase was accompanied by a small decrease in the share of MSW sent to landfill (Figure 5.3), though it is not clear to what extent the higher charges contributed to this trend. One factor that may have blunted the incentive effect is the lack of weighing bridges at many landfills (EEA, 2013). Also, charge rates are relatively low compared to other European countries (Figure 5.7).

Figure 5.7. **Municipal landfill charges in selected OECD countries, 2013**

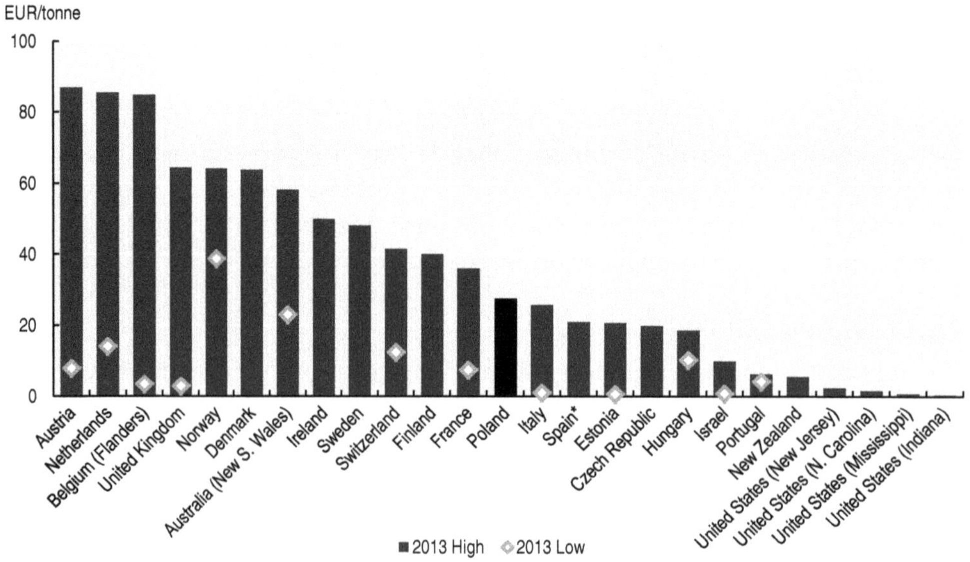

* Catalonia, 2013, Castile-La Mancha, 2007.

Source: OECD (2014), *OECD Database on Instruments Used for Environmental Policy and Natural Resources Management.*

StatLink http://dx.doi.org/10.1787/888933197858

The landfill charges are paid by landfill operators and are transferred to the following institutions, to support environmental investment:

- National Fund for Environmental Protection and Water Management (14 %)
- voivodship funds (26 %)
- provincial (poviat) budgets (10 %)
- municipal budgets (50%).

Several economic instruments have been introduced for packaging. Since 2002, companies responsible for packaging waste have had to pay product charges if they failed to achieve the required recovery and recycling levels; the charges are based on the amount of shortfall (Section 4). Separate rates are set for aluminium, glass, natural textiles, paper, plastic and wood packaging. In 2012, some PLN 1.1 million in these fees was paid to the marshals' offices (CSO, 2013).

In 2012, a mineral extraction tax for copper ore was introduced; information on potential results in terms of resource efficiency or waste generation was unavailable.

Poland's experience in the use of economic instruments provides a good base for further policy efforts in this area. A recent study for the European Commission has identified several areas for action, including increasing landfill charges to create stronger incentives for recovery and recycling of MSW and other waste streams (Box 5.5). A mineral extraction fee is in place, but does not seem to have a significant incentive effect. An increase of this fee for aggregates extraction could discourage the high use of construction materials, which have been the main area of growth for domestic materials consumption: this could play an important role in promoting greater materials efficiency. In early 2014, the MoE was studying options to increase environmental taxes and charges.

Box 5.5. **Opportunities to strengthen economic instruments on materials and waste**

A 2014 study for the European Commission reviewing opportunities to increase environmental taxes and charges in EU countries identifies several opportunities in Poland related to materials consumption and waste disposal:

- A tax on the extraction of aggregates, including sand, gravel, gypsum, limestone and other stones. By increasing the price of raw materials, the tax could strengthen the market for recycled materials, including those from construction and demolition. The tax would also tackle Poland's consumption of non-metallic minerals, which has grown rapidly to become the largest component of DMC (see Section 2.1).
- An increase in landfill taxes to help meet the EU's 2020 targets for recyclable materials (glass, metal, paper and plastic) as well as those for biological waste.
- A tax on single-use carrier bags to reduce littering, including marine litter.

Source: Hogg et al. (2014).

6.5. *Financing and programming waste management investment*

Total investment

From 2000 to 2012, Poland invested a total of about EUR 2.4 billion (in constant 2005 prices) in waste management, soil and groundwater (Figure 5.8). Total investment peaked

Figure 5.8. **Outlays of fixed assets for waste management and soil protection, 2000-12**

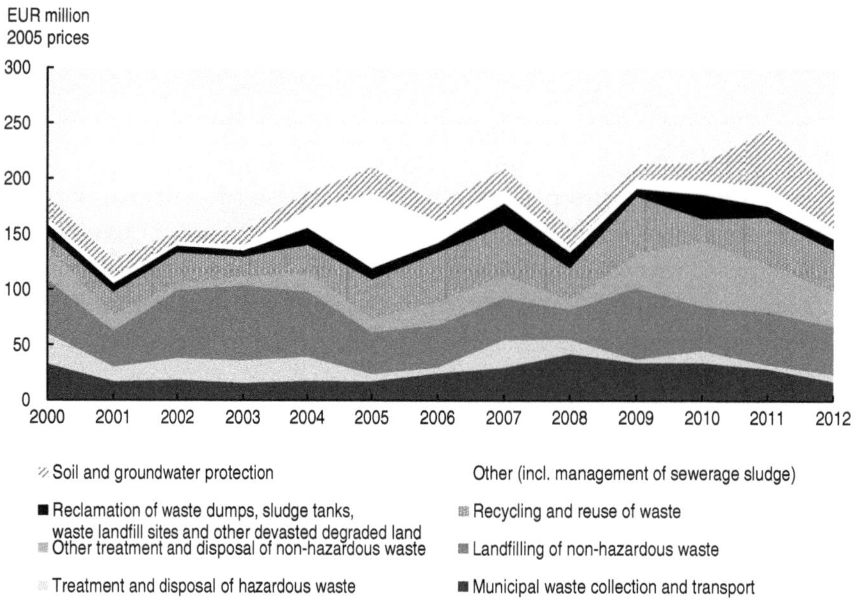

Source: CSO (2014), "Environmental Protection", *Local Data Bank* (database).

StatLink http://dx.doi.org/10.1787/888933197862

at EUR 246 million in 2011, falling to EUR 191 million in 2012 (in constant 2005 prices). Investment in treatment and disposal of non-hazardous waste made up 40% of the total in 2012, followed by other recycling and reuse and by soil and groundwater, at about 18% each.

Poland has increased financing for waste management facilities, addressing the recommendation of the 2003 OECD review to mobilise public and private resources to meet investment needs related to EU accession.

Financing sources

For all waste investment, enterprises' and municipalities' own resources provided 50% of the financing in 2012. Resources from abroad – mainly EU funds – and the national environmental fund each provided about 20%, with domestic credits and loans providing a further 7%. Other resources, including regular government budgets, provided only very small shares of total financing.

The NFEPWM and voivodship funds provide a large portion of financing via loans, though typically a portion of a loan they provide to municipalities and other public borrowers is turned into a grant upon successful completion of a project. One constraint on loan financing is that municipalities face government-imposed limits on debt financing.

The main source of EU funding was OPIE 2007-13. Co-financed by the EU and managed jointly by the national and voivodship funds, it was the largest programme for spending EU cohesion funds not only in Poland but in Europe overall. EUR 1.43 billion was allocated to waste management and soil protection, of which the EU funded EUR 1.2 billion. The amount for waste was equivalent to 4.4% of total cohesion funding available to Poland for the period (Ministry of Regional Development, 2007).

The role of EU funds, which are provided via grants, has been particularly strong for the construction of composting and related facilities, including MBT plants, where in 2012 they provided one-third of all investment resources. Many investments in this area have combined EU funds with national funding. An example is seen in Pomerania voivodship, where these mainly public sources were blended to finance new treatment facilities (Box 5.6).

Box 5.6. **Financing waste investment in Pomerania**

Pomerania, a voivodship in northern Poland that includes the city of Gdańsk, has divided its municipalities into seven waste management regions of at least 150 000 inhabitants each, across which 15 MSW treatment facilities are in operation, most of them recently built or expanded MBT plants. The total biological treatment capacity of all operating MBT installations is 202 000 tonnes per year. Financing came mainly from EU operational programmes and Poland's environmental funds:

- PLN 376 million (about EUR 90 million) in grants from OPIE 2007-13
- PLN 180 million in loans from the National Fund for Environmental Protection and Water Management
- PLN 56 million in loans from Regional Funds for Environmental Protection and Water Management
- PLN 33 million in grants from Pomerania's Regional Operational Programme 2007-13.

Most projects use a combination of these financing sources, with the national fund and OPIE supporting larger projects and the regional funds smaller ones. The amounts include funding for construction and other costs, including landfill closure in the waste management regions.

Source: Regional Fund for Environmental Protection and Water Management in Gdańsk.

Programming new investments

In early 2014, the MoE, drawing on an assessment by the World Bank for the new OPIE, estimated that over EUR 6 billion in investment was needed for MSW management over 2014-20 (Table 5.7). Among the areas for attention are further improvements in waste recycling and composting.

Table 5.7. **Estimate of investment needs for MSW facilities, 2014-20**

Type of facility	PLN (million)	EUR (million)
Collection points for recyclable waste	1 940	462
Waste sorting facilities	2 160	514
Composting and fermentation plants for biological waste	3 960	943
Incineration plants	18 720	4 457
Total	26 780	6 376

Note: PLN converted to EUR using early 2014 exchange rates.
Source: MoE; WB and MRD (2013).

Under this scenario, about 70% of the expended investment would go for MSW incineration plants with energy recovery. The estimate is based on construction of incinerator capacity to treat 30% of MSW at a cost of about EUR 1 000 per tonne of capacity.

This would be equivalent to more than 20 facilities the size of the incinerator now being built at Poznań. Six new incinerator projects have already been approved, and construction has begun. The next largest area of investment, composting and fermentation plants, represents about 15% of the total expenditure. Here, the goal is to more than triple existing capacity to treat separately collected biodegradable waste (about 35% of MSW).

These projects, however, require a major increase in financing: average annual investment for 2014-20 should be about four times the level in 2012. About PLN 9.1 billion (EUR 2.1 billion) may be available from the national and voivodship funds.

Preliminary allocations for OPIE 2014-20 indicate that EUR 863 million will be available for waste management, mainly for MSW collection and treatment facilities. This means that private financing will be needed for at least half the investment proposed. The Poznań incinerator is being financed via a public-private partnership (PPP), but it required extensive negotiations with the private partner, as often seen in such projects worldwide (Box 5.7).

Box 5.7. **Using public-private partnerships for large investment projects**

Despite efforts to encourage PPPs for investment in large waste facilities, as yet only one is under way, for the incinerator with energy recovery in Poznań. This project uses a so-called hybrid model blending national public support, EU funds and private investment.

The city of Poznań started the application procedure for the EU cohesion funds in 2004. Between August and October 2009, it carried out a public consultation on siting, and in 2010 it obtained approval regarding the environmental impact assessment and the location. In 2011, the city started the tendering procedure to select a private partner. The process lasted until 2013, when an agreement was signed with SITA Zielona Energia, a partnership created by SITA Polska and Marguerite Waste Polska. The PPP agreement is divided into the construction period (43 months from the signing of the PPP agreement) and the operation period (25 years from completion of construction, scheduled for late 2016). Total net capital expenditure is PLN 725 million (EUR 173 million), with PLN 352 million in co-financing from EU cohesion funds.

As this was the first major PPP project for waste management in Poland, negotiations were lengthy. The change in municipal responsibilities for waste in 2013 created delays, as did the hybrid approach to financing, combining private investment with EU funds and a municipal guarantee. The private partner's desire for confidentiality on aspects of the project also created tensions. In addition, the project was controversial and faced some public opposition.

Studying this and other experiences, the Polish PPP Centre, an industry-supported body, analysed PPPs in the waste sector (Centrum PPP, 2013). Its recommendations include:

- undertaking a strong initial financial analysis of potential risk, possible impact of the project on the municipal budget, assumptions regarding supply of and demand for waste streams, and clear understanding which risks can and will be assumed by the private partner and which will remain with public entities
- ensuring early application and sufficient lead time if EU funds are involved, as well as adequate consideration of co-financing
- setting out clear criteria for initial qualification and final selection, giving adequate weight to the experience and financial capacity.

Box 5.7. **Using public-private partnerships for large investment projects** *(cont.)*

A joint analysis by the World Bank and the Ministry of Regional Development highlighted similar issues, including the limited capacity of public authorities to manage and implement PPP financing for large and complex projects, which also is linked to long project preparation periods. Around the world, it found, preparing PPP projects for infrastructure is "expensive, risky and time consuming". A dedicated preparation facility can provide expertise and upfront resources for preparation (WB and MRD, 2013).

Source: WB and MRD (2013).

Poland should thus consider giving priority to building facilities for the collection and sorting of recyclable waste and the management of biodegradable municipal waste in order to focus investment on the EU's 2020 requirements in these areas.

That would allow lessons to be drawn from Poznań and other recent incinerator projects. It is true that the EU called for an end to the landfilling of waste in the 2011 Roadmap to a Resource Efficient Europe and other documents, and Poland would likely need further incinerator capacity to reach this objective. This is not a legally binding target, however, unlike those for recyclable and biodegradable waste. Costly investment in incineration capacity needs to be programmed carefully, to avoid crowding out investment related to the binding targets and to ensure that incinerators do not compete for recyclable waste or other potential recovery mechanisms, including refuse-derived fuel. Poland lacks sufficient MSW treatment capacity, true, but long-term planning should not overlook the fact that several countries in Europe currently have an overcapacity of waste incinerators.

Notes

1. Act of 14 December 2012 on waste (Journal of Laws of 2013, item 21, with later amendments).
2. The 2020 target, however, refers to "household" waste, not all MSW.
3. See *www.sp2000.fr*.
4. Producer obligations are based mainly on the Act of 13 June 2013 on Packaging and Packaging Waste Management (since 1 January 2014) and the Act of 11 May 2001 on Economic Operators' Obligations in the Scope of Managing Certain Types of Waste and on Product Charges (before 1 January 2014).
5. Rates are calculated as percentages of the mass of tyres introduced to the market the preceding year.

References

Adamczyk, L. and T. Schoenfelder (2014), ATMOTERM S.A., personal communication, May.

ADEME (2010), Collection Repères: Automobiles – Données 2010, *www2.ademe.fr/servlet/KBaseShow?sort=-1&cid=96&m=3&catid=19686.*

Andrykiewicz, A. et al. (2012), "The Assessment and Use of Integrated Product Policy in Poland", Management Systems in Production Engineering, No. 4 (8).

BiPro (2013a), *Country Factsheet Poland*, prepared for the European Commission, *http://ec.europa.eu/environment/waste/framework/pdf/PL_factsheet_FINAL.pdf.*

BiPro (2013b), *Roadmap for Poland*, prepared for the European Commission, *http://ec.europa.eu/environment/waste/framework/pdf/PL_Roadmap_FINAL.pdf.*

Cała, M. et al. (2013), *Mining Waste Management in the Baltic Sea Region. Min-Novation project*, AGH University of Science and Technology, Kraków, Poland.

CEE Bankwatch (2014), *Krakow waste incinerator, Poland*, accessed May 2014, *http://bankwatch.org/our-work/projects/krakow-waste-incinerator-poland.*

Centrum PPP (2013), *Partnerstwo publiczno-prywatne w gospodarce odpadami* – Public-Private Partnership In waste management, Warsaw, *www.centrum-ppp.pl/templates/download/crido_odpady.pdf.*

CSO (2013), *Environment 2013*, Central Statistical Office, Warsaw.

European Commission (2012), *Environment: Commission urges Poland to ensure proper disposal of end-of-life vehicles* (press release), European Commission, Brussels, *http://europa.eu/rapid/press-release_IP-12-293_en.htm?locale=en.*

European Commission (2011), *Environment: Commission urges Poland to comply with EU waste legislation* (press release), European Commission, Brussels, *http://europa.eu/rapid/press-release_IP-11-1275_en.htm.*

EEA (2013), *Municipal waste management in Poland*, February, European Environment Agency, Copenhagen, *www.eea.europa.eu/publications/managing-municipal-solid-waste.*

EEA (2011) *Survey of resource efficiency policies in EEA member and cooperating countries. Country profile: Poland*, European Environment Agency, Copenhagen, *www.eea.europa.eu/themes/economy/resource-efficiency/resource-efficiency-policies-country-profiles.*

Eurostat (2014), statistical portal, *http://epp.eurostat.ec.europa.eu/portal/page/portal/statistics/search_database.*

Fischer, C. et al. (2012), "Overview of the use of landfill taxes in Europe", *ETC/SCP Working paper* 1, European Topic Centre on Sustainable Consumption and Production, *http://scp.eionet.europa.eu/publications/WP2012_1.*

GIOS (2014), *Zbiorcza informacja na temat zawartości rejestru bezpośrednich zagrożeń szkodą w środowisku i szkód w środowisku za rok 2013* (Consolidated information on content of the register of direct damage risk in environment and environmental damage in 2013), February, Chief Inspectorate for Environmental Protection, Warsaw.

GIOS (2013), *Raport z przeprowadzonego przez Inskekcje Ochroney Srodowiska Ogólnokrajowego cyklu kontrolnego przestrzegania przez gminy przepisów znowelizowanej ustawy z dnia 13 września 1996 r.* Chief Inspectorate for Environmental Protection, Warsaw.

Hogg, D. (2014), Study on Environmental Fiscal Reform Potential in 12 EU Member States: Final Report to DG Environment of the European Commission, Eunomia Research & Consulting Ltd, Bristol *http://ec.europa.eu/environment/integration/green_semester/pdf/EFR-Final%20Report.pdf.*

Jarzab, M. (2011), *Analizauregulowanprawnych w zakresieselektywnejzbiórkiodpadów w Polsce i UE* (Analysis of legal regulations in the field of selective collection of waste in Poland and UE), RegRec, Zgorzelec *www.regrec.eu/index.php?option=com_content&view=article&id=19%3Aanaliza-i-ocena-kompetencji-oraz-struktury-organizacyjnej-w-zarzdzaniu-gospodark-odpadami-w-powiecie-zgorzeleckim&catid=3%3Adokumenty&Itemid=16&lang=pl.*

Korkozowicz, M. (2014), REBA Organizacja Odzysku SA, personal communication.

Kraj, I. (2014),"Wiadomości z Warszawy. Sąsiedzi wysypiska idą na ratusz!", Se.pl, 13 April,*www.se.pl/wydarzenia/warszawa/wiadomosci-z-warszawy-sasiedzi-wysypiska-ida-na-ratusz_391854.html.*

Mehlhart, G. et al (2011), *European second-hand car market analysis: Final Report*, Öko-Institut e.V. and COWI for the European Commission, *http://ec.europa.eu/clima/policies/transport/vehicles/docs/2010_2nd_hand_car_en.pdf.*

Ministry of Economy (2010), "Programme of Asbestos Abatement", Minstry o fEconomy, Warsaw, *www.mg.gov.pl/Bezpieczenstwo+gospodarcze/Program+Oczyszczania+Kraju+z+Azbestu.*

MoE (2014), "Keep Your Soul Unpolluted": Summing-up the Campaign, Ministry of the Environment, Warsaw, *www.mos.gov.pl/artykul/123_13908.html?j=en,* accessed May 2014.

MoE (2013a), Response to the questionnaire on implementation of the Waste Framework Directive for the years 2010-2012, Ministry of the Environment, Warsaw, *www.mos.gov.pl/artykul/4230_sprawozdania/21712_sprawozdanie_rzeczypospolitej_polskiej_z_wykonania_dyrektywy_parlamentu_europejskiego_i_rady_2008_98_we_z_dnia_19_listopada_2008_r_w_sprawie_odpadow_oraz_uchylajacej_niektore_dyrektywy_dz_u_l_312_z_22_11_2008_r_str_3_za_lata_2010_2012.html.*

MoE (2013b), *Response to the questionnaire for the OECD Environmental Performance Review of Poland*, Ministry of the Environment, Warsaw.

MoE (2011), *Implementation Report: National Waste Management Plan 2010* (for the period from 1 January 2009 to 31 December 2010), Ministry of the Environment, Warsaw, *www.mos.gov.pl/kategoria/2435_sprawozdania*.

MoE (2010), *The National Waste Management Plan 2014*, Ministry of the Environment, Warsaw.

MoE (2008), *The National Environmental Policy for 2009-2012 and its 2016 Outlook*, Ministry of the Environment, Warsaw.

Ministry of Infrastructure and Development (2014), *Sprawozdanie roczne z realizacji POIiŚ za 2013 rok, zatwierdzone przez Komitet Monitorujący Program uchwałą nr 3/2014 z dnia 3 czerwca 2014 r.* (Annual report on implementation of the OPI&E for 2013, approved by the Program Monitoring Committee), *www.pois.gov.pl/AnalizyRaportyPodsumowania/Strony/default.aspx*.

Ministry of Regional Development (2007), *Operational Programme Infrastructure and Environment, the National Strategic Reference Framework for the years 2007-2013*, Ministry of Regional Development, Warsaw.

OECD (2014), *OECD Economic Surveys: Poland 2014*, OECD Publishing, Paris, *http://dx.doi.org/10.1787/eco_surveys-pol-2014-en*.

OECD (2011), *OECD Environmental Performance Reviews: Portugal 2011*, OECD Publishing, Paris, *http://dx.doi.org/10.1787/19900090*.

OECD (2010), *OECD Environmental Performance Reviews: Ireland 2010*, OECD Publishing, Paris, *http://dx.doi.org/10.1787/19900090*.

OECD (2009), "State-Owned Enterprises and the Principle of Competitive Neutrality", Competition Law and Policy, OECD Publishing, Paris.

OECD (2003), *OECD Environmental Performance Reviews: Poland 2003*, OECD Publishing, Paris, *http://dx.doi.org/10.1787/9789264100961-en*.

OECD (2001), *Extended Producer Responsibility: A Guidance Manual for Governments*, OECD Publishing, Paris, *http://dx.doi.org/10.1787/9789264189867-en*.

Przygoński, P. (2014), The Polish Chamber of Waste Management (PIGO, Polska Izba Gospodarki Odpadami), personal communication, May.

Schneider, J. et al. (2010), *End of life vehicles: Legal aspects, national practices and recommendations for future successful approach*, Umweltbundesamt GmbH for the European Parliament, *http://ec.europa.eu/environment/waste/pdf/study/elv.pdf*.

Tyczkowski, J. (2014), *Rekopol*, personal communication, May.

World Bank (2011), *Solid Waste Management in Bulgaria, Croatia, Poland and Romania, a cross-country analysis of sector challenges towards EU harmonization*, World Bank, Washington DC, *https://openknowledge.worldbank.org/handle/10986/2754*.

WB and MRD (2013), *Ex-Ante Assessment of Financial Instruments for the Proposed Operational Programme on Infrastructure and Environment 2014-20 in Selected Sectors*, World Bank and Polish Ministry of Regional Development, Washington DC and Warsaw.

Zubik, M. (2013), "Wysypisko na Bielanach jeszcze 3 lata. Potem nowe w Zielonce", Gazeta.pl, 6 December, *http://warszawa.gazeta.pl/warszawa/1,34862,15084249,Wysypisko_na_Bielanach_jeszcze_3_lata__Potem_nowe.html*.

Zubik, M. (2014), "Czy firmy śmieciowe wybrano w Warszawie legalnie? Będzie wyrok", Gazeta.pl, 10 April (and related articles), *http://warszawa.gazeta.pl/warszawa/1,34889,15772353,Czy_firmy_smieciowe_wybrano_w_Warszawie_legalnie_.html#TRrelSST*.

ANNEX I

*Selected data**

* The statistical data for Israel are supplied by and under the responsibility of the relevant Israeli authorities. The use of such data by the OECD is without prejudice to the status of the Golan Heights, East Jerusalem and Israeli settlements in the West Bank under the terms of international law.

Figure I.A. **Selected economic data* – Economic context**

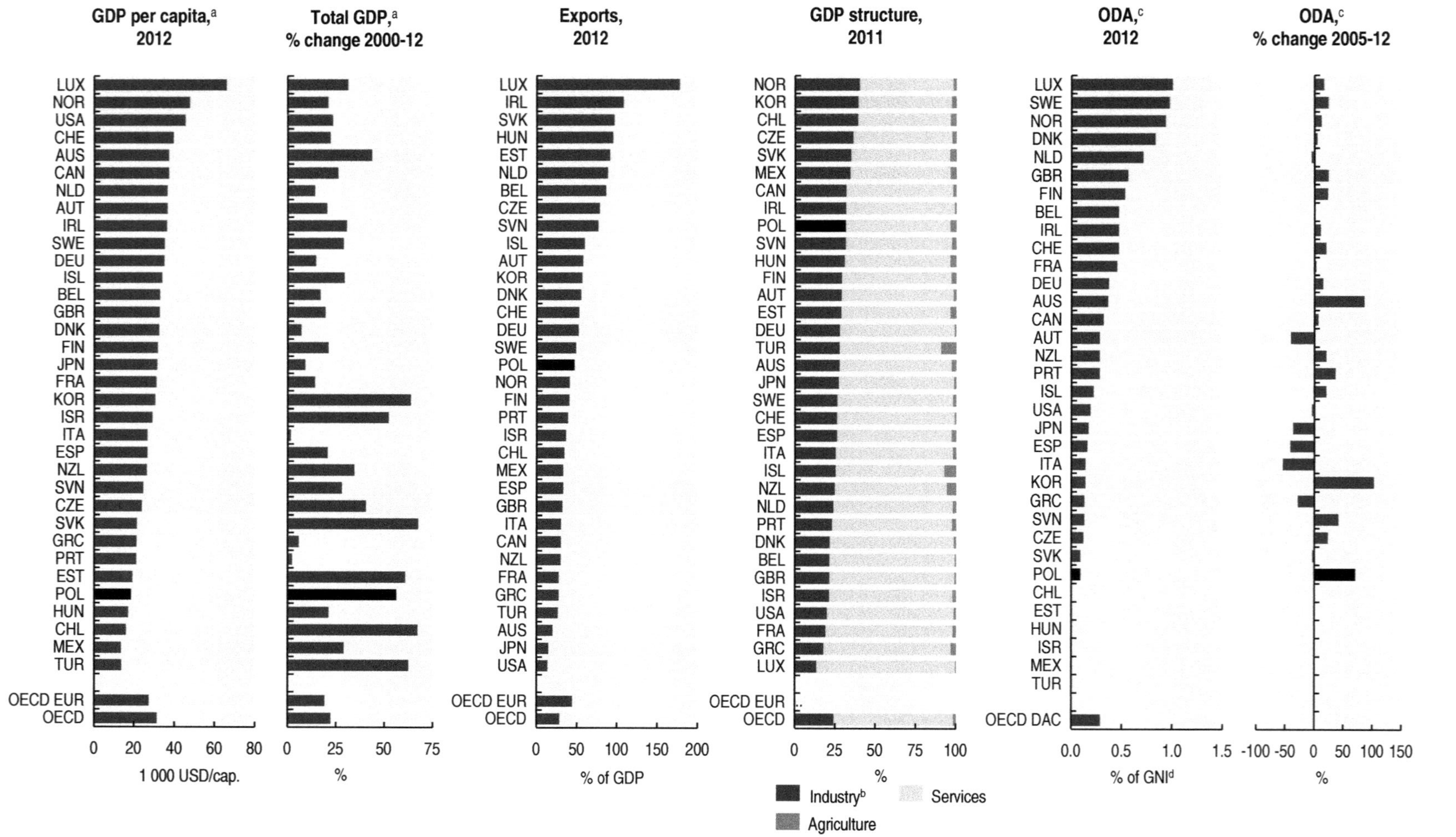

*) Data refer to the indicated year or to the latest available year. They may include provisional figures and estimates. Partial totals are indicated by shaded fill.

a) GDP at 2005 prices and purchasing power parities.

b) Includes mining and quarrying, manufacturing, gas, electricity and water, and construction.

c) Official development assistance by member countries of the OECD Development Assistance Committee. Total net disbursements at constant 2012 USD. CZE, ISL, KOR, POL, SVK and SVN became DAC members after 2005.

d) Gross national income.

Source: OECD (2014), *OECD Economic Outlook No. 95* (database); OECD (2014), *OECD Environment Statistics* (database); OECD (2014), *OECD International Development Statistics* (database).

Figure I.A. **Selected economic data* – Energy**

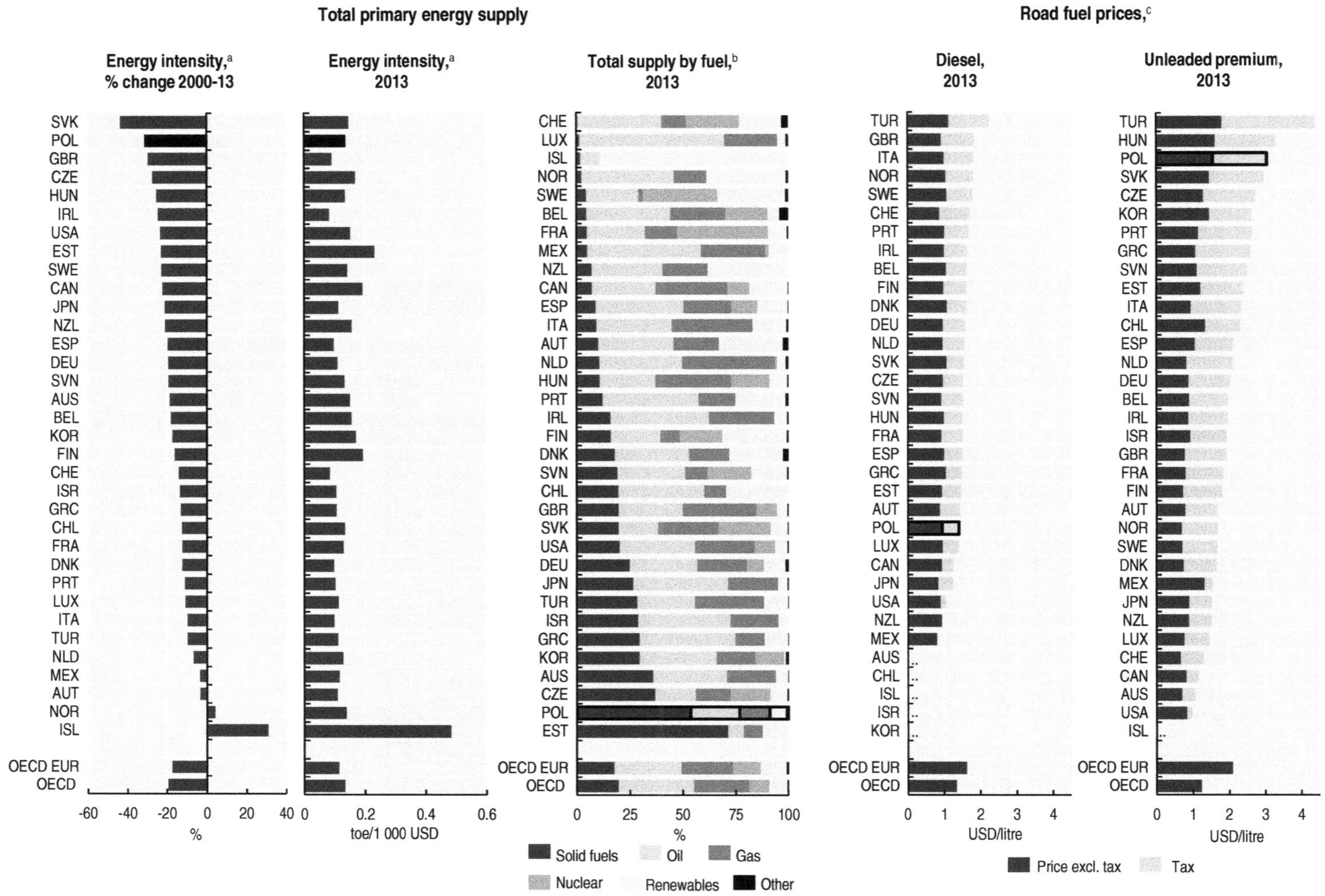

*) Data refer to the indicated year or to the latest available year. They may include provisional figures and estimates. Partial totals are indicated by dotted borders.

a) Total primary energy supply per unit of GDP expressed at 2005 prices and purchasing power parities.

b) The breakdown excludes trade of electricity and heat.

c) Diesel fuel: automotive diesel for commercial use, current USD; unleaded petrol: unleaded premium (RON 95), except JPN (unleaded regular), USD at current prices and purchasing power parities.

Source: IEA (2014), *IEA Energy Prices and Taxes Statistics* (database); IEA (2014), *IEA World Energy Statistics and Balances* (database).

Figure I.A. **Selected economic data* – Transport**

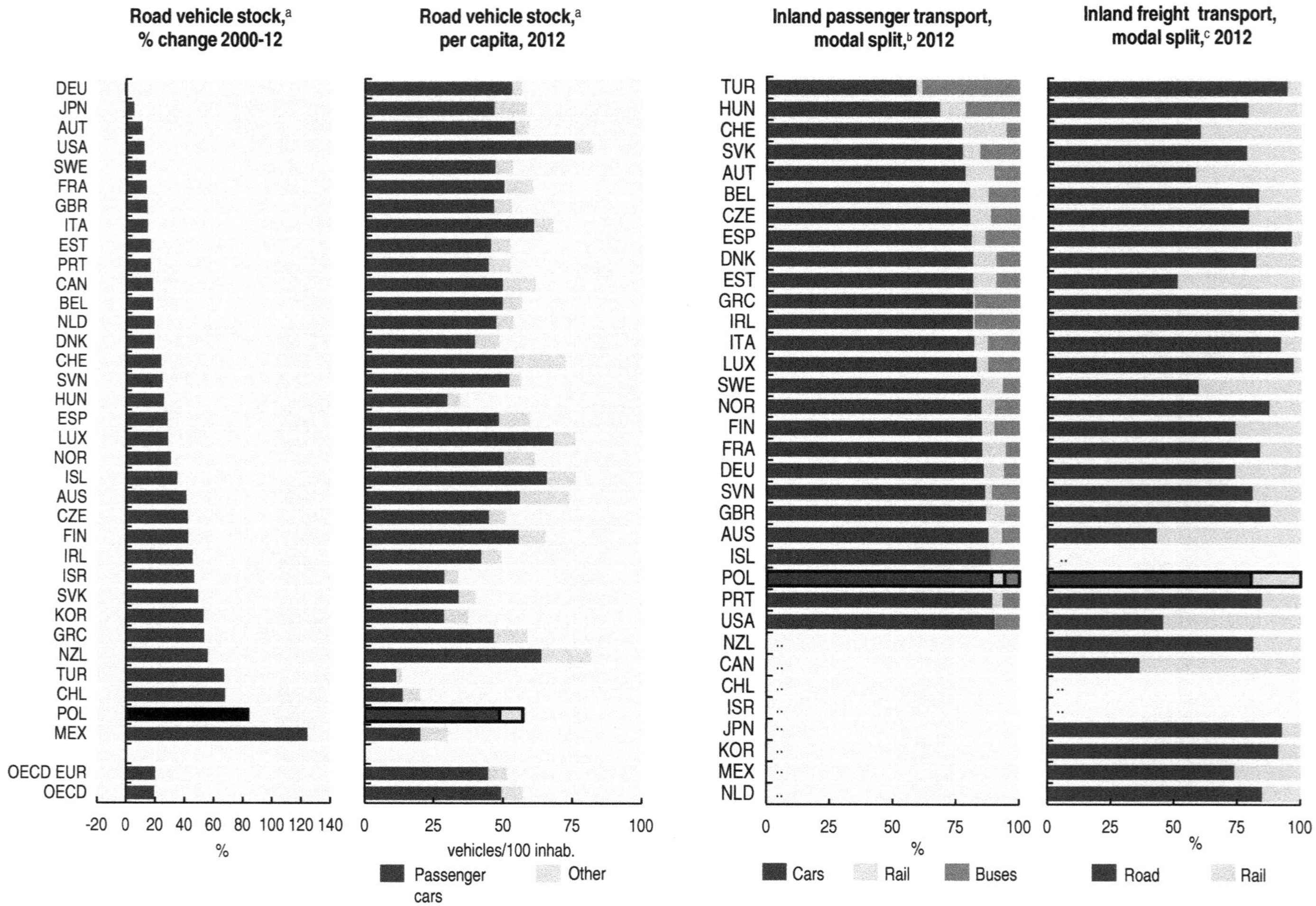

*) Data refer to the indicated year or to the latest available year. They may include provisional figures and estimates. Partial totals are indicated by dotted borders.

a) Motor vehicles with four or more wheels.

b) Based on data expressed in passenger/km.

c) Based on value expressed in tonne/km.

Source: Eurostat (2014), *Transport Statistics* (database); OECD (2013), *Environment at a Glance 2013: OECD Indicators*; OECD/ITF (2014), *ITF Transport Outlook 2013: Funding Transport.*

Figure I.B. Selected social data* – Social context

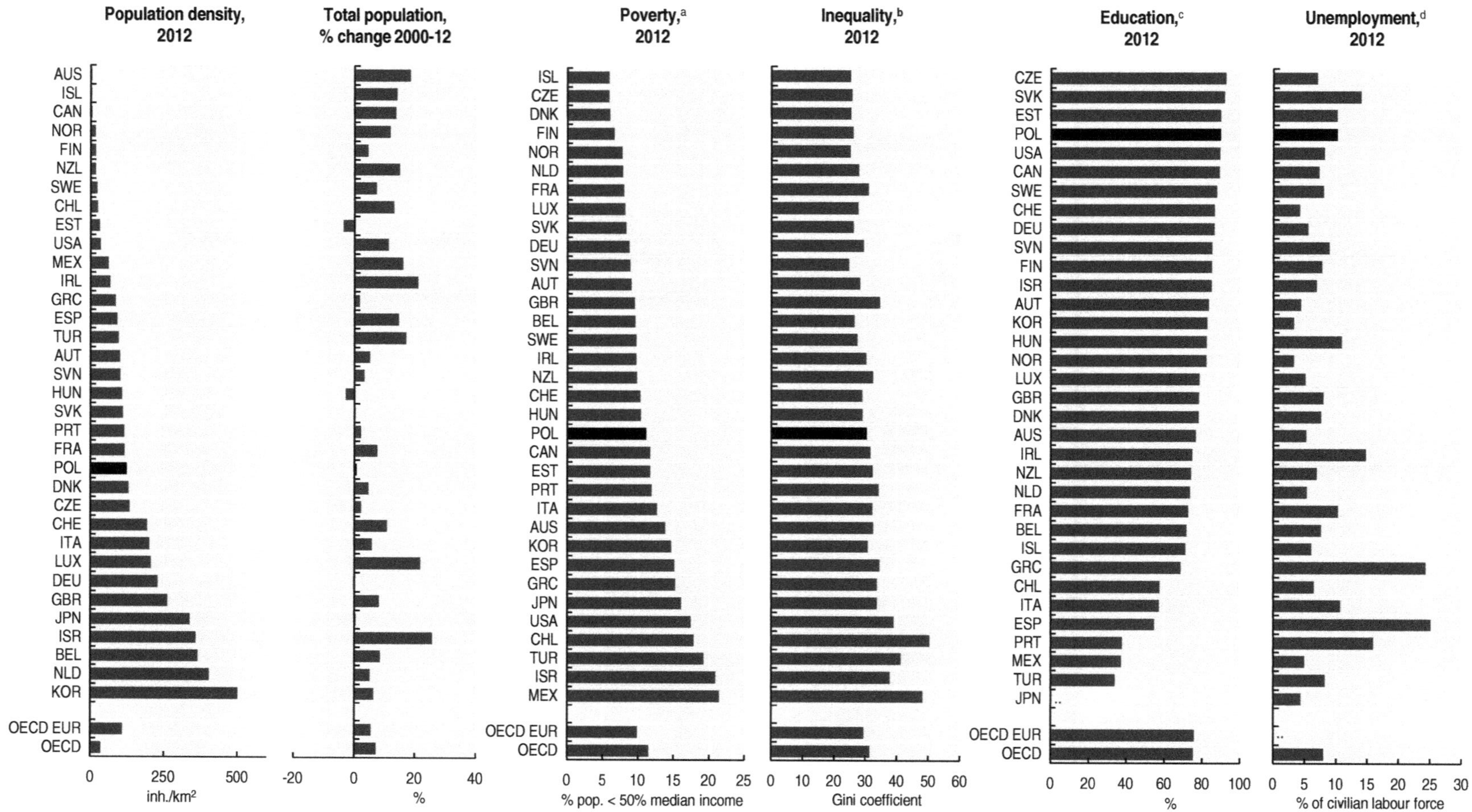

*) Data refer to the indicated year or to the latest available year. They may include provisional figures and estimates. Partial totals are indicated by dotted borders.

a) Share of population with an income under 50% of the median income after taxes and transfers. OECD and OECD EUR: average of rates.

b) Ranging from 0 (equal) to 100 (inequal) income distribution, based on total disposable income (incl. all incomes, taxes and benefits) for the entire population. OECD and OECD EUR: average of rates.

c) Share of population aged 25-64 years with at least upper secondary education. OECD and OECD EUR: average of rates.

d) Harmonised unemployment rates.

Source: OECD (2014), *OECD Education Statistics* (database); *OECD Environment Statistics* (database), *OECD Main Economic Indicators* (database), *OECD Social and Welfare Statistics* (database).

Figure I.C. **Selected environmental data* – Air**

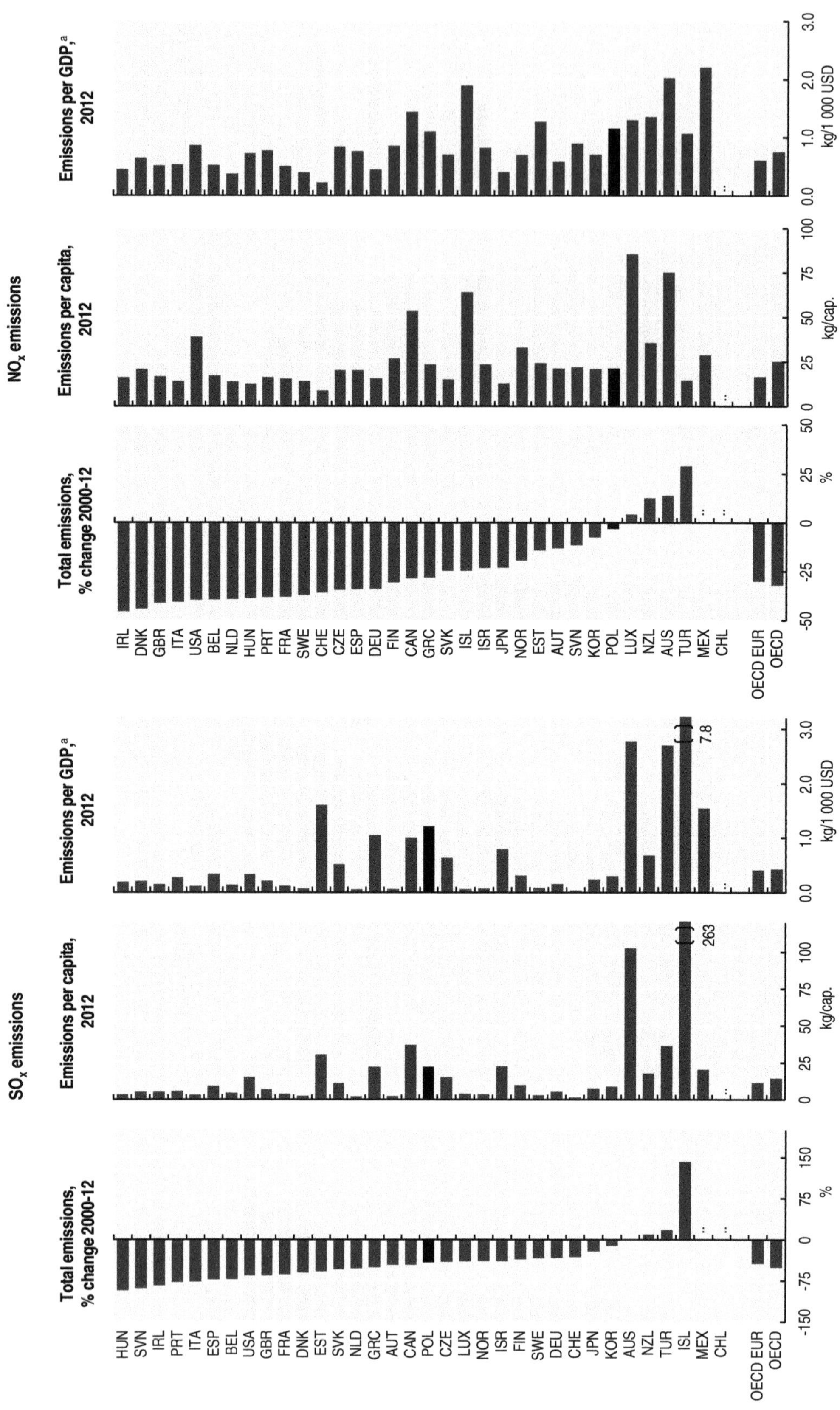

*) Data refer to the indicated year or to the latest available year. They may include provisional figures and estimates. Partial totals are indicated by dotted borders.

a) GDP at 2005 prices and purchasing power parities.

ISL: SO$_x$ emissions include emissions from geothermal energy. LUX: NO$_x$ emissions exclude emissions from "fuel tourism".

Source: OECD (2014); *OECD Environment Statistics* (database).

Figure I.C. **Selected environmental data* – Climate**

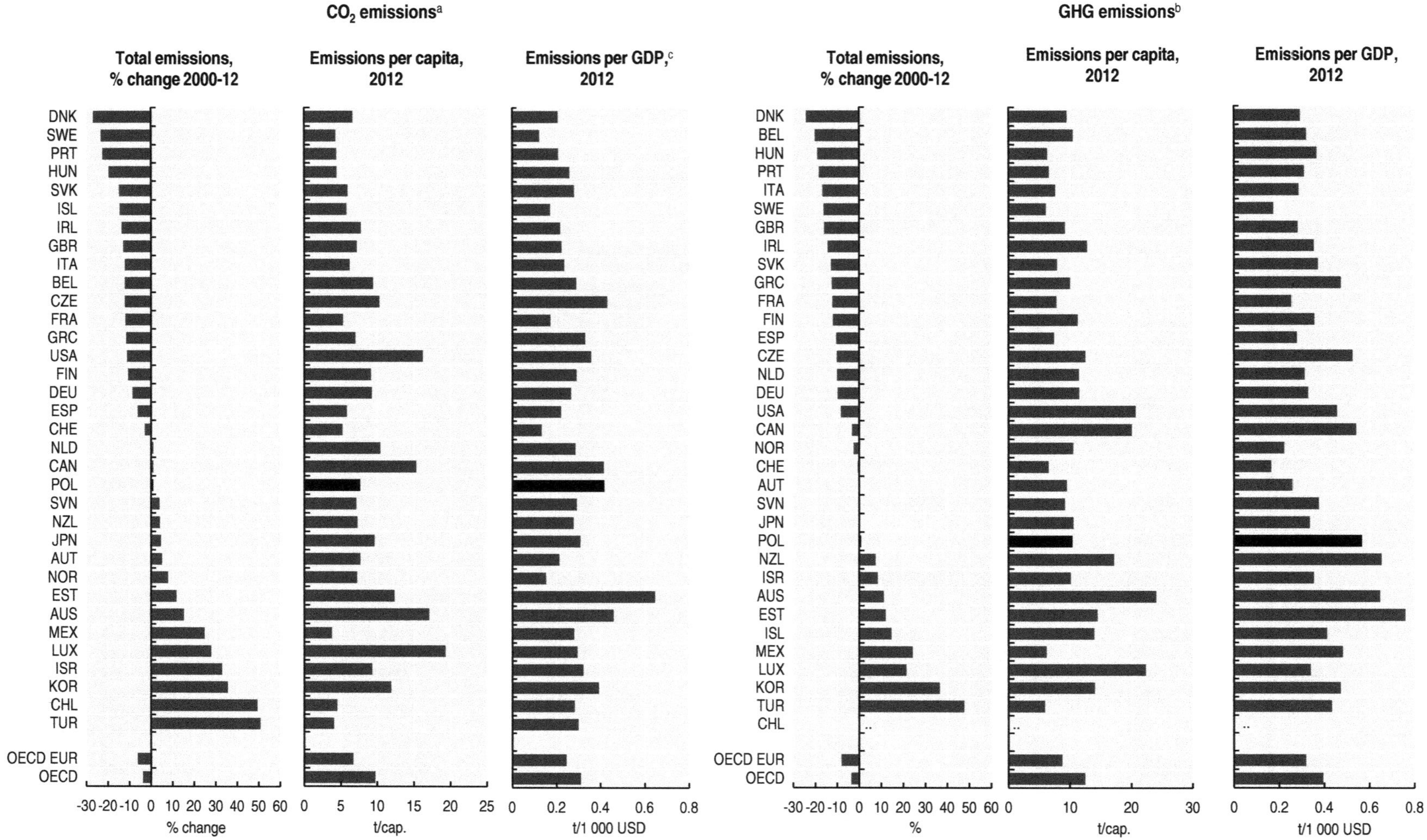

*) Data refer to the indicated year or to the latest available year. They may include provisional figures and estimates. Partial totals are indicated by dotted borders.

a) Emissions from energy use only; excluding international marine and aviation bunkers; sectoral approach.

b) Excluding emissions/removals from land use, land-use change and forestry. ISR: 2000 data exclude F-gases.

c) GDP at 2005 prices and purchasing power parities.

Source: IEA (2014), *IEA CO_2 Emissions from Fuel Combustion Statistics* (database); OECD (2014), *OECD Environment Statistics* (database).

Figure I.C. **Selected environmental data* – Biodiversity conservation and sustainable use**

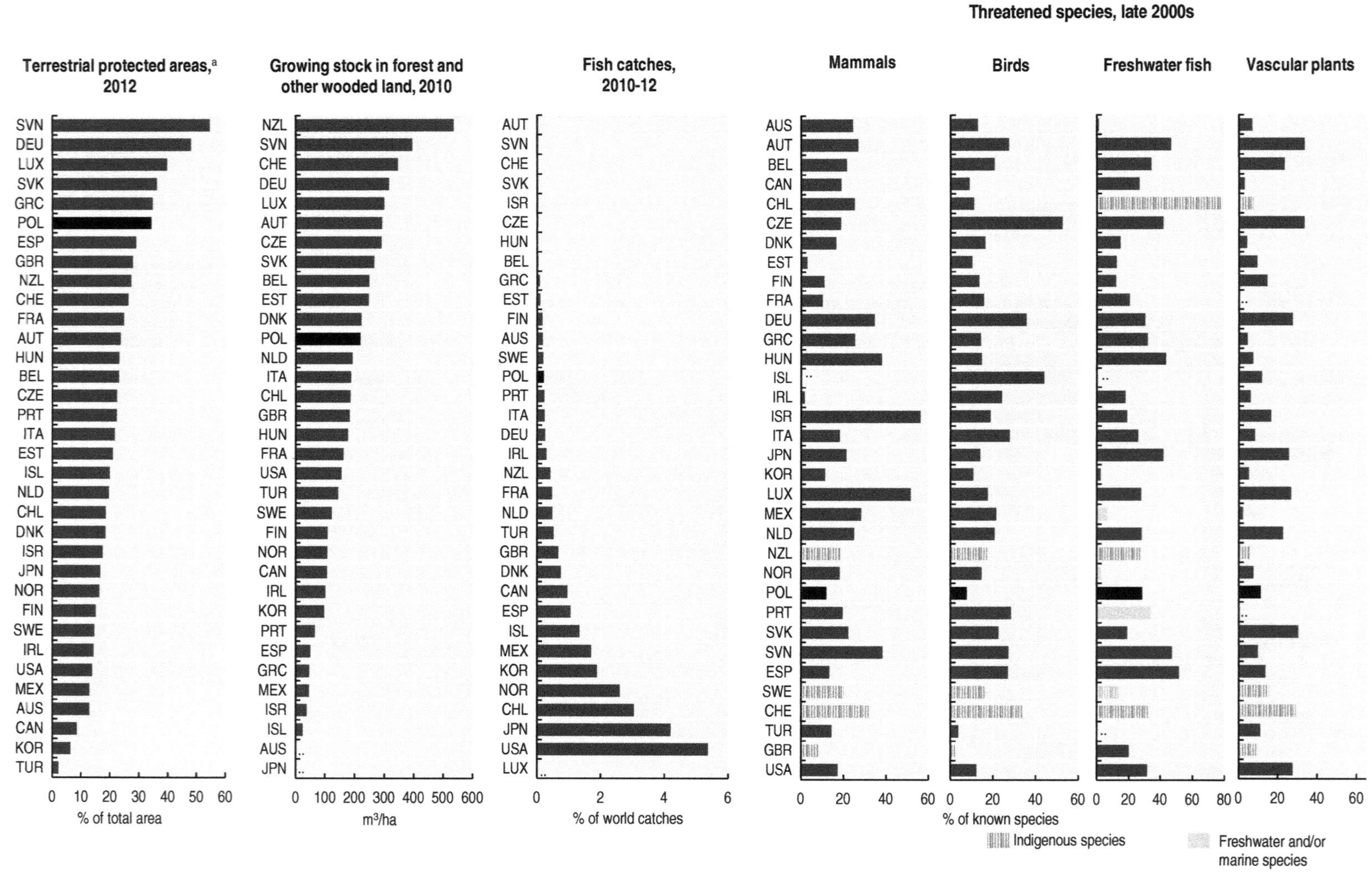

*) Data refer to the indicated year or to the latest available year. They may include provisional figures and estimates.

a) Nationally designated terrestrial protected areas recorded in the World Database on Protected Areas (WDPA). National classifications may differ.

Source: FAO (2014), *Global Capture Production* (database); FAO (2010), *Global Forest Resources Assessment 2010*; OECD (2014), *OECD Environment Statistics (database)*; UNSTATS (2014), *Millennium Development Goals Indicators* (database).

Figure I.C. **Selected environmental data* – Water and land**

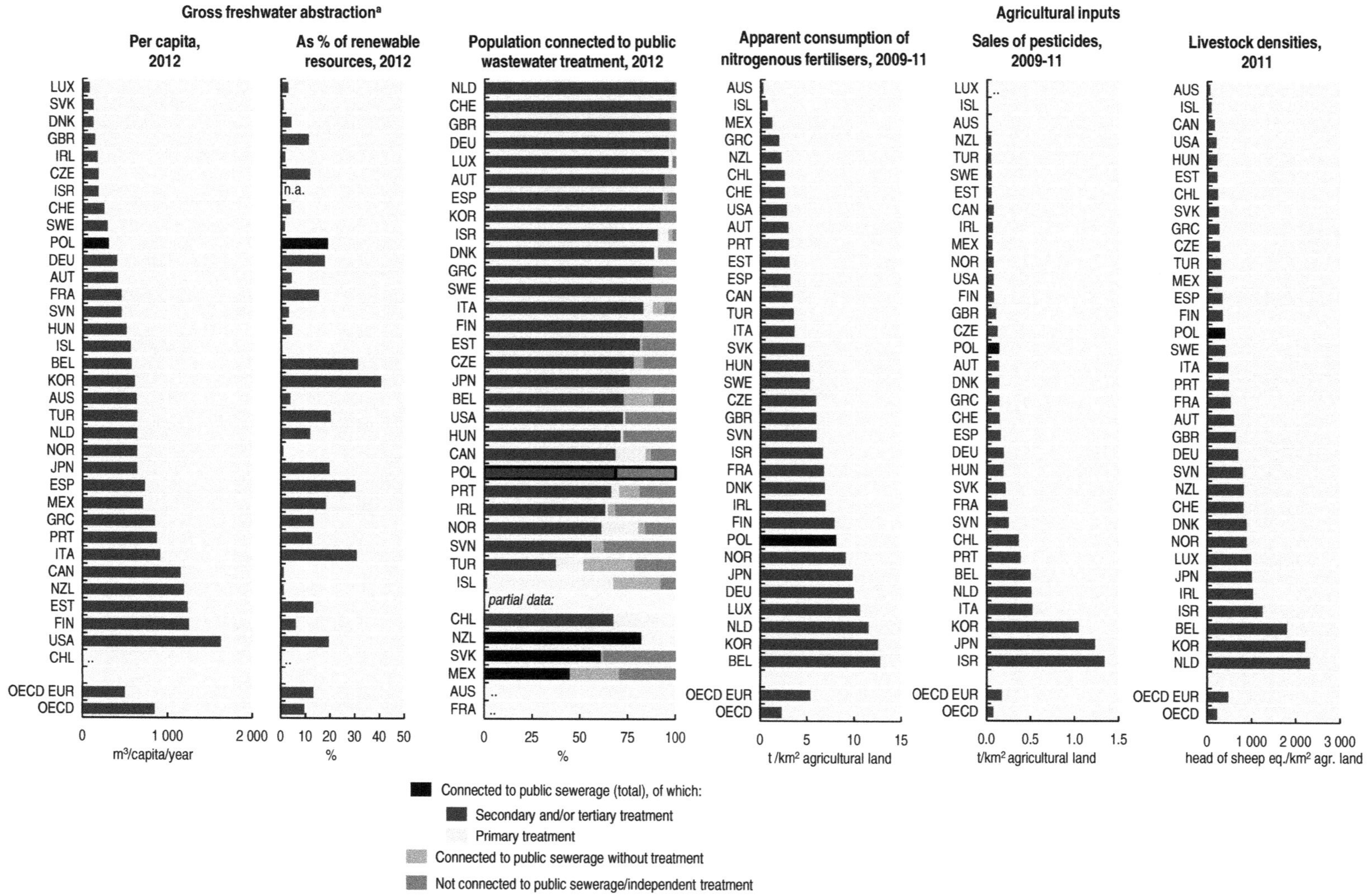

*) Data refer to the indicated year or to the latest available year. They may include provisional figures and estimates. Partial totals are indicated by dotted borders.

a) For some countries, data refer to water permits and not to actual abstractions.

GBR: Water abstraction and public wastewater treatment: England and Wales only; pesticides use: Great Britain only.

Source: OECD (2014), *OECD Environment Statistics* (database).

Figure I.C. **Selected environmental data* – Material productivity and waste**

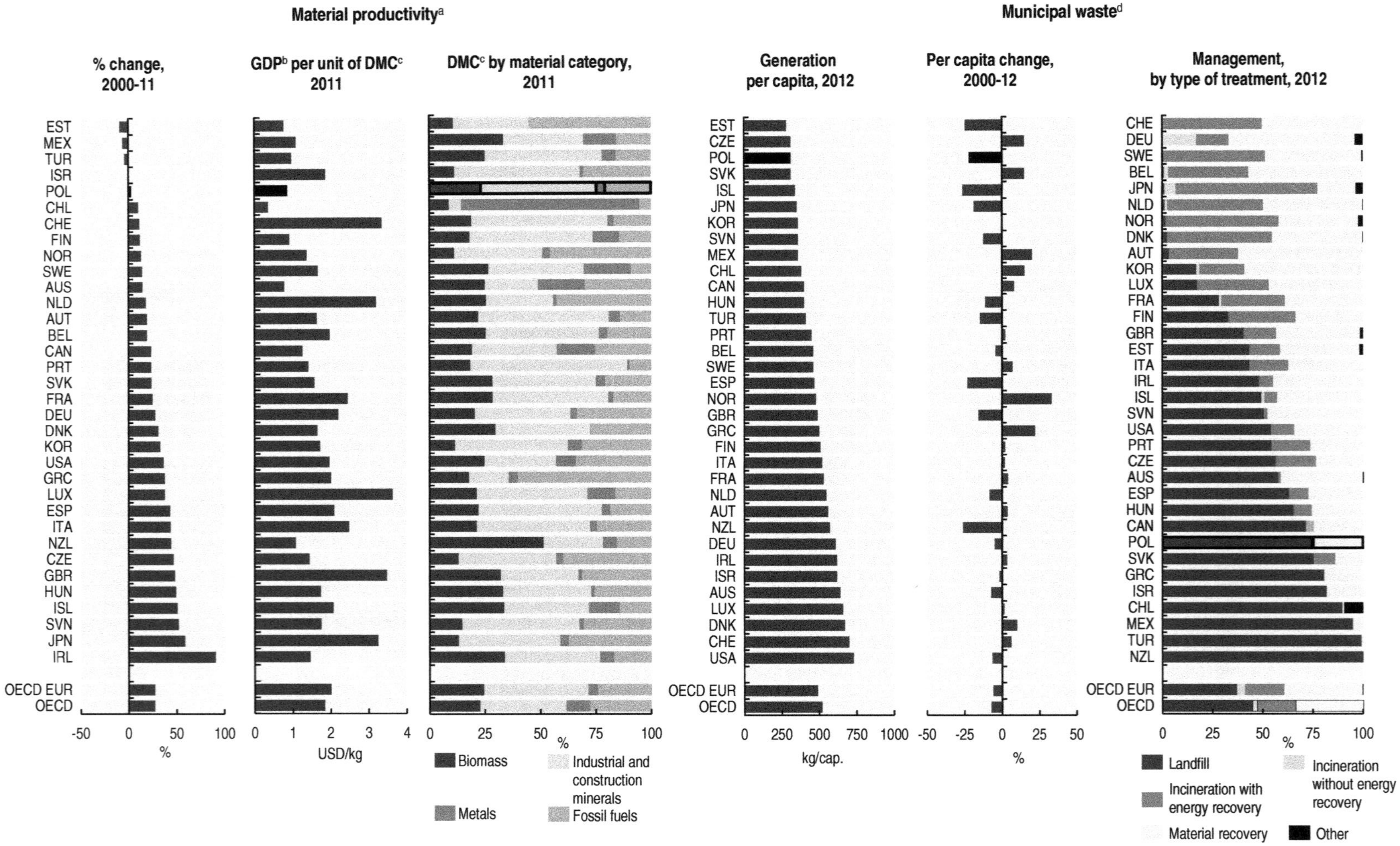

*) Data refer to the indicated year or to the latest available year. They may include provisional figures and estimates. Partial totals are indicated by dotted borders.

a) Amount of GDP generated per unit of materials used, ratio of GDP to domestic material consumption (DMC).

b) GDP at 2005 prices and purchasing power parities.

c) DMC equals the sum of domestic extraction of raw materials used by an economy and their physical trade balance (imports minus exports of raw materials and manufactured products).

d) Waste collected by or for municipalities and includes household, bulky and commercial waste, and similar waste handled at the same facilities. CAN: household waste only and total incineration; NZL: landfilled waste only.

Source: OECD (2014), *OECD Environment Statistics* (database).

ANNEX II

Actions taken on recommendations from the 2003 OECD Environmental Performance Review of Poland

Recommendations	Actions taken
	1. Environmental Management
Further implement the polluter pays and user pays principles to make provision of environmental services more efficient and contribute to their financing, taking into account social considerations.	From 2007 to 2008, the landfill charge for municipal waste was raised sharply (Chapter 5). Levels of charges and fees on air and water pollution, water abstraction and waste landfilling have not been high enough to provide an incentive to reduce pollution and use water efficiently, and related revenue remains insufficient to cover the cost of environmental services (Chapter 3).
Increase and maintain environmental expenditure at levels necessary to implement the EU environmental acquis, using more private funding (e.g. user charges) and EU funding for environmental investments.	Between 2006 and 2011, total public and business environmental expenditure increased from 1.6% of GDP to 1.9%. Between 2002 and 2011, total investment in environmental protection nearly doubled, with particularly strong growth after 2007 due to large inflows of EU funds. Poland aims to increase private sector participation in water and waste infrastructure under the recently amended public-private partnership law (Chapter 3).
Further enhance the transparency, accountability and effectiveness of environment funds (national, regional and local).	Since 2009, the National Fund for Environmental Protection and Water Management (NFEPWM) has taken a more transparent and results-oriented approach of four-year funding cycles. It developed a strategy reflecting its priority programmes, the rules for co-financing projects and selection criteria. A joint strategy with the 16 Voivodship Funds for Environmental Protection and Water Management was developed to improve co-ordination (Chapter 3).
Expand the use of economic instruments to improve the cost-effectiveness of environmental management; assess the potential role of tradeable emissions permits.	Poland has increased transport fuel taxes and broadened the energy tax base. Excise taxes on coal were introduced in 2012 and on natural gas in 2013. However, a wide range of exemptions remains. Poland has participated in the EU Emissions Trading System (EU ETS) since its launch in 2005. The NFEPWM has increasingly supported investment in energy efficiency and renewables, in particular under a green investment programme using the proceeds from sales of surplus of assigned amount units from the Kyoto commitment period 2008-12. Quotas for renewables and high-efficiency combined heat and power (CHP) have been implemented using tradable certificate systems, and since 2013 a white certificate system to achieve energy savings has been in effect for energy suppliers (Chapter 3).
Further strengthen enforcement of environmental regulations, expanding the role and capacity of the Inspectorate for Environmental Protection and of prosecutors, in line with new responsibilities (e.g. implementation of IPPC, decentralisation of environmental management responsibilities).	Since 2010, a compliance monitoring and enforcement management system (a so-called "control system"), has been in place. Poland's environmental compliance assurance system has been strengthened through the decentralisation of compliance monitoring and inspections, but has also been made more efficient by streamlining inspection procedures, reducing administrative burdens and increasing the effectiveness of non-compliance responses (Chapter 2).
Strengthen integration of environmental objectives into spatial planning and enhance the coherence of local and regional plans.	Limited progress has been made in spatial planning at subnational levels. Only 28% of land is covered by binding local land use plans and many individual construction permits are issued on a case-by-case basis. To prevent encroachment on protected areas, protected area administrations must show that development would have detrimental environmental effects. The national parks administration often lacks the capacity to make the case. A National Spatial Development Concept 2030 was adopted by the Council of Ministers in December 2011. It identifies the following broad objectives: protect public interest; establish an efficient spatial planning system; ensure the rule of law in spatial planning and land use developments; introduce site-specific instruments consistent with the development policy; create favourable conditions for business activity (Chapter 2, Chapter 4).

Recommendations	Actions taken
Strengthen the use of quantitative indicators to assess pressures on the environment and the effectiveness of policy responses.	Every four years, the Chief Inspectorate for Environmental Protection publishes an environmental indicator report based on the OECD pressure-state-response model (Chapter 2). Further efforts are needed to improve the accuracy of waste data and develop environmental accounting (e.g. economy-wide material flow accounts, environmental goods and services sector, ecosystem services) (Chapter 3, Chapter 4, Chapter 5).
Air	
Finalise and implement the national air management strategy and related sectoral action plans, with appropriate review mechanisms.	The National Air Management Strategy was implemented through the provisions of the Environmental Protection Law of 2001, which define the principles of the air quality assessment and management system. In line with EU requirements, detailed air protection programmes are developed in areas where air quality standards are not met.
Continue efforts to reduce emissions of SO_X, NO_X, NMVOCs, particulates and toxic organic chemicals from both stationary and mobile sources, in order to meet national and international commitments and minimise local air pollution hotspots and chronic photochemical oxidant pollution.	Poland met the 2010 targets on emissions of SO_2, NO_X, NMVOCs and NH_3 under the National Emission Ceilings Directive. In 2012, PM_{10} and $PM_{2.5}$ concentrations exceeded recommended levels at many sites. Urban exposure to ozone air pollution has decreased, and Polish levels were lower than the EU average in the early 2010s (Chapter 1). In 2013, Poland joined the Climate and Clean Air Coalition, focused on reducing emissions of short-lived climate pollutants such as black carbon, methane and hydrofluorocarbons.
Further enhance the role of economic instruments (e.g. emission trading, extended use of excise duty on non-automotive fuels) in the policy mix to improve the cost-effectiveness of environmental management.	Poland has broadened the energy tax base. Excise taxes on coal were introduced in 2012 and on natural gas in 2013. However, a wide range of exemptions remains. Poland has participated in the EU ETS since its launch in 2005. The NFEPWM has increasingly supported investment in energy efficiency and renewables, in particular under a green investment programme using the proceeds from sales of surplus of assigned amount units from the Kyoto commitment period 2008-12. Quotas for renewables and high-efficiency CHP have been implemented using tradable certificate systems, and inc 2013 a white certificate system to achieve energy savings was introduced for energy suppliers (Chapter 3).
Further integrate environmental concerns into energy policies, including through promotion of energy efficiency, progressive removal of environmentally harmful subsidies, and strengthening of incentives for cleaner production.	The 2009 Energy Policy of Poland to 2030 aims at mitigating the power sector's environmental impact by improving energy efficiency and diversifying the energy mix. It includes a target of increasing the share of renewables to 15% of gross final energy consumption by 2020. The 2014 Energy Security and the Environment Strategy's objective is "to create conditions for the development of a competitive and efficient energy sector while respecting the principles of sustainable development and respect for the environment". Under the 2012 EU Directive on Energy Efficiency (2012/27/EU), Poland has set an indicative target for 2020 of stabilising primary energy consumption at about the 2010 level. Financial incentives, primarily through preferential loans, have been provided to support end-use energy efficiency, as well as renewable energy production. A broad range of exemptions to the payment of excise taxes on energy remains. Other than these exemptions, direct support to the hard-coal industry and rebates on diesel fuel tax for farming are the main types of subsidies for fossil fuels. Subsidies to the coal industry have been framed by EU rules since Poland's accession, and state aid is no longer given for operating costs (Chapter 1, Chapter 3).
Accelerate the modernisation of air quality monitoring networks and streamline their administration.	The air quality monitoring system has been further strengthened over the last decade in line with EU requirements. In 2007, it was enlarged to include heavy metals (As, Ni, Cd) and benzo(a)pyrene. In 2010, $PM_{2.5}$ measurement was introduced. Several regional inspectorates modernised their monitoring equipment and established new stations that improve the assessment system in areas of increased pressures (Chapter 2).
Water	
Mobilise financing needed to upgrade and extend both urban and rural sewerage, waste water treatment and drinking water supply infrastructure, giving consideration to greater involvement of the private sector.	Since 2002, the near doubling of investment in wastewater management has helped increase the share of population connected to sewage treatment plants, which grew by 12 percentage points to 69% in 2012. However, Poland is unlikely to meet the 2015 deadline for implementing the Urban Waste Water Treatment Directive due to planning deficiencies and a financing gap. The national municipal wastewater treatment programme, adopted in 2003 to fulfil the directive requirements, is being revised for the fourth time and should address these issues. Although the share of population with access to water supply had grown to 88% by 2012, there are wide variations between regions and between rural and urban areas. In recent years, there has been progress in inter-municipal co-operation to provide infrastructure for water treatment, often involving joint applications for EU funds or other external finance. However, the fragmentation of the water and sanitation sector, the dominance of municipally owned utilities and the tendency of municipalities to set below-cost tariffs to protect local monopolies have deterred further private involvement. Poland aims to increase private sector participation in water and waste infrastructure under the recently amended public-private partnership law (Chapter 3).

Recommendations	Actions taken
Apply the user pays and polluter pays principles more fully for water services, taking into account social considerations.	The principle of recovery of cost for water services was laid down in the Water Law in 2011. Water users are required to cover the costs of water resource use by bearing the charges for water abstraction and pollution discharges provided for by the Environmental Protection Law. Revenue from charges on water abstraction and effluent discharges remains insufficient to cover the cost of water and sanitation services. Major water users are exempt from water abstraction fees, notably for aquaculture, irrigation and mining, and, subject to certain conditions, for power generation cooling and hydropower.
Pursue implementation of EU legislation and implementation of the new institutional framework for water management established by the 2001 Water Act.	In line with the Water Framework Directive, river basin management plans were adopted in 2011. Despite several amendments, Polish water legislation has shortcomings in transposition and implementation of EU legislation (e.g. Urban Waste Water Treatment Directive and Nitrates Directive). Discussions about clarifying and streamlining the institutional arrangements in the water sector have been going on for some time but no decisions have yet been reached (Chapter 1, Chapter 2, Chapter 3).
Focus water management priorities, with clear quantified objectives and time limits, while paying particular attention to minimising the costs of meeting environmental quality targets.	As part of river basin management plans, Poland reported programmes of measures to achieve good status of water bodies. Their effectiveness has not yet been evaluated (Chapter 1).
Continue to implement flood prevention and mitigation programmes and plans, in particular by protecting flood plains and natural buffer zones.	In line with the EU Floods Directive, watercourses posing a potential flooding threat were identified and flood-prone areas were mapped. A forecasting and warning system is being developed. Management plans to reduce flood damage have to be developed.
Introduce measures to promote use of phosphate-free detergents (e.g. product charges, phase-out).	In line with European legislation, limitations of phosphorus content in washing machine detergents have applied since 30 June 2013. Limitations concerning dishwasher detergents will apply from 1 January 2017.
	Waste
Implement the national waste management plan, establishing a mechanism for regular review of progress.	The National Waste Management Plan 2006 (NWMP 2006, published in 2002) was updated by the NWMP 2010 (published in 2006), which was in turn revised by the NWMP 2014 (published in 2010). The national plans include provisions for monitoring results. Regular implementation reports have detailed progress towards targets and have identified shortfalls. Their conclusions help strengthen continuity across the plans (Chapter 5).
Strictly enforce technical standards for landfills and urgently close a number of substandard sites; reinforce enforcement of prohibitions against illegal dumping.	By early 2014, the Ministry of the Environment reported, substandard landfills had stopped operations, though preparation of closure plans and investment for closure were still under way for many. The Chief Inspectorate for Environmental Protection issues guidelines on landfills for the voivodship inspectorates (Chapter 5).
Review possible approaches to increasing private and public financing of the upgrading and expansion of waste management facilities; address the large financing gap expected due to implementation of EU waste legislation and domestic legislation on land contamination.	Since 2002, the NFEPWM, its counterparts at the voivodship level and EU funds have supported investment in municipal waste treatment capacity. From 2007 to 2008 the landfill charge for municipal waste was raised sharply. Since 2006 all importers of used vehicles, including individuals, have had to contribute to the NFEPWM; the revenue is used to support authorised recycling. Municipal waste management requires a major increase in financing: average annual investment for 2014-20 should be about four times the level in 2012. Despite efforts to encourage public-private partnerships for investment in large waste facilities, as yet only one is under way. Since 2013, municipalities have been responsible for municipal waste management. They have to set and collect fees from residents and service sector businesses to cover the full costs of municipal waste collection and treatment (Chapter 5).
Continue to improve the system for regulating the movement and treatment of hazardous waste, expanding the capacity to destroy PCBs and obsolete pesticides.	By 2011, Poland had eliminated obsolete pesticides at 95% of the more than 200 repository sites around the country. In mid-2014, pesticides remained at three sites where legal issues over ownership held up final removal and treatment. Poland has also made important progress in removing and treating oil, liquids, capacitors and other products containing PCBs. The 2002 and 2006 NWMPs called for removing PCB-containing equipment in use by July 2010 and treating PCB-containing waste. These targets were not fully met. By early 2014, treatment of former PCB equipment had been completed in 11 of 16 voivodships and continued in the remaining 5 (Chapter 5).
Strengthen measures to increase municipal waste recovery rates, with stronger initiatives by authorities concerning separate collection and the creation of sustainable recycling markets.	Since 2013, municipalities have been responsible for municipal waste management and required to organise separate collection of recyclable waste. Preliminary results show improved separate waste collection. Extended producer responsibility systems have played an important role in establishing infrastructure and increasing separate collection, recovery and recycling of six waste streams, including packaging, tyres and batteries. In 2013, Poland reformed its law on packaging waste to reduce the "grey zone" of improper accounting and consolidate administrative roles (Chapter 5).

Recommendations	Actions taken
Nature and biodiversity	
Ensure proper implementation and monitoring of the National Biodiversity Strategy, including through strengthened institutional co-ordination at all administration levels and improved measurement of status and trends of biodiversity across the country.	Supervision of implementation of the National Biodiversity Strategy and its Action Programme for 2007-13 was entrusted to a steering committee appointed by the environment minister. Its 24 members represent all the entities identified in the Action Programme as being responsible for particular tasks, as well as representatives of financing institutions, scientific bodies and non-government organisations (NGOs).
Ensure that development projects and programmes respect Natura 2000 designations and management concepts, and redouble efforts to organise consultations at the local level on Natura 2000 proposals, especially when sites are outside existing protected areas.	Pursuant to the 2004 Nature Conservation Act, all plans, programmes and planned developments likely to have a significant impact on Natura 2000 sites are subject to environmental impact assessment (EIA). Principles for conducting such assessments are set out in the 2008 EIA Act. In case of negative impact on the site, consent can only be given on certain conditions (absence of alternative solutions; imperative reasons of overriding public interest; compensatory measures ensuring coherence of Natura 2000). Consultations during the process of Natura 2000 site designation are regulated by the Nature Conservation Act. Councils of local administrative units have 30 days to give their opinion on the proposed sites (Chapter 2, Chapter 4).
Improve conservation in Landscape Parks through incentives and legal mechanisms to encourage private owners or leaseholders within these parks to respect biodiversity conservation objectives; ensure integration of Landscape Park conservation plans into local land use planning.	Apart from consultations under the EIA Act, stakeholders are given the option to participate in the preparation of management plans through the creation of local co-operation groups.
Develop diverse, thriving rural economies that value biodiversity (e.g. through green tourism, environmentally sound agriculture, efficient use of agri-environmental and less favoured area programmes); remove perverse incentives such as the reduced VAT on agricultural pesticides.	Since 2004, the Rural Development Plan has included agri-environmental programmes and support for afforestation of agricultural land, for agricultural activity in less favoured areas, for organic farming and for farmers who contribute to nature conservation activities in protected areas. VAT rates on pesticides were increased from 0% in 2004 to 7% in 2010 and 8% in 2011, but pesticides continue to be taxed at reduced rates.
Establish protected areas in the marine environment and expand efforts to protect marine biodiversity.	Seventeen Natura 2000 sites have been designated in marine waters. The sites also have Baltic Sea Protected Areas status under the Helsinki Commission (HELCOM).
2. Towards sustainable development **Integration of environmental concerns into economic decisions**	
Further decouple environmental pressures from economic growth to reduce pollution intensity and improve resource efficiency of the economy.	Between 2000 and 2012, Poland achieved a significant but relative decoupling of GHG emissions from economic growth. The energy and carbon intensities of the economy decreased faster than in most OECD countries. Material productivity has varied with the cycles of investment in infrastructure. Progress has been made in decoupling waste generation, water withdrawal and emissions of several air pollutants from economic growth. Environmental pressures from nutrients have not been decoupled from agricultural production (Chapter 1).
Consider economic, environmental and social aspects in setting national priorities at the strategic, planning, programming and budgeting levels.	Full transposition of Directive 2001/42/EC on the assessment of the effects of certain plans and programmes on the environment was achieved in 2008. Over the years, strategic environmental assessment (SEA) has evolved from merely fulfilling the formal requirement of environmental assessment to a practical tool which contributes to the integration of environmental considerations in the planning process (Chapter 2).
At project level, ensure the integration of environmental concerns through EIA and spatial planning and develop sharing of best practices among regions and municipalities.	Developments in general must conform to the local land use plan, if there is one, though some exemptions are provided for by EIA regulations. Opportunities exist to further improve and harmonise the methodology for conducting EIA, and to make the process more transparent by facilitating public participation at all stages (Chapter 2).
Continue to integrate environmental concerns into sectoral fiscal and price signals; extend taxation of fuels used by stationary sources, differentiating tax rates to internalise environmental externalities.	Poland has increased transport fuel taxes and broadened the energy tax base. Since 2007, the tax differential between diesel and petrol has narrowed. Excise taxes on coal were introduced in 2012 and on natural gas in 2013. However, a wide range of exemptions remains (Chapter 3).
Prioritise implementation of cost-effective measures to improve the energy efficiency of large stationary sources and to reduce the carbon intensity of the energy supply (e.g. through progressive removal of environmentally harmful subsidies).	Poland has transposed the EU directive on limitating air emissions of certain pollutants from large combustion plants (2001/80/EC) and participates in the EU ETS. In July 2014, the Sejm (Parliament) adopted draft amendments to the 2001 Environmental Protection Law to implement the Industrial Emissions Directive (2010/75/EU). Some installations will be covered by a transitional national plan that will move the deadline for compliance to 2020 (Chapter 2). The carbon intensity of the energy supply has decreased due to modernisation, improved efficiency and a moderate shift to natural gas and renewable energy sources (primarily biomass) (Chapter 1).

Recommendations	Actions taken
Further promote capacity building and networking for local development initiatives integrating economic, social and environmental concerns (e.g. Local Agenda 21) in urban and rural development.	No reported action.
	Sectoral integration: Transport
Fully implement exhaust emission control, automotive fuel quality control and in use-vehicle inspections to reduce road vehicle emissions.	Poland has implemented fuel quality and vehicle emission standards and monitoring obligations pursuant to EU legislation.
Fully integrate environmental considerations into Poland's road transport infrastructure development (e.g. the Trans-European Network), using environmental impact assessment and strategic environmental assessment; in particular, ensure consistency with the Habitats Directive and with the sustainable development scenario of Poland's 2001 National Transport Plan.	SEA is carried out for any draft policies, strategies, plans or programmes (including on transport), setting out the framework for future implementation of projects likely to have a significant effect on the environment. The body that elaborates the draft document is also responsible for preparing the environmental report (which has to include information concerning impact on the Natura 2000 area) and for ensuring opportunities for public participation. The high speed rail programme was subject to SEA. Any projects likely to have a significant or potentially significant effect on the environment (including most transport investment projects) require prior EIA. The process also involves assessment of the project's impact on Natura 2000 sites (Chapter 2, Chapter 4).
Establish priorities for scheduling and financing transport infrastructure investments.	With support from EU funds, the GDP share of transport investment rose from 0.7% in 2000 to 2.5% in 2011. Roads have accounted for 90% of transport infrastructure investment. Under the Operational Programme Infrastructure and Environment 2007-13, more than EUR 5 billion of EU funds was allocated to modernise and expand railway infrastructure, develop intelligent transport systems and promote intermodal transport. However, absorption of EU funds for rail infrastructure has been challenging. Rail investment was prioritised in the 2011 Multi-Annual Programme of Railway Investments to 2013 of the Transport Development Strategy. However, the funding allocated to the programme was repeatedly scaled down (Chapter 3).
Implement demand management measures for both passenger and freight transport (e.g. park and ride, combined freight transport, tighter parking control in city centres).	The 2011 Act on Public Transport requires cities with more than 50 000 inhabitants to develop plans for sustainable public transport development based on demand analysis. Corresponding plans for regional public transport and for long-distance public transport are to be developed by voivodships and the Ministry of Infrastructure and Development. Measures to restrict access and parking in city centres are implemented in Kraków, Sopot, Szczecin, Opole, Chorzów and Poznań. Public transport is promoted through passenger information systems and integrated train, bus and tram tickets. Some cities, such as Gdańsk, Kraków, Wrocław and Poznań, have introduced bicycle transport development programmes. Promotion of cycling is also part of the Operational Programme Development of Eastern Poland.
Facilitate sharing of cities' experiences improving urban public transport, with appropriate national administrative support for local authorities.	Thirty-four Polish mayors have signed the Covenant of Mayors, a movement involving local and regional authorities who voluntarily commit to increasing energy efficiency and use of renewable energy sources on their territories to meet and exceed the EU's 20% CO_2 reduction objective by 2020 (*www.covenantofmayors.eu/index_en.html*). In addition, Poland's Chamber of Urban Transport, the supporting body for developing sustainable public transport plans at local level, provides information, consulting and training services and has published developer guidelines.
Review and revise transport taxes and charges, with a view to better internalising the environmental externalities of various transport modes.	Since 2006, a fee of PLN 500 has applied to the importation of any vehicle, to support authorised recycling of end-of-life vehicles. The one-off tax levied on the sale or import of passenger vehicles is not explicitly linked to environmental performance. In 2009, it was raised from 3.1% to 18.6% for cars with capacity greater than 2 000 cm^3. There is no recurrent tax on car ownership. Since 2011 an electronic road toll system for vehicles above 3.5 tonnes has been in place, with per kilometre rates differentiated according to Euro emission standards. There are also tolls for all road users on specific sections of motorways and national roads (Chapter 3).
	3. International commitments
Adopt and implement a coherent national climate protection policy which identifies priority policy measures based on their cost-effectiveness (e.g. in terms of cost per unit of avoided emissions) and is co-ordinated with energy and transport policies (e.g. taking ancillary benefits into account).	Poland has no specific national climate change policy beyond its EU targets. In 2011, it started work on a National Programme for the Development of a Low-Emission Economy, to encourage development and use of low emission technology to promote growth and competitiveness. A draft document is expected to be completed in 2015. The government adopted a National Adaptation Strategy in October 2013. It assessed climate change impacts and found these to be primarily negative, notably in terms of water resources, flooding and increasing temperatures. The strategy accordingly calls for "climate proofing" spatial planning and infrastructure decisions, especially in transport and energy (Chapter 3).

Recommendations	Actions taken
Ratify relevant Protocols to the UN-ECE Convention on Long-range Transport of Air Pollutants, and pursue their reduction targets (e.g. for SO_X, NOx, VOCs, NH3) through the national air management strategy.	Poland has ratified the 1988 Sofia Protocol to the 1979 Convention on Long-range Transboundary Air Pollution concerning the Control of Emissions of Nitrogen Oxides or their Transboundary Fluxes, and the 1984 Geneva Protocol on Long-term Financing of the Co-operative Programme for Monitoring and Evaluation of the Long-range Transmission of Air Pollutants in Europe. It has not ratified the 1999 Gothenburg Protocol to Abate Acidification, Eutrophication and Ground-level Ozone, the 1998 Aarhus Protocol on Persistent Organic Pollutants, the 1998 Aarhus Protocol on Heavy Metals, or the 1994 Oslo Protocol on Further Reduction of Sulphur Emissions. Nor has it signed the 1991 Geneva Protocol concerning the Control of Emissions of Volatile Organic Compounds or their Transboundary Fluxes, or the 1985 Helsinki Protocol on the Reduction of Sulphur Emissions or their Transboundary Fluxes by at least 30 per cent. Upon accession to the EU, Poland became subject to ceilings under the National Emission Ceilings Directive that are equal to those in the Gothenburg Protocol. Poland has met the 2010 targets of the directive (Chapter 1).
Complete investment in municipal waste water treatment stations and strengthen measures to reduce nutrient run-off from agriculture, as necessary, to comply with pollution reduction commitments made in the framework of HELCOM.	Since 2002, the near doubling of investment in wastewater management has helped increase the share of population connected to sewage treatment plants and reduce nutrient inputs to the Baltic Sea. The national municipal wastewater treatment programme, adopted in 2003 to fulfil the Urban Waste Water Treatment Directive requirements, is the main instrument for compliance with pollution reduction commitments made in the framework of HELCOM. In addition, measures taken to prevent and reduce nitrate pollution from agricultural sources include spatial and temporal limitation of fertiliser application and increased manure storage capacity. Their effect on water quality has not yet been evaluated (Chapter 1).
Strengthen monitoring and inspection of fish catches (in harbours, on ships, by satellite) and work to improve information collection on by-catch and discards in offshore fisheries; take further steps to reduce fishing capacity.	Under Council Regulation (EC) 812/2004 laying down measures concerning incidental catches of cetaceans in fisheries, Poland is required to set up a monitoring system. The 2004 Fisheries Act implements the provisions of the Common Fisheries Policy and defines the procedure concerning the granting of permits to perform fishing activities; rational fisheries practices, including the protection of marine living resources; and supervision and control over fishing activities and marketing of fisheries products. Poland has implemented EU fisheries control provisions (Regulation 1224/2009 establishing a Community control system for ensuring compliance with the rules of the Common Fisheries Policy). Each year, the Ministry of Agriculture and Rural Development approves the Polish control action programme for the Baltic Sea. A fishing effort adjustment plan was adopted in 2010.
Strengthen enforcement against illegal trade in ozone-depleting substances, endangered species and hazardous waste.	Customs officers have been designated in each customs office to co-ordinate environmental issues. Eighteen customs officers have been trained to prevent illegal trade in ozone-depleting substances. The 2004 Nature Conservation Act implements the EU Wildlife Trade Regulations and the provisions of the Washington Convention on International Trade in Endangered Species of Wild Fauna and Flora (CITES). A CITES Working Group was established, including representatives of the ministries dealing with environment, scientific authority and finance, as well as customs, police, veterinary inspection, judiciary, NGOs and zoological and botanical gardens. Over the review period, Poland strengthened enforcement of hazardous waste shipments. Major cases of illegal waste shipments have not been found in recent years (Chapter 5).
Ensure better integration of environmental concerns into development projects financed by international and EU funding.	Under the Operational Programme Infrastructure and Environment 2007-13, transport infrastructure was the top priority with 69% of funding, followed by environment (including water management) at 16% and energy-related projects at 8% (including 5% for improving energy security). In the next phase (2014-20), environmental protection represents 14% of allocations and the low-emission economy 6%. Thus the focus on climate-related support is greater than in the previous programming period, though transport once again receives the greatest share of funds. Transport infrastructure projects receiving EU funding are subject to EIA (Chapter 3).

Source: Country submission; OECD Environment Directorate.

ANNEX III

Abbreviations

CAP	Common Agricultural Policy
CBD	Convention on Biological Diversity
CCS	Carbon capture and storage
CO_2	Carbon dioxide
CSO	Central Statistical Office
DGSF	Directorate-General of State Forests
DMC	Domestic material consumption
EAFRD	European Agricultural Fund for Rural Development
EC	European Commission
EEA	European Environment Agency
EGS	Environmental goods and services
EIA	Environmental impact assessment
ELVs	End-of-life vehicles
EMAS	EU Eco-Management and Audit Scheme
EPR	Extended producer responsibility
ESE	Energy Security and the Environment Strategy
ETS	Emissions trading system
EU	European Union
EUR	Euro
FAO	Food and Agriculture Organization
FSC	Forest Stewardship Council
GDEP	General Directorate for Environmental Protection
GDP	Gross domestic product
GHG	Greenhouse gas
GIOS	Chief Environmental Protection Inspectorate
IEA	International Energy Agency
IOS	Inspectorate for Environmental Protection
IUCN	International Union for Nature Conservation
LP	Lasy Państwowe - State Forests
MBT	Mechanical-biological treatment
MoE	Ministry of the Environment
MRD	Ministry of Regional Development
MSW	Municipal solid waste
NBS	National Biodiversity Strategy

NDS	National Development Strategy
NEC	National Emission Ceilings
NEP	National Environmental Policy
NFEPWM	National Fund for Environmental Protection and Water Management
NFP	National Forest Policy
NGO	Non-government organisation
NIK	Supreme Audit Office
NMVOC	Non-methane volatile organic compound
NO_x	Nitrogen oxides
NWMP	National Waste Management Plan
OPIE	Operational Programme Infrastructure and Environment
PAHs	Polycyclic aromatic hydrocarbons
PCBs	Polychlorinated biphenyls
PCT	Patent Co-operation Treaty
PEFC	Programme for the Endorsement of Forest Certification
PM	Particulate matters
PPP	Public-private partnership
PRO	Producer responsibility organisation
RCL	Government Legislation Centre
RDEP	Regional Directorate for Environmental Protection
RDF	Refuse-derived fuel
RDP	Rural Development Plan
RDSF	Regional Directorates of State Forests
R&D	Research and development
SEA	Strategic environmental assessment
SMEs	Small and medium-sized enterprises
SO_x	Sulphur oxides
STRATEG	System of Indicators for Monitoring and Programming of the Development Policy
TPES	Total primary energy supply
UNECE	United Nations Economic Commission for Europe
UNFCCC	United Nations Framework Convention on Climate Change
USD	United States Dollar
VAT	Value added tax
VFEPWM	Voivodship Fund for Environmental Protection and Water Management
WEEE	Waste electrical and electronic equipment
WFD	EU Water Framework Directive
WHO	World Health Organization
WIOS	Regional Environmental Protection Inspectorate

ORGANISATION FOR ECONOMIC CO-OPERATION AND DEVELOPMENT

The OECD is a unique forum where governments work together to address the economic, social and environmental challenges of globalisation. The OECD is also at the forefront of efforts to understand and to help governments respond to new developments and concerns, such as corporate governance, the information economy and the challenges of an ageing population. The Organisation provides a setting where governments can compare policy experiences, seek answers to common problems, identify good practice and work to co-ordinate domestic and international policies.

The OECD member countries are: Australia, Austria, Belgium, Canada, Chile, the Czech Republic, Denmark, Estonia, Finland, France, Germany, Greece, Hungary, Iceland, Ireland, Israel, Italy, Japan, Korea, Luxembourg, Mexico, the Netherlands, New Zealand, Norway, Poland, Portugal, the Slovak Republic, Slovenia, Spain, Sweden, Switzerland, Turkey, the United Kingdom and the United States. The European Commission takes part in the work of the OECD.

OECD Publishing disseminates widely the results of the Organisation's statistics gathering and research on economic, social and environmental issues, as well as the conventions, guidelines and standards agreed by its members.

ÉDITIONS OCDE, 2, rue André-Pascal, 75775 PARIS CEDEX 16
(97 2015 13 1 P) ISBN 978-92-64-08190-1 – 2015-17

www.ingramcontent.com/pod-product-compliance
Ingram Content Group UK Ltd.
Pitfield, Milton Keynes, MK11 3LW, UK
UKHW051501290926
15471UKWH00008B/1338